Lecture Notes in Computer Science 14138

The series Lecture Notes in Computer Science (LNCS), including its subseries Lecture Notes in Artificial Intelligence (LNAI) and Lecture Notes in Bioinformatics (LNBI), has established itself as a medium for the publication of new developments in computer science and information technology research, teaching, and education.

LNCS enjoys close cooperation with the computer science R & D community, the series counts many renowned academics among its volume editors and paper authors, and collaborates with prestigious societies. Its mission is to serve this international community by providing an invaluable service, mainly focused on the publication of conference and workshop proceedings and postproceedings. LNCS commenced publication in 1973.

Laure Petrucci · Jeremy Sproston
Editors

Formal Modeling and Analysis of Timed Systems

21st International Conference, FORMATS 2023
Antwerp, Belgium, September 19–21, 2023
Proceedings

 Springer

Editors
Laure Petrucci ⓘ
Université Sorbonne Paris Nord
Villetaneuse, France

Jeremy Sproston ⓘ
University of Turin
Turin, Italy

ISSN 0302-9743   ISSN 1611-3349 (electronic)
Lecture Notes in Computer Science
ISBN 978-3-031-42625-4   ISBN 978-3-031-42626-1 (eBook)
https://doi.org/10.1007/978-3-031-42626-1

This Springer imprint is published by the registered company Springer Nature Switzerland AG
The registered company address is: Gewerbestrasse 11, 6330 Cham, Switzerland

Paper in this product is recyclable.

Preface

This volume contains the proceedings of the 21st International Conference on Formal Modeling and Analysis of Timed Systems (FORMATS), held on September 19–21, 2023, in Antwerp, Belgium. The conference was co-located with three others, CONCUR, FMICS, and QEST, held together as part of the CONFEST 2023 event.

FORMATS is an annual conference which aims at promoting the study of fundamental and practical aspects of timed systems, and bringing together researchers from different disciplines that share interests in the modelling, design, and analysis of timed computational systems. The conference aims at attracting researchers interested in real-time issues in hardware design, performance analysis, real-time software, scheduling, semantics, and verification of real-time, hybrid, and probabilistic systems.

In total, 21 paper submissions were received and distributed for review amongst a Programme Committee comprising 32 members. All papers received at least three reviews and were then discussed by the committee members. Following the discussion, nine papers (43%) were accepted for inclusion in the scientific program. The conference specifically solicited papers for a featured track on "Monitoring of cyber-physical systems". Two of the accepted papers fell within this category.

For the second time in FORMATS, authors of accepted papers that included computational results or tools were invited to submit accompanying artifacts for evaluation. This was to allow independent reproduction of the results stated in the papers, thereby strengthening the quality of the published papers. Three artifacts were submitted, representing a third of all accepted papers. These artifacts were evaluated by a separate Artifact Evaluation Committee, comprising 17 members, chaired by Arnd Hartmanns (University of Twente, The Netherlands) and Paolo Zuliani (Università di Roma "La Sapienza", Italy). All artifacts received at least four reviews and all three artifacts passed the acceptance criteria. The corresponding papers display an "Artifact Evaluated" badge in these proceedings.

FORMATS 2023 also included two invited talks from Nicolas Markey (CNRS and IRISA, Université de Rennes, France) and Jaco van de Pol (Aarhus University, Denmark). An accompanying paper for the former and the abstract for the latter are included in these proceedings.

In June 2023, the FORMATS community learned the tragic news of the passing of Sergiy Bogomolov of Newcastle University, who co-chaired FORMATS 2022 and was an emerging leader in the timed and hybrid systems research community. A special memorial session to celebrate Sergiy's life and contributions to the field was organised at FORMATS 2023 by Martin Fränzle and Taylor Johnson and included invited talks from close collaborators and friends.

Finally, we would like to thank all those who contributed to FORMATS 2023. These include the Program Committee, the additional reviewers, and the Artifact Evaluation Committee, who we thank for their professionalism and dedication displayed in the reviewing, discussion, and artifact evaluation phases. We also thank the Steering Committee, in particular the Steering Committee chair Martin Fränzle, and the organisational committee behind CONFEST 2023. Finally, we would also like to thank DENSO and Springer for their generous sponsorship of FORMATS, Springer for their support with publishing the proceedings, and EasyChair for providing the paper submission and review system.

July 2023   Laure Petrucci
                                                                         Jeremy Sproston

Organization

Program Committee Chairs

Laure Petrucci   Université Sorbonne Paris Nord & CNRS, France
Jeremy Sproston   University of Turin, Italy

Artifact Evaluation Committee Chairs

Arnd Hartmanns   University of Twente, The Netherlands
Paolo Zuliani   Università di Roma "La Sapienza", Italy

Special Track Chair

Masaki Waga   Kyoto University, Japan

Steering Committee

Rajeev Alur   University of Pennsylvania, USA
Eugene Asarin   Paris Cité University, France
Martin Fränzle (Chair)   Universität Oldenburg, Germany
Thomas A. Henzinger   IST Austria, Austria
Joost-Pieter Katoen   RWTH Aachen University, Germany
Kim G. Larsen   Aalborg University, Denmark
Oded Maler (Founding Chair, 1957–2018)   CNRS, France
Pavithra Prabhakar   Kansas State University, USA
Mariëlle Stoelinga   University of Twente, The Netherlands
Wang Yi   Uppsala University, Sweden

Program Committee

Alessandro Abate   University of Oxford, UK
Parosh Aziz Abdulla   Uppsala University, Sweden
Marcello M. Bersani   Politecnico di Milano, Italy

Patricia Bouyer	CNRS and ENS Paris-Saclay, France
Franck Cassez	Windranger Labs, Australia
Pedro R. D'Argenio	Universidad Nacional de Córdoba - CONICET, Argentina
Jyotirmoy Deshmukh	University of Southern California, USA
Catalin Dima	Université Paris Est - Créteil, France
Miriam García Soto	Complutense University of Madrid, Spain
Gilles Geeraerts	Université libre de Bruxelles, Belgium
Taylor T. Johnson	Vanderbilt University, USA
Jan Kretinsky	Technical University of Munich, Germany
Engel Lefaucheux	Inria Nancy, Loria, Université de Lorraine, France
Jun Liu	University of Waterloo, Canada
Manuel Mazo Jr.	Delft University of Technology, The Netherlands
Benjamin Monmege	Aix-Marseille Université, France
Dejan Nickovic	Austrian Institute of Technology AIT, Austria
Nicola Paoletti	King's College London, UK
Laure Petrucci	Université Sorbonne Paris Nord & CNRS, France
Kristin Yvonne Rozier	Iowa State University, USA
Krishna S.	IIT Bombay, India
Ocan Sankur	Université de Rennes, CNRS, France
Sadegh Soudjani	Newcastle University, UK
Jeremy Sproston	University of Turin, Italy
Jiri Srba	Aalborg University, Denmark
B. Srivathsan	Chennai Mathematical Institute, India
Nathalie Sznajder	Sorbonne Université, CNRS, LIP6, France
Patrick Totzke	University of Liverpool, UK
Stavros Tripakis	Northeastern University, USA
Enrico Vicario	University of Florence, Italy
Masaki Waga	Kyoto University, Japan
Naijun Zhan	Institute of Software, Chinese Academy of Sciences, China

Additional Reviewers

Arif, Muhammad Fareed
Aurandt, Alexis
Benjamin, Patrick
Bollig, Benedikt
Kazemi, Milad
Kuipers, Tom
Madnani, Khushraj
Perez, Guillermo

Potomkin, Kostiantyn
Prokop, Maximilian
Rieder, Sabine
Ting, Gan
Varacca, Daniele
Yakovlev, Alex
Zhao, Hengjun

Artifact Evaluation Committee

Omid Akbarzadeh	Newcastle University, UK
Jaime Arias	CNRS & Université Sorbonne Paris Nord, France
Sougata Bose	University of Liverpool, UK
Francesca Cairoli	University of Trieste, Italy
Hongkai Chen	Stony Brook University, USA
Alexandros Evangelidis	Technical University of Munich, Germany
Martijn Goorden	Aalborg University, Denmark
Amit Gurung	Kyoto University, Japan
Dylan Marinho	Université de Lorraine, France
Yiming Meng	University of Waterloo, Canada
Sayan Mukherjee	Université Libre de Bruxelles, Belgium
Amirmohammad Nazari	University of Southern California, USA
Julie Parreaux	Aix-Marseille Université, France
Fedor Shmarov	University of Manchester, UK
Ben Wooding	Newcastle University, UK

Encoding Planning and Games in SAT and QBF (Invited Talk)

Jaco van de Pol[1,2] and Irfansha Shaik[2]

[1] Department of Computer Science, Aarhus University, Aarhus, Denmark
jaco@cs.au.dk
[2] Formal Methods and Tools, University of Twente, Enschede, The Netherlands

Abstract. We will first review the concise encoding of planning problems in SAT and QBF. Then we will illustrate how the Quantum Circuit Layout problem can be encoded and solved as a planning problem. Finally, we will consider the encoding of some board games in QBF.

Planning problems can be specified by predicates on objects, indicating the initial state, the goal states, and the preconditions and effects of possible actions that can be applied to the objects. A reduction of planning problems to propositional SAT proceeds in two steps: first, all predicates are *grounded* to propositions, by instantiating them for all concrete object combinations; second, the transition formulas are *unrolled* to obtain a formula encoding a plan of some bounded length. The size of the resulting formula depends on the length of the plan and on the number of object combinations. Alternatively, one can encode planning problems more concisely in QBF, Quantified Boolean Formulas.

We will discuss a number of well-known techniques to reduce the size of the formulas. *Parallel plans* apply independent actions simultaneously, to reduce the required plan length. *Compact QBF encoding* a path of length n is expressed as a formula of size $\log(n)$, at the expense of adding extra quantifier alternations. *Lifted QBF encoding* avoids the grounding step by using quantifiers. While SAT is "only" NP-complete, QBF is PSPACE-complete; its complexity increases with the number of quantifier alternations. On the other hand, SAT formulas can be exponentially larger than their QBF counterparts.

Next, we will study the Quantum Circuit Layout problem: a circuit of quantum gates on *logical qubits* must be compiled to operations on *physical qubits* of some quantum platform. The platform can only apply binary operations on physical qubits that are connected, which requires the introduction of extra swap-operations on qubits. The goal is to minimize the number of required swaps. We express Quantum Circuit Layout as a classical planning problem, and show how *parallel plans* scale the instances one can solve with a SAT solver.

Finally, quantifier alternations in QBF can also be used to encode the turns in a two-player game. We show a concise *Lifted QBF encoding* of board games, which grows logarithmically in the number of squares on the board. We use a QBF solver to solve (small instances of) board games including generalized Tic-Tac-Toe, Connect-4, Hex, Break-Through, Domineering, and Evader-Pursuer.

Contents

Invited Talk

Computing the Price of Anarchy in Atomic Network Congestion Games (Invited Talk)

Nicolas Markey[✉]

IRISA, CNRS & Inria & Univ. Rennes, Rennes, France
nmarkey@irisa.fr

Abstract. Network congestion games are a simple model for reasoning about routing problems in a network. They are a very popular topic in algorithmic game theory, and a huge amount of results about existence and (in)efficiency of equilibrium strategy profiles in those games have been obtained over the last 20 years.

In particular, the price of anarchy has been defined as an important notion for measuring the inefficiency of Nash equilibria. Generic bounds have been obtained for the price of anarchy over various classes of networks, but little attention has been put on the effective computation of this value for a given network. This talk presents recent results on this problem in different settings.

1   Atomic Network Congestion Games

Congestion games have been introduced by Rosenthal in 1973 [28,29] as a model for reasoning about traffic-routing or resource-sharing problems [27,36]. *Network* congestion games [22,30] are played by n players on a weighted graph $G = \langle V, E, l \rangle$, where l labels the edges of G with non-decreasing functions (called *latency functions*): each player has to select a route in this graph from their source state to their target state; for each edge they use, they have to pay $l(k)$, where k is the total number of players using the same edge. These games are called *atomic* as opposed to non-atomic ones, where each player can route arbitrarily-small parts of their load along different paths. In the sequel, we focus on the *symmetric* setting, where all players have the same source- and target vertices.

Example 1. Figure 1 represents an atomic network congestion game: it is made of a graph, with a state s_0 as the source state of the four players (represented by the four tokens in that state), and s_1 as their target state. Edges $s_0 \to l$ and $r \to s_1$ are labelled with the identity function $k \mapsto k$, meaning that the cost of using each of these edges is equal to the number of players using it; in this example, the cost of the other edges is a constant.

This paper is based on joint works with Nathalie Bertrand, Aline Goeminne, Suman Sadhukhan, Ocan Sankur, and benefited from discussions with Arthur Dumas and Stéphane Le Roux. These works have received fundings from ANR projects TickTac and BisoUS.

L. Petrucci and J. Sproston (Eds.): FORMATS 2023, LNCS 14138, pp. 3–12, 2023.
https://doi.org/10.1007/978-3-031-42626-1_1

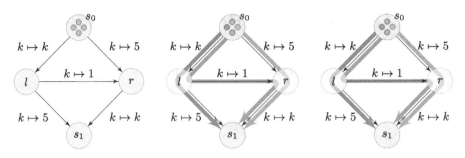

Fig. 1. An example of a congestion game with four players.

Fig. 2. One player going to s_1 via l, and three players via r.

Fig. 3. One player going via l, one via r, and two using the transverse edge.

Figure 2 displays a round of this game, where one player takes the path $\pi_l \colon s_0 \to l \to s_1$, and the other three take $\pi_r \colon s_0 \to r \to s_1$; the cost for the former player is 6, while it is 8 for the other three. Figure 3 shows another profile of strategies, with one player taking π_l, one player taking π_r, and the remaining two using $\pi_{lr} \colon s_0 \to l \to r \to s_1$. In that case, edges $s_0 \to l$ and $r \to s_1$ are used by three players, hence they have a cost of 3; the first two players thus have to pay 8, while the cost for the other two is 7.

In symmetric atomic network congestion games, all agents are indistinguishable. A strategy profile can thus be represented as a vector $\mathsf{p} = (p_\pi)_{\pi \in \mathsf{Paths}}$, where Paths is the set of all paths from source to target, and p_π is the number of players selecting path π in that profile. For a strategy profile $\mathsf{p} = (p_\pi)_{\pi \in \mathsf{Paths}}$ and a path ρ, we write $\mathsf{p} + \rho$ to denote the strategy profile obtained from p by incrementing p_ρ; $\mathsf{p} - \rho$ is defined similarly, assuming that ρ occurs in p. The *flow* of a strategy profile p is the vector $\mathsf{flow}(\mathsf{p}) = (q_e)_{e \in E}$ such that for each edge e, q_e is the number of players using edge e in the profile p. The cost a following path ρ in a strategy profile p is then defined as $\mathsf{cost}_\mathsf{p}(\rho) = \sum_{e \in \rho} l(q_e)$. The social cost of a strategy profile is then defined as follows: $\mathsf{cost}(\mathsf{p}) = \sum_{\rho \in \mathsf{Paths}} p_\rho \cdot \mathsf{cost}_\mathsf{p}(\rho) = \sum_{e \in E} q_e \cdot l(q_e)$.

In congestion games, two kinds of behaviours of the players are of particular interest:

- the *social optima*, which minimise the *total cost* of the whole set of players: formally, p is a social optimum if $\mathsf{cost}(\mathsf{p})$ is less than or equal to $\mathsf{cost}(\mathsf{p}')$ for any profile p';
- the *Nash equilibria*, which correspond to selfish behaviours, each player aiming at minimising their *individual cost* given the strategies of the other players: formally, p is a Nash equilibrium if for any ρ occurring in p and any ρ', it holds $\mathsf{cost}_\mathsf{p}(\rho) \leq \mathsf{cost}_{\mathsf{p}+\rho'-\rho}(\rho')$.

Social optima represent collaborative behaviours that would be played if the players had to share the total cost, while Nash equilibria correspond to selfish behaviours.

Example 1 (contd). Consider again the network congestion game of Fig. 1. It is easy to check that the social optimum is achieved when two players take π_l and the other two take π_r: the total cost is 28.

Finding Nash equilibria is more difficult. First notice that the social optimum obtained above is not a Nash equilibrium: if one of the players taking π_l decided to take π_{lr}, their cost would be 6 instead of 7. (Notice that this does not improve the social optimum since the two players taking π_r would see their cost increase).

The strategy profile of Fig. 3 is a Nash equilibrium: it can be checked that no players can lower their cost by switching to another path; the total cost (also called *social cost*) of this Nash equilibrium is 30. Notice that another Nash equilibrium exists in this game: when all the players take π_{lr}, each of them pays a cost of 9, and switching to one of the other two paths would give the same cost; the social cost of this Nash equilibrium is 36.

In his seminal papers [28,29], Rosenthal shows that congestion games always admit Nash equilibria, by exhibiting a *potential function*, which decreases when any player individually switches to a better strategy. As shown in Example 1, Nash equilibria are in general not unique, and they may have different social costs. Koutsoupias and Papadimitriou defined the *price of anarchy* as the ratio between the social cost of the worst Nash equilibrium and the social optimum [23]: it measures how bad selfish behaviours can be compared to an optimal collaborative solution. Symmetrically, with a more optimistic point of view, the *price of stability* is the ratio between the best Nash equilibrium and the social optimum, and measures the minimal cost of moving from a collaborative solution to a selfish one [2].

An impressive amount of results have been obtained about (network) congestion games during the last 25 years:

- numerous variations on the model have been studied: atomic vs. non-atomic players [32], weighted players [16] with splittable or unsplittable flows [31], sequential or simultaneous choices [26], ... Several restrictions on the graphs have been used to obtain certain results, such as series-parallel graphs [15,19] or graphs with only parallel links [23,25]. Mixed-strategy Nash equilibria have also been been considered, see e.g. [10,25].
- the complexity of computing *some* Nash equilibrium has been studied. Since Nash equilibria always exist and are made of one path per player, the problem is in TFNP; it is actually in FPTIME if all players have the same source and target states, and PLS-complete otherwise [14]. The existence of a Nash equilibrium whose social cost lies below (resp. above) a given threshold (which is the decision problem associated to the computation of a best (resp. worst) Nash equilibrium) is NP-complete [34], even for series-parallel graphs. We call this problem *constrainted Nash-equilibrium problem* in the sequel;
- in some cases, the price of anarchy can be proven to be bounded, independently of the graph: this is the case for instance in atomic network congestion games with linear latency functions, where the price of anarchy can be at most 5/2 [6,10]; under the series-parallel restriction, the price of anarchy is bounded by 2 [19].

2   Computing the Prices of Anarchy and Stability

In contrast to the topics listed above, the problem of computing the prices of anarchy and stability of a *given* network has received little attention [11,12]. We address this problem by developing techniques to compute best and worst Nash equilibria and social optima for atomic network congestion games in three different settings: first, for series-parallel networks with linear latency functions, we compute a representation of Nash equilibria and social (local) optima for any number of players; second, in a more *dynamic* (sometimes called *sequential*) setting where the players can adapt their route along the way, for piecewise-affine latency functions, we develop an exponential-space algorithm for solving the constrained Nash-equilibrium problem; third, we extend these results to timed network games.

2.1   Series-Parallel Networks with Linear Latency Functions

Using the notations above, we see strategy profiles as $|\mathsf{Paths}|$-dimensional vectors $(p_\pi)_{\pi \in \mathsf{Paths}}$, and their associated flows as $|E|$-dimensional vectors $(q_e)_{e \in E}$.

The flow of the social optima are the flows $(q_e)_{e \in E}$ such that $\sum_{e \in E} q_e \cdot l(q_e)$ is minimal over all flows. As we assume that l is linear, we get a quadratic expression to minimize, which is intractable. Instead, we focus on social *local* optima, which are only optimal among the profiles obtained by changing a single strategy. We prove that a flow $(q_e)_{e \in E}$ is locally optimal if, and only if, for all paths ρ and ρ' such that $q_e > 0$ for all $e \in \rho$, it holds

$$\text{for all } \rho, \rho', \text{ if } q_e > 0 \text{ for all } e \in \rho, \text{ then } \sum_{e \in \rho \setminus \rho'} l(2q_e - 1) \leq \sum_{e \in \rho' \setminus \rho} l(2q_e + 1).$$

Similarly, flows of Nash equilibria p characterized as vectors $(q_e)_{e \in E}$ satisfying

$$\text{for all } \rho, \rho', \text{ if } \rho \in \mathsf{p}, \text{ then } \sum_{e \in \rho \setminus \rho'} l(q_e) \leq \sum_{e \in \rho' \setminus \rho} l(q_e + 1).$$

It follows:

Theorem 1 ([8,33]). For any atomic network congestion game G with linear latency functions, the sets $\mathsf{SLO}(G)$ of all social local optima, and $\mathsf{NE}(G)$ of all Nash equilibria, as well as the sets of corresponding flows, are semi-linear [17].

When restricting to series-parallel graphs (which are graphs obtained from the trivial single-edge graph by series- and parallel compositions) [35]), we can prove that both sets of flows expand in a unique direction δ: in other terms, they can be written as $B \cup \bigcup_{i \in I k \geq 0} b_i + k \cdot \delta$, for finite sets B and I.

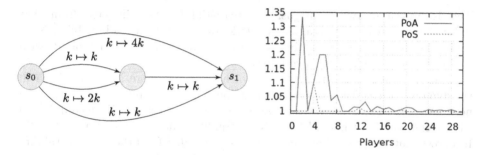

Fig. 4. Evolution of prices of anarchy and stability as a function of the number of players

One consequence of this is that, in our setting, the prices of anarchy and stability converges to 1 when the number of players tends to infinity. It also allows us to compute finite representations of the sets of all social local optima and Nash equilibria, which in turn can be used to compute the prices of anarchy and stability. Figure 4 displays an example of such a computation on a 4-path example for up to 30 players.

2.2   Dynamic Network Congestion Games

Dynamic network congestion games are a refined version of network congestion games with two main changes: first, the number of players using a given edge is now measured *synchronously*, considering that the load of an edge depends on time [3,20]; second, the players do not choose simple paths but adaptive (pure) strategies, that depend on the other players' past moves: this provides a way of reacting to strategy deviations *during the course of the game* [5,13,26].

Example 1 (contd). Consider again the network congestion game of Example 1, and in particular the strategy profile of Fig. 3: the edge $r \to s_1$ is used by strategies π_r and π_{lr}, but considering that the players move synchronously, this edge is traversed at the second step in π_r and at the third step in π_{lr}; there is no congestion effect between the single player following path π_r and the two players following π_{lr}; in that case, all three of them will pay a cost of 6.

Strategies may now depend on what the other players have been playing (but the players are still anonymous). Considering again the example of Fig. 3, the players can now decide to go to l, and depending on the number of players in l and in r, choose to go directly to s_1 or take the edge $l \to r$.

We call *blind strategies* the special case of strategies that we used in the previous section, which follow a single path independently of the other players' moves. We prove:

Theorem 2 ([7,33])**.** Any dynamic network congestion game admits a (blind) Nash equilibrium.

This is proven in two steps: using a potential function inspired from that of [28,29], we prove that dynamic network congestion games admit blind Nash equilibria (considering only blind deviations); we then prove that blind Nash equilibria are also plain Nash equilibria.

Actually, there exist networks in which there are more Nash equilibria in the dynamic setting than in the classical one. Figure 5 displays an example of a network congestion game in which, for three players, there is a Nash equilibrium with social cost 36, while all blind Nash equilibria have cost at least 37 [7,33]. It follows that the price of anarchy is in general higher (and the price of stability is lower) in the dynamic setting than when restricting to blind strategies.

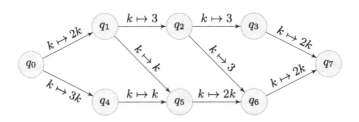

Fig. 5. A network congestion game in which blind Nash equilibria are sub-optimal

Since Nash equilibria always exist, the prices of anarchy and stability are always defined. They can be computed by solving the constrained social-optimum (resp. Nash equilibrium) problem, which asks whether some strategy profile (resp. Nash equilibrium) has social cost satisfying a given linear inequality.

Theorem 3 ([7,33]). The constrained social-optimum problem can be solved in polynomial space. The constrained Nash-equilibrium problem can be solved in exponential space. The prices of anarchy and stability of a given atomic network congestion game can be computed in exponential space.

Notice that such complexity results cannot be achieved by just building the explicit game on the graph of configurations, since this graph would have size $|V|^n$ (with n given in binary).

In this dynamic setting, it is usually more relevant to consider subgame-perfect equilibria, which rule out non-credible threats. It is open whether subgame perfect always exist in dynamic network congestion games. Adapting techniques developed in [9], we get:

Theorem 4 ([7,33]). The constrained subgame-perfect-equilibrium problem can be solved in double-exponential time.

3   Timed Network Games

Several works have proposed to add a real-time dimension to network congestion games. In some of those extensions, congestion affects time (instead of cost), with the aim of minimizing the total time to reach the target state [20,21,24]. For the case where congestion affects the cost, the class of timed network games is introduced in [3,4]: following the semantics of timed automata [1], in a timed network game the players can decide to take a transition, or to spend time in the state they are visiting. Transitions are immediate and have no cost, but their availability depends on time; states are decorated with latency functions indicating the cost for spending one time unit in that state, as a function of the load of that state.

Example 6. Figure 6 represents a timed network game: vertices are labelled with their latency functions, and edges are decorated with intervals indicating the time at which they can be traversed.

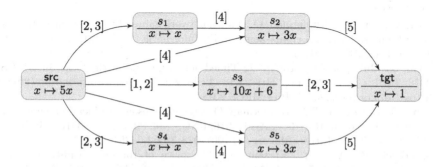

Fig. 6. Example of a timed network game

An example of a (blind) strategy π_1 in that timed network game consists in letting 1.3 time units elapse in src, then go to state s_3, and go to tgt at time 2. Another example π_2 could propose to stay in src until time 4, then go to s_5, and reach tgt at time 5.

If two players follow those strategies π_1 and π_2, the first one will have a total cost of 24.2 (namely, $(5 \times 2) \times 1.3 + (10 \times 1 + 6) \times 0.7$) when entering tgt, while the second one will have a total cost of 29.5 (in details, $(5 \times 2) \times 1.3 + (5 \times 1) \times 2.7 + (3 \times 1) \times 1$).

In this framework, *boundary* blind strategies, which are blind strategies that always take transitions at one of the boundaries of their timing constraints, have been identified as an important subclass of strategies: any timed network game has a boundary social optimum, and a boundary Nash equilibrium (among blind strategies). However, best and worst blind Nash equilibria need not be boundary [3].

Focusing on the computation of best and worst Nash equilibria, the results of the previous section can be extended in discrete time, for non-blind strategies, as follows:

Theorem 5 ([18]). *In* discrete-time *timed network games, the constrained social-optimum problem can be solved in polynomial space, and the constrained Nash-equilibrium problem can be solved in exponential space. The prices of anarchy and stability of a given timed network game can be computed in exponential space.*

References

1. Alur, R., Dill, D.L.: A theory of timed automata. Theor. Comput. Sci. **126**(2), 183–235 (1994)
2. Anshelevich, E., Dasgupta, A., Kleinberg, J., Tardos, É., Wexler, T., Roughgarden, T.: The price of stability for network design with fair cost allocation. In: FOCS 2004, pp.. 295–304. IEEE Comp. Soc. Press, (2004). https://doi.org/10.1109/FOCS.2004.68
3. Avni, G., Guha, S., Kupferman, O.: Timed network games. In: MFCS 2017. LIPIcs, vol. 84, pp. 37:1–37:16. Leibniz-Zentrum für Informatik (2017). https://doi.org/10.4230/LIPIcs.MFCS.2017.37
4. Avni, G., Guha, S., Kupferman, O.: Timed network games with clocks. In: MFCS 2018. LIPIcs. vol. 117, pp. 23:1–23:18. Leibniz-Zentrum für Informatik (2018). https://doi.org/10.4230/LIPIcs.MFCS.2018.23
5. Avni, G., Henzinger, T.A., Kupferman, O.: Dynamic resource allocation games. In: Gairing, M., Savani, R. (eds.) SAGT 2016. LNCS, vol. 9928, pp. 153–166. Springer, Heidelberg (2016). https://doi.org/10.1007/978-3-662-53354-3_13
6. Awerbuch, B., Azar, Y., Epstein, A.: The price of routing unsplittable flow. In: STOC 2005, pp. 57–66. ACM Press (2005). https://doi.org/10.1145/1060590.1060599
7. Bertrand, N., Markey, N., Sadhukhan, S., Sankur, O.: Dynamic network congestion games. In: FSTTCS 2020. LIPIcs 182, pp. 40:1–40:16. Leibniz-Zentrum für Informatik (2020). https://doi.org/10.4230/LIPIcs.FSTTCS.2020.40
8. Bertrand, N., Markey, N., Sadhukhan, S., Sankur, O.: Semilinear representations for series-parallel atomic congestion games. In: FSTTCS 2022. LIPIcs, vol. 250, pp. 32:1–32:20. Leibniz-Zentrum für Informatik (2022). https://doi.org/10.4230/LIPIcs.FSTTCS.2022.32
9. Brihaye, Th., Bruyère, V., Goeminne, A., Raskin, J.-F., Van den Bogaard, M.: The complexity of subgame perfect equilibria in quantitative reachability games. In CONCUR 2019. LIPIcs, vol. 140, pp. 13:1–13:16. Leibniz-Zentrum für Informatik (2019). https://doi.org/10.4230/LIPIcs.CONCUR.2019.13
10. Christodoulou, G., Koutsoupias, E.: The price of anarchy of finite congestion games. In STOC 2005, pp. 67–73. ACM Press (2005). https://doi.org/10.1145/1060590.1060600
11. Colini-Baldeschi, R., Cominetti, R., Mertikopoulos, P., Scarsini, M.: When is selfish routing bad? The price of anarchy in light and heavy traffic. Operations Res. **68**(2):411–434 (2020). https://doi.org/10.1287/opre.2019.1894
12. Cominetti, R., Dose, V., Scarsini, M.: The price of anarchy in routing games as a function of the demand. Math. Program (2023). https://doi.org/10.1007/s10107-021-01701-7 (to appear)
13. Correa, J.R., de Jong, J., de Keizer, B., Uetz, M.: The inefficiency of Nash and subgame-perfect equilibria for network routing. Math. Operat. Res. **44**(4), 1286–1303 (2019). https://doi.org/10.1287/moor.2018.0968

14. Fabrikant, A., Papadimitriou, Ch.H., Talwar, K.: The complexity of pure Nash equilibria. In STOC 2004, pp. 604–612. ACM Press (2004). https://doi.org/10.1145/1007352.1007445

15. Fotakis, D.: Congestion games with linearly independent paths: convergence time and price of anarchy. In: Monien, B., Schroeder, U.-P. (eds.) SAGT 2008. LNCS, vol. 4997, pp. 33–45. Springer, Heidelberg (2008). https://doi.org/10.1007/978-3-540-79309-0_5

16. Fotakis, D., Kontogiannis, S., Spirakis, P.G.: Selfish unsplittable flows. Theor. Comput. Sci. **348**(2-3), 226–239 (2005). https://doi.org/10.1016/j.tcs.2005.09.024

17. Ginsburg, S., Spanier, E.: Semigroups, Presburger formulas, and languages. Pac. J. Math. **16**(2), 285–296 (1966)

18. Goeminne, A., Markey, N., and Sankur, O.: Non-blind strategies in timed network congestion games. In: FORMATS 2022. LNCS, vol. 13465, pp. 183–199. Springer (2022). https://doi.org/10.1007/978-3-031-15839-1_11

19. Hao, B., Michini, C.: Inefficiency of pure nash equilibria in series-parallel network congestion games. In: WINE 2022, LNCS, vol. 13778, pp. 3–20. Springer (2022). https://doi.org/10.1007/978-3-031-22832-2_1

20. Hoefer, M., Mirrokni, V.S., Röglin, H., Teng, S.-H.: Competitive routing over time. Theor. Comput. Sci. **412**(39), 5420–5432 (2011). https://doi.org/10.1016/j.tcs.2011.05.055

21. Koch, R., Skutella, M.: Nash equilibria and the price of anarchy for flows over time. Theory Comput. Syst. **49**(1), 71–97 (2011). https://doi.org/10.1007/s00224-010-9299-y

22. Kontogiannis, S., Spirakis, P.: Atomic selfish routing in networks: a survey. In: Deng, X., Ye, Y. (eds.) WINE 2005. LNCS, vol. 3828, pp. 989–1002. Springer, Heidelberg (2005). https://doi.org/10.1007/11600930_100

23. Koutsoupias, E., Papadimitriou, C.: Worst-case equilibria. In: Meinel, C., Tison, S. (eds.) STACS 1999. LNCS, vol. 1563, pp. 404–413. Springer, Heidelberg (1999). https://doi.org/10.1007/3-540-49116-3_38

24. Koutsoupias, E., Papakonstantinopoulou, K.: Contention issues in congestion games. In: Czumaj, A., Mehlhorn, K., Pitts, A., Wattenhofer, R. (eds.) ICALP 2012. LNCS, vol. 7392, pp. 623–635. Springer, Heidelberg (2012). https://doi.org/10.1007/978-3-642-31585-5_55

25. Mavronicolas, M., Spirakis, P.G.: The price of selfish routing. Algorithmica **48**(1), 91–126 (2007). https://doi.org/10.1007/s00453-006-0056-1

26. Paes Leme, R., Syrgkanis, V., Tardos, É.: The curse of simultaneity. In: ITCS 2012, pp. 60–67. ACM Press (2012). https://doi.org/10.1145/2090236.2090242

27. Pigou, A.C.: The economics of welfare. MacMillan and Co. (1920)

28. R. W. Rosenthal. A class of games possessing pure-strategy Nash equilibria. *International Journal of Game Theory*, 2(1):65–67, 1973

29. Rosenthal, R.W.: The network equilibrium problem in integers. Networks **3**(1), 53–59 (1973). https://doi.org/10.1002/net.3230030104

30. Roughgarden, T.: Routing games. In: Algorithmic Game Theory, chapter 18, pp. 461–486. Cambridge University Press (2007)

31. Roughgarden, T., Tardos, É.: How bad is selfish routing? J. of the ACM **49**(2), 236–259 (2002). https://doi.org/10.1145/506147.506153

32. Roughgarden, T., Tardos, É.: Bounding the inefficiency of equilibria in non-atomic congestion games. Games Econ. Behav. **47**(2), 389–403 (2004). https://doi.org/10.1016/j.geb.2003.06.004

33. Sadhukhan, S.: A Verification Viewpoint on Network Congestion Games. PhD thesis, Université Rennes 1, France (2021)

34. Sperber, H.: How to find Nash equilibria with extreme total latency in network congestion games? Math. Methods Operat. Res. **71**(2), 245–265 (2010). https://doi.org/10.1007/s00186-009-0293-6
35. Valdes, J., Tarjan, R.E., Lawler, E.L.: The recognition of series-parallel digraphs. In STOC 1979, pp. 1–12. ACM Press (1979). https://doi.org/10.1145/800135.804393
36. Wardrop, J.G.: Some theoretical aspects of road traffic research. Proc. Inst. Civil Eng. **1**(3), 325–362 (1952). https://doi.org/10.1680/ipeds.1952.11259

FORMATS 2023 Main Track

Causal Reversibility for Timed Process Calculi with Lazy/Eager Durationless Actions and Time Additivity

Marco Bernardo[⊠] and Claudio A. Mezzina

Dipartimento di Scienze Pure e Applicate, Università di Urbino, Urbino, Italy
marco.bernardo@uniurb.it

Abstract. A reversible computing system features backward computations along which the effects of forward ones are undone when needed. This is accomplished by reverting executed actions from the last one. Since the last performed action may not be uniquely identifiable in a concurrent system, causal reversibility is considered: an executed action can be undone provided that all of its consequences have been undone already. We investigate causal reversibility in a timed setting by defining a reversible calculus in the style of Phillips and Ulidowski in which action execution is separated from time passing, actions can be lazy or eager, and time is described via numeric delays subject to time additivity. We show that the calculus meets causal reversibility through an adaptation of the technique of Lanese, Phillips, and Ulidowski that ensures a proper treatment of action laziness/eagerness as well as time-additive delays.

1 Introduction

In the 60's it was observed that irreversible computations cause heat dissipation into circuits because any logically irreversible manipulation of information, such as bit erasure or computation path merging, must be accompanied by a corresponding entropy increase [21,3]. Therefore, any logically reversible computation, in which no information is canceled, may be potentially carried out without releasing any heat, as verified in [7] and given a physical foundation in [15]. This suggested that low energy consumption could be achieved by resorting to *reversible computing*, in which there is no information loss because computation can go not only forward, but also backward by undoing the effects of the forward direction when needed. Nowadays, reversible computing has several applications such as biochemical reaction modeling [33,34], parallel discrete-event simulation [31,37], robotics [26], control theory [38], fault-tolerant systems [13,40,22,39], and concurrent program debugging [16,24].

Reversibility in a computing system has to do with the possibility of reverting the last performed action. In a sequential computing system this is very simple because at each step only one action is executed, hence the only challenge is how to store the information needed to reverse that action. As far as concurrent

© The Author(s), under exclusive license to Springer Nature Switzerland AG 2023
L. Petrucci and J. Sproston (Eds.): FORMATS 2023, LNCS 14138, pp. 15–32, 2023.
https://doi.org/10.1007/978-3-031-42626-1_2

and distributed systems are concerned, a critical aspect of reversibility is that there may not be a total order over executed actions, hence the last performed action may not be uniquely indentifiable. This led to the introduction of the notion of *causal reversibility* [12], according to which a previously executed action can be undone provided that all of its consequences, if any, have been undone beforehand. It is worth noting that the concept of causality is used in place of the concept of time to decide whether an action can be undone or not.

In a pure nondeterministic process algebraic setting, two distinct approaches have been developed to deal with causal reversibility. The *dynamic* approach of [12,20], which is adequate for very expressive calculi and programming languages, attaches external stack-based memories to process terms so as to record all the executed actions. In contrast, the *static* approach of [32], which is convenient for handling labeled transition systems and basic process calculi, makes all process algebraic operators static – in particular action prefix and choice – so that they are kept within the derivative process term of any transition. The two approaches have been shown to be equivalent in terms of labeled transition system isomorphism [23] and the common properties they exploit to ensure causal reversibility have been systematically studied in [25].

When timed systems are considered, other notions of reversibility may come into play. This is the case with *time reversibility* for stochastic processes like continuous-time Markov chains [19]. It ensures that the stochastic behavior of a *shared-resource* computing system remains the same when the direction of time is reversed and is instrumental to develop performance evaluation methods that cope with state space explosion and numerical stability problems. In [5] causal reversibility and time reversibility have been jointly investigated in the setting of a Markovian process calculus defined according to the static approach of [32], where every action is extended with a positive real number quantifying the rate of the corresponding exponentially distributed random duration.

In this paper we address the reversibility of *real-time* computing systems. Unlike [5], time flows *deterministically*, instead of stochastically, and is described *orthogonally* to actions, i.e., through a specific delay prefix operator, instead of being integrated within actions. In the rich literature of deterministically timed process calculi – timed CSP [36], temporal CCS [29], timed CCS [41], real-time ACP [2], urgent LOTOS [9], CIPA [1], TPL [17], ATP [30], TIC [35], and PAFAS [11] – the differences are due to the following time-related options:

- *Durationless actions* versus *durational actions*. In the first case, actions are instantaneous events and time passes in between them; hence, functional behavior and time are *orthogonal*. In the second case, every action takes a certain amount of time to be performed and time passes only due to action execution; hence, functional behavior and time are *integrated*.
- *Relative time* versus *absolute time*. Assume that timestamps are associated with the events observed during system execution. In the first case, each timestamp refers to the time instant of the previous observation. In the second case, all timestamps refer to the starting time of the system execution.

– *Global clock* versus *local clocks*. In the first case, a single clock governs time passing. In the second case, several clocks associated with the various system parts elapse independently, although defining a unique notion of global time.

In addition, there are several different interpretations of action execution in terms of whether and when the execution can be delayed:

– *Eagerness*: actions must be performed as soon as they become enabled, i.e., without any delay, thereby implying that their execution is *urgent*.
– *Laziness*: after getting enabled, actions can be delayed arbitrarily long before they are executed.
– *Maximal progress*: enabled actions can be delayed unless they are independent of the external environment, in which case their execution is urgent.

The two major combinations of the aforementioned options yield the *two-phase functioning principle*, according to which actions are durationless, time is relative, and there is a single global clock, and the *one-phase functioning principle*, according to which actions are durational, time is absolute, and several local clocks are present. In [10] the two principles have been investigated under the various action execution interpretations through a bisimilarity-preserving encoding from the latter principle to the former, whilst the inverse encoding was provided in [4] along with a pair of encodings for the case of stochastic delays.

In this paper we focus on the two-phase functioning principle, yielding action transitions separated from delay transitions like in temporal CCS [29], and develop a reversible timed process calculus with lazy/eager actions, whose syntax and semantics adhere to the static approach of [32]. Then we show that the calculus is causally reversible through notions of [12] and the technique of [25]. The following adaptations turn out to be necessary with respect to [32,12,25]:

– Similar to executed actions, which are decorated with communication keys so as to remember who synchronized with whom when going backward [32], elapsed delays have to be decorated with keys to ensure that all subprocesses of an alternative or parallel composition go back in time in a well-paired way, as time cannot solve choices or decide which parallel process advances [29].
– The necessary condition for reversibility known as loop property [12,32,25], which establishes the presence of both a forward transition and a backward transition with the same label between any pair of connected states, has to deal with delay transitions too, in a way consistent with time additivity [29].
– Conflicting transitions, from which concurrent transitions [12] are then derived, and causal equivalence [12], which is needed to identify computations differing for the order of concurrent action transitions, have to be extended with additional conditions specific to delay transitions.
– Backward transitions independence, one of the properties studied in [25] to ensure causal reversibility, has to be paired with a novel property, which we have called backward triangularity, due to time additivity [29]. Furthermore, the semantic rules implementing laziness and maximal progress have to be carefully designed to guarantee the parabolic lemma [12,25].

Table 1. Syntax of forward processes (top) and reversible processes (bottom)

$$P, Q ::= \underline{0} \mid a . P \mid (n) . P \mid P + Q \mid P \,\|_L\, Q$$
$$R, S ::= P \mid a[i] . R \mid (n)^{[i]}. R \mid R + S \mid R \,\|_L\, S$$

This paper is organized as follows. In Sect. 2 we present the syntax and the semantics of our reversible timed process calculus. In Sect. 3 we prove that the calculus satisfies causal reversibility and illustrate some examples. In Sect. 4 we conclude with final remarks and directions for future work.

2   Reversible Timed Process Calculus: Actions Vs Delays

In this section we present the syntax and the semantics of RTPC – Reversible Timed Process Calculus, which are inspired by temporal CCS [29] and tailored for a reversible setting according to the static approach of [32].

Given a countable set $\mathcal{A}$ of actions – ranged over by a, b – including an invisible or silent action denoted by τ, the syntax of RTPC is shown in Table 1. A standard *forward process* P is one of the following: the terminated process $\underline{0}$; the action-prefixed process $a . P$, which is able to perform an action a and then continues as process P; the delay-prefixed process $(n) . P$, which lets $n \in \mathbb{N}_{>0}$ time units pass and then continues as process P; the nondeterministic choice $P + Q$; or the parallel composition $P \,\|_L\, Q$, indicating that processes P and Q execute in parallel and must synchronize only on actions in $L \subseteq \mathcal{A} \setminus \{\tau\}$.

We assume *time determinism* [29], i.e., time passing cannot solve choices or decide which parallel process advances, hence the same amount of time must pass in all subprocesses of a nondeterministic choice or parallel composition. Under eagerness, the execution of all actions is urgent and $\underline{0}$ cannot let time pass. Under laziness, action execution can be delayed arbitrarily long and $\underline{0}$ lets time pass. Under maximal progress, only the execution of τ is urgent, because τ cannot be involved in synchronizations, and $\underline{0}$ lets time pass.

A *reversible process* R is built on top of forward processes. The syntax of reversible processes differs from the one of forward processes due to the fact that, in the former, action and delay prefixes are decorated. As in [32], each action prefix is decorated with a *communication key* i belonging to a countable set $\mathcal{K}$. A process of the form $a[i] . R$ expresses that in the past the process synchronized with the environment on a and this synchronization was identified by key i. Keys are thus attached only to executed actions and are necessary to remember who synchronized with whom when undoing actions; keys could be omitted in the absence of parallel composition. Similarly, $(n)^{[i]}. R$ means that n time units elapsed in the past. Here communication keys are needed to ensure time determinism in the backward direction, so that all subprocesses go back in time in the same way; keys could be omitted in the absence of choice and parallel composition.

We denote by $\mathcal{P}$ the set of processes generated by the production for R in Table 1, while we use predicate std(_) to identify the standard forward processes

Table 2. Structural operational semantic rules for RTPC action transitions

$$(\text{Act1}) \ \frac{\text{std}(R)}{a \, . \, R \xrightarrow{a[i]}_{\text{a}} a[i] \, . \, R} \qquad\qquad (\text{Act1}^\bullet) \ \frac{\text{std}(R)}{a[i] \, . \, R \dashrightarrow_{\text{a}}^{a[i]} a \, . \, R}$$

$$(\text{Act2}) \ \frac{R \xrightarrow{b[j]}_{\text{a}} R' \quad j \neq i}{a[i] \, . \, R \xrightarrow{b[j]}_{\text{a}} a[i] \, . \, R'} \qquad (\text{Act2}^\bullet) \ \frac{R \dashrightarrow_{\text{a}}^{b[j]} R' \quad j \neq i}{a[i] \, . \, R \dashrightarrow_{\text{a}}^{b[j]} a[i] \, . \, R'}$$

$$(\text{Act3}) \ \frac{R \xrightarrow{b[j]}_{\text{a}} R'}{\delta(n,i) \, . \, R \xrightarrow{b[j]}_{\text{a}} \delta(n,i) \, . \, R'} \qquad (\text{Act3}^\bullet) \ \frac{R \dashrightarrow_{\text{a}}^{b[j]} R'}{\delta(n,i) \, . \, R \dashrightarrow_{\text{a}}^{b[j]} \delta(n,i) \, . \, R'}$$

$$(\text{Cho}) \ \frac{R \xrightarrow{a[i]}_{\text{a}} R' \quad \text{npa}(S)}{R + S \xrightarrow{a[i]}_{\text{a}} R' + S} \qquad (\text{Cho}^\bullet) \ \frac{R \dashrightarrow_{\text{a}}^{a[i]} R' \quad \text{npa}(S)}{R + S \dashrightarrow_{\text{a}}^{a[i]} R' + S}$$

$$(\text{Par}) \ \frac{R \xrightarrow{a[i]}_{\text{a}} R' \quad a \notin L \quad i \notin \text{keys}_{\text{a}}(S)}{R \,\|_L S \xrightarrow{a[i]}_{\text{a}} R' \,\|_L S} \quad (\text{Par}^\bullet) \ \frac{R \dashrightarrow_{\text{a}}^{a[i]} R' \quad a \notin L \quad i \notin \text{keys}_{\text{a}}(S)}{R \,\|_L S \dashrightarrow_{\text{a}}^{a[i]} R' \,\|_L S}$$

$$(\text{Coo}) \ \frac{R \xrightarrow{a[i]}_{\text{a}} R' \quad S \xrightarrow{a[i]}_{\text{a}} S' \quad a \in L}{R \,\|_L S \xrightarrow{a[i]}_{\text{a}} R' \,\|_L S'} \quad (\text{Coo}^\bullet) \ \frac{R \dashrightarrow_{\text{a}}^{a[i]} R' \quad S \dashrightarrow_{\text{a}}^{a[i]} S' \quad a \in L}{R \,\|_L S \dashrightarrow_{\text{a}}^{a[i]} R' \,\|_L S'}$$

that can be derived from the production for P in the same table. For example, $a \, . \, (5) \, . \, b \, . \, \underline{0}$ is a standard forward process that can perform action a, let 5 time units pass, and then execute b, while $a[i] \, . \, (5)^{[j]} \, . \, b \, . \, \underline{0}$ is a non-standard reversible process that can either go back by 5 time units and undo action a, or perform action b. Note that $a \, . \, (5)^{[j]} \, . \, b \, . \, \underline{0}$ and $a \, . \, (5) \, . \, b[j] \, . \, \underline{0}$ are not in $\mathcal{P}$ because a future action or delay cannot precede a past one in the description of a process.

Let $\mathcal{A}_\mathcal{K} = \mathcal{A} \times \mathcal{K}$ and $\mathbb{N}_\mathcal{K} = \mathbb{N}_{>0} \times \mathcal{K}$, with $\mathcal{L} = \mathcal{A}_\mathcal{K} \cup \mathbb{N}_\mathcal{K}$ ranged over by ℓ. Let $\delta(n,i)$ denote $(n)^{[i]}$ or $\langle n^i \rangle$, with the use of the latter being explained later and terms of the form $\langle n^i \rangle \, . \, R$ being added to the syntax thus yielding $\mathcal{P}'$. The semantics for RTPC is the labeled transition system $(\mathcal{P}', \mathcal{L}, \longmapsto)$. The transition relation $\longmapsto \, \subseteq \mathcal{P}' \times \mathcal{L} \times \mathcal{P}'$ is given by $\longmapsto \, = \longrightarrow \cup \dashrightarrow$ where in turn the *forward transition relation* is given by $\longrightarrow \, = \longrightarrow_{\text{a}} \cup \longrightarrow_{\text{d}}$ and the *backward transition relation* is given by $\dashrightarrow \, = \dashrightarrow_{\text{a}} \cup \dashrightarrow_{\text{d}}$. In the definitions of the transition relations, we make use of the set $\text{keys}_{\text{a}}(R)$ of action keys in a process $R \in \mathcal{P}'$:

$$\text{keys}_{\text{a}}(P) = \emptyset$$
$$\text{keys}_{\text{a}}(a[i] \, . \, R) = \{i\} \cup \text{keys}_{\text{a}}(R)$$
$$\text{keys}_{\text{a}}(\delta(n,i) \, . \, R) = \text{keys}_{\text{a}}(R)$$
$$\text{keys}_{\text{a}}(R + S) = \text{keys}_{\text{a}}(R) \cup \text{keys}_{\text{a}}(S)$$
$$\text{keys}_{\text{a}}(R \,\|_L S) = \text{keys}_{\text{a}}(R) \cup \text{keys}_{\text{a}}(S)$$

as well as of predicate $\text{npa}(\_)$ to establish whether the considered process $R \in \mathcal{P}'$ contains no past actions (note that $\text{std}(R)$ ensures $\text{npa}(R)$):

$$\begin{aligned}
\text{npa}(P) &= \texttt{true} \\
\text{npa}(a[i] \,.\, R) &= \texttt{false} \\
\text{npa}(\delta(n,i) \,.\, R) &= \text{npa}(R) \\
\text{npa}(R + S) &= \text{npa}(R) \wedge \text{npa}(S) \\
\text{npa}(R \,\|_L\, S) &= \text{npa}(R) \wedge \text{npa}(S)
\end{aligned}$$

The *action transition relations* $\longrightarrow_a \subseteq \mathcal{P}' \times \mathcal{A}_\mathcal{K} \times \mathcal{P}'$ and $\dashrightarrow_a \subseteq \mathcal{P}' \times \mathcal{A}_\mathcal{K} \times \mathcal{P}'$ are the least relations respectively induced by the forward rules in the left part of Table 2 and by the backward rules in the right part of the same table.

Rule ACT1 handles processes of the form $a \,.\, P$, where P is written as R subject to $\texttt{std}(R)$. In addition to transforming the action prefix into a transition label, it generates a key i that is bound to the action a thus yielding the label $a[i]$. As can be noted, according to [32] the prefix is not discarded by the application of the rule, instead it becomes a key-storing part of the target process that is necessary to offer again that action after coming back. Rule ACT1$^\bullet$ reverts the action $a[i]$ of the process $a[i] \,.\, R$ provided that R is a standard process, which ensures that $a[i]$ is the only past action that is left to undo.

The presence of rules ACT2 and ACT2$^\bullet$ is motivated by the fact that rule ACT1 does not discard the executed prefix from the process it generates. In particular, rule ACT2 allows a process $a[i] \,.\, R$ to execute if R itself can execute, provided that the action performed by R picks a key j different from i so that all the action prefixes in a sequence are decorated with distinct keys. Rule ACT2$^\bullet$ simply propagates the execution of backward actions from inner subprocesses that are not standard as long as key uniqueness is preserved, in such a way that past actions are overall undone from the most recent one to the least recent one. Rules ACT3 and ACT3$^\bullet$ play an analogous propagating role in a delay context; executed actions and elapsed delays are not required to feature different keys.

Unlike the classical rules for nondeterministic choice [28], according to [32] rule CHO does not discard the part of the overall process that has not contributed to the executed action. If process R does an action, say $a[i]$, and becomes R', then the entire process $R + S$ becomes $R' + S$ as the information about $+ S$ is necessary for offering again the original choice after coming back. Once the choice is made, only the non-standard process R' can proceed further, with process S – which is standard or contains past delays – constituting a dead context of R'. Note that, in order to apply rule CHO, at least one of R and S must contain no past actions, meaning that it is impossible for two processes containing past actions to execute if they are composed by a choice operator. Rule CHO$^\bullet$ has precisely the same structure as rule CHO, but deals with the backward transition relation; if R' is standard, then the dead context S will come into play again. The symmetric variants of CHO and CHO$^\bullet$, in which it is S to move, are omitted.

The semantics of parallel composition is inspired by [18]. Rule PAR allows process R within $R \,\|_L\, S$ to individually perform an action $a[i]$ provided $a \notin L$. It is also checked that the executing action is bound to a fresh key $i \notin \texttt{keys}_a(S)$, thus ensuring the uniqueness of communication keys across parallel composition too. Rule COO instead allows both R and S to move by synchronizing on any action in the set L as long as the communication key is the same on both sides, i.e., $i \in \mathsf{keys_a}(R') \cap \mathsf{keys_a}(S')$. The resulting cooperation action has the same name and the same key. Rules PAR$^\bullet$ and COO$^\bullet$ respectively have the same structure as PAR and COO. The symmetric variants of PAR and PAR$^\bullet$ are omitted.

To illustrate the need of communication keys, consider for instance the standard forward process $(a \, . \, P_1 \, \|_\emptyset \, a \, . \, P_2) \, \|_{\{a\}} (a \, . \, P_3 \, \|_\emptyset \, a \, . \, P_4)$, which may evolve to $(a[i] \, . \, P_1 \, \|_\emptyset \, a[j] \, . \, P_2) \, \|_{\{a\}} (a[i] \, . \, P_3 \, \|_\emptyset \, a[j] \, . \, P_4)$ after doing a forward $a[i]$-transition followed by a forward $a[j]$-transition. When going backward, in the absence of communication keys i and j we could not know that the a preceding P_1 (resp. P_2) synchronized with the a preceding P_3 (resp. P_4).

The *delay transition relations* $\longrightarrow_\mathrm{d} \subseteq \mathcal{P}' \times \mathbb{N}_\mathcal{K} \times \mathcal{P}'$ and $\dashrightarrow_\mathrm{d} \subseteq \mathcal{P}' \times \mathbb{N}_\mathcal{K} \times \mathcal{P}'$ are the least relations respectively induced by the forward rules in the left part of Table 3 and by the backward rules in the right part of the same table.

Rules IDLING1 and IDLING2 encode laziness: $\underline{0}$ can let time pass and every action can be delayed arbitrarily long. Rules IDLING1 and IDLING3 encode maximal progress: $\underline{0}$ can let time pass and every action other than τ can be delayed arbitrarily long. Rules IDLING1$^\bullet$, IDLING2$^\bullet$, and IDLING3$^\bullet$ play the corresponding roles in the backward direction; all the six rules are dropped under eagerness. Note that the three forward rules introduce a dynamic delay prefix $\langle n^i \rangle$ in the target process, which is then removed from the source process by the three backward rules. The need for $\langle n^i \rangle$ will be illustrated in Example 1.

The pairs of rules DELAY1 and DELAY1$^\bullet$, DELAY2 and DELAY2$^\bullet$, and DELAY3 and DELAY3$^\bullet$ are respectively the delay counterparts of the pairs of rules ACT1 and ACT1$^\bullet$, ACT2 and ACT2$^\bullet$, and ACT3 and ACT3$^\bullet$. We remind that executed actions and elapsed delays are allowed to share the same keys.

Rules TADD1 and TADD2 encode *time additivity* [29], i.e., several consecutive delays can jointly elapse as a single delay and, on the other hand, a single delay can be split into several shorter delays that elapse consecutively. Rules TADD1$^\bullet$ and TADD2$^\bullet$ play the corresponding roles in the backward direction.

Rules TCHO1 and TCOO encode time determinism. Time advances in the same way in the two subprocesses of a choice or a parallel composition, without making any decision. Rule TCHO2 is necessary for dealing with the case in which the nondeterministic choice has already been resolved due to the execution of an action by R. Rules TCHO1$^\bullet$, TCOO$^\bullet$, and TCHO2$^\bullet$ play the corresponding roles in the backward direction. The symmetric variants of TCHO2 and TCHO2$^\bullet$, in which it is S to move, are omitted.

To illustrate the need of communication keys also for delays, consider the standard forward process $(n) \, . \, \underline{0} \, \|_\emptyset (n) \, . \, \underline{0}$, which may evolve to $(n)^{[i]} . \, \underline{0} \, \|_\emptyset (n)^{[i]} . \, \underline{0}$ after that delay n has elapsed. When going backward under laziness or maximal progress, in the absence of key i it may happen that $\underline{0}$ in either subprocess lets n time units pass backward – due to IDLING1$^\bullet$ – with this pairing with undoing delay n in the other subprocess – due to DELAY1$^\bullet$ – which results in a process where one delay n can elapse forward again whereas the other one cannot. The presence of keys forces the idling of either $\underline{0}$ to synchronize with the idling of the other $\underline{0}$. The same situation would take place with $+$ in lieu of $\|_\emptyset$. In contrast,

Table 3. Structural operational semantic rules for RTPC delay transitions

(IDLING1) $\underline{0} \xrightarrow{(n)^{[i]}}_d \langle n^i \rangle . \underline{0}$	(IDLING1$^\bullet$) $\langle n^i \rangle . \underline{0} \dashrightarrow_d \underline{0}$ with $(n)^{[i]}$
(IDLING2) $\dfrac{\mathtt{std}(R)}{a . R \xrightarrow{(n)^{[i]}}_d \langle n^i \rangle . a . R}$	(IDLING2$^\bullet$) $\dfrac{\mathtt{std}(R)}{\langle n^i \rangle . a . R \overset{(n)^{[i]}}{\dashrightarrow}_d a . R}$
(IDLING3) $\dfrac{\mathtt{std}(R) \quad a \neq \tau}{a . R \xrightarrow{(n)^{[i]}}_d \langle n^i \rangle . a . R}$	(IDLING3$^\bullet$) $\dfrac{\mathtt{std}(R) \quad a \neq \tau}{\langle n^i \rangle . a . R \overset{(n)^{[i]}}{\dashrightarrow}_d a . R}$
(DELAY1) $\dfrac{\mathtt{std}(R)}{(n) . R \xrightarrow{(n)^{[i]}}_d (n)^{[i]} . R}$	(DELAY1$^\bullet$) $\dfrac{\mathtt{std}(R)}{(n)^{[i]} . R \overset{(n)^{[i]}}{\dashrightarrow}_d (n) . R}$
(DELAY2) $\dfrac{R \xrightarrow{(n)^{[j]}}_d R'}{a[i] . R \xrightarrow{(n)^{[j]}}_d a[i] . R'}$	(DELAY2$^\bullet$) $\dfrac{R \overset{(n)^{[j]}}{\dashrightarrow}_d R'}{a[i] . R \overset{(n)^{[j]}}{\dashrightarrow}_d a[i] . R'}$
(DELAY3) $\dfrac{R \xrightarrow{(m)^{[j]}}_d R' \quad j \neq i}{\delta(n,i) . R \xrightarrow{(m)^{[j]}}_d \delta(n,i) . R'}$	(DELAY3$^\bullet$) $\dfrac{R \overset{(m)^{[j]}}{\dashrightarrow}_d R' \quad j \neq i}{\delta(n,i) . R \overset{(m)^{[j]}}{\dashrightarrow}_d \delta(n,i) . R'}$
(TADD1) $\dfrac{R \xrightarrow{(m)^{[j]}}_d R' \quad \mathtt{std}(R) \quad j \neq i}{(n) . R \xrightarrow{(n+m)^{[i]}}_d (n)^{[i]} . R'}$	(TADD1$^\bullet$) $\dfrac{R \overset{(m)^{[j]}}{\dashrightarrow}_d R' \quad \mathtt{std}(R') \quad j \neq i}{(n)^{[i]} . R \overset{(n+m)^{[i]}}{\dashrightarrow}_d (n) . R'}$
(TADD2) $\dfrac{\mathtt{std}(R) \quad n = n_1 + n_2}{(n) . R \xrightarrow{(n_1)^{[i]}}_d (n_1)^{[i]} . (n_2) . R}$	(TADD2$^\bullet$) $\dfrac{\mathtt{std}(R) \quad n = n_1 + n_2}{(n_1)^{[i]} . (n_2) . R \overset{(n_1)^{[i]}}{\dashrightarrow}_d (n) . R}$
(TCHO1) $\dfrac{R \xrightarrow{(n)^{[i]}}_d R' \quad S \xrightarrow{(n)^{[i]}}_d S'}{\mathtt{npa}(R + S)}{R + S \xrightarrow{(n)^{[i]}}_d R' + S'}$	(TCHO1$^\bullet$) $\dfrac{R \overset{(n)^{[i]}}{\dashrightarrow}_d R' \quad S \overset{(n)^{[i]}}{\dashrightarrow}_d S'}{\mathtt{npa}(R + S)}{R + S \overset{(n)^{[i]}}{\dashrightarrow}_d R' + S'}$
(TCHO2) $\dfrac{R \xrightarrow{(n)^{[i]}}_d R'}{\neg\mathtt{npa}(R) \quad \mathtt{npa}(S)}{R + S \xrightarrow{(n)^{[i]}}_d R' + S}$	(TCHO2$^\bullet$) $\dfrac{R \overset{(n)^{[i]}}{\dashrightarrow}_d R'}{\neg\mathtt{npa}(R) \quad \mathtt{npa}(S)}{R + S \overset{(n)^{[i]}}{\dashrightarrow}_d R' + S}$
(TCOO) $\dfrac{R \xrightarrow{(n)^{[i]}}_d R' \quad S \xrightarrow{(n)^{[i]}}_d S'}{R \,\|_L\, S \xrightarrow{(n)^{[i]}}_d R' \,\|_L\, S'}$	(TCOO$^\bullet$) $\dfrac{R \overset{(n)^{[i]}}{\dashrightarrow}_d R' \quad S \overset{(n)^{[i]}}{\dashrightarrow}_d S'}{R \,\|_L\, S \overset{(n)^{[i]}}{\dashrightarrow}_d R' \,\|_L\, S'}$

the problem does not show up under eagerness. In that case, elapsed delays can be uniformly decorated, for example with † like in [5].

Process syntax prevents future actions or delays from preceding past ones. However, this is not the only necessary limitation, because not all the processes generated by the considered grammar are semantically meaningful. On the one hand, in the case of a choice at least one of the two subprocesses has to contain no past actions, hence for instance $a[i] . \underline{0} + b[j] . \underline{0}$ is not admissible as it indicates that both branches have been selected. On the other hand, key uniqueness must be enforced within processes containing past actions, so for example $a[i] . b[i] . \underline{0}$ and $a[i] . \underline{0} \parallel_{\emptyset} b[i] . \underline{0}$ are not admissible either.

In the following we thus consider only *reachable processes*, whose set we denote by $\mathbb{P}$. They include processes from which a computation can start, i.e., standard forward processes, as well as processes that can be derived from the previous ones via finitely many applications of the semantic rules. Given a reachable process $R \in \mathbb{P}$, if $\mathrm{npa}(R)$ then $\mathrm{keys}_a(R) = \emptyset$ while $\mathrm{keys}_a(R') \neq \emptyset$ for any other process R' reachable from R in which at least one of the actions occurring in R has been executed, as that action has been equipped with a key inside R'.

We conclude by showing the validity of time determinism and time additivity. The former holds in the forward direction up to the keys associated with the considered delay, which is formalized via syntactical substitutions of delay keys, because DELAY1 creates a fresh key (whereas DELAY1$^\bullet$ uses the existing one). As for the latter, two distinct processes may be reached in the forward direction because elapsed delays are kept within processes. This is illustrated in Fig. 1 by the 2-delay forward transition on the right and the two consecutive 1-delay forward transitions on the left. Dually, in the backward direction, the starting processes may be different, as exemplified by the 2-delay backward transition on the right and the two consecutive 1-delay backward transitions on the left.

Proposition 1 (time determinism). *Let $R, S_1, S_2 \in \mathbb{P}$, $n \in \mathbb{N}_{>0}$, $i_1, i_2 \in \mathcal{K}$, and $j \in \mathcal{K}$ be not occurring associated with past delays in S_1 and S_2. Then:*

- *If $R \xrightarrow{(n)^{[i_1]}}_d S_1$ and $R \xrightarrow{(n)^{[i_2]}}_d S_2$, then $S_1\{^j/_{i_1}\} = S_2\{^j/_{i_2}\}$.*
- *If $R \dashrightarrow^{(n)^{[i_1]}}_d S_1$ and $R \dashrightarrow^{(n)^{[i_2]}}_d S_2$, then $S_1 = S_2$.* ∎

Proposition 2 (time additivity). *Let $R, R', S, S' \in \mathbb{P}$, $n, h \in \mathbb{N}_{>0}$, $i \in \mathcal{K}$, and $m_1, \ldots, m_h \in \mathbb{N}_{>0}$ be such that $\sum_{1 \leq l \leq h} m_l = n$. Then:*

- *$R \xrightarrow{(n)^{[i]}}_d S$ iff $R \xrightarrow{(m_1)^{[i_1]}}_d \cdots \xrightarrow{(m_h)^{[i_h]}}_d S'$.*
- *$R \dashrightarrow^{(n)^{[i]}}_d S$ iff $R' \dashrightarrow^{(m_1)^{[i_1]}}_d \cdots \dashrightarrow^{(m_h)^{[i_h]}}_d S$.* ∎

3   Causal Reversibility of RTPC

We now prove the causal reversibility of RTPC. This means that each reachable process of RTPC is able to backtrack *correctly*, i.e., without encountering previously inaccessible states, and *flexibly*, i.e., along any path that is causally equivalent to the one undertaken in the forward direction. This is accomplished through the notion of concurrent transitions of [12] and the technique of [25].

A necessary condition for reversibility is the *loop property* [12,32,25]. It establishes that each executed action can be undone and that each undone action can be redone, which in a timed setting needs to be extended to delays. Therefore, when considering the states associated with two arbitrary reachable processes,

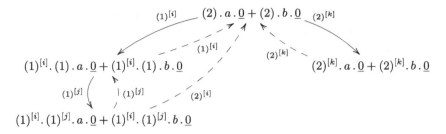

Fig. 1. Time additivity and loop property (only delay transitions are depicted)

either there is no transition between them, or there is a pair of identically labeled transitions such that one is a forward transition from the first to the second state while the other is a backward transition from the second to the first state.

To be precise, due to time additivity, a delay transition in one direction may be matched by a sequence of delay transitions in the opposite direction, such that the label of the former is equal to the sum of the labels of the latter. This can be seen in Fig. 1. Each of the four 1-delay transitions on the left and of the two 2-delay transitions on the right is matched by a single identically labeled delay transition in the opposite direction, whereas the 2-delay backward transition on the left is matched only by a sequence of two 1-delay forward transitions.

Proposition 3 (loop property). *Let $R, S \in \mathbb{P}$, $a[i], (n)^{[i]} \in \mathcal{L}$, $h \in \mathbb{N}_{>0}$, and $m_1, \ldots, m_h \in \mathbb{N}_{>0}$ be such that $\sum_{1 \leq l \leq h} m_l = n$. Then:*

- $R \xrightarrow{a[i]}_{\mathsf{a}} S$ *iff* $S \dashrightarrow^{a[i]}_{\mathsf{a}} R$.
- *If* $R \xrightarrow{(n)^{[i]}}_{\mathsf{d}} S$ *then* $S \dashrightarrow^{(n)^{[i]}}_{\mathsf{d}} R$.
- $R \xrightarrow{(n)^{[i]}}_{\mathsf{d}} S$ *iff* $S \dashrightarrow^{(m_1)^{[i_1]}}_{\mathsf{d}} \ldots \dashrightarrow^{(m_h)^{[i_h]}}_{\mathsf{d}} R$.
- $R \dashrightarrow^{(n)^{[i]}}_{\mathsf{d}} S$ *iff* $S \xrightarrow{(m_1)^{[i_1]}}_{\mathsf{d}} \ldots \xrightarrow{(m_h)^{[i_h]}}_{\mathsf{d}} R$. ■

Given a transition $\theta : R \xmapsto{\ell} S$ with $R, S \in \mathbb{P}$, we call R the *source* of θ and S its *target*. If θ is a forward transition, i.e., $\theta : R \xrightarrow{\ell} S$, we denote by $\bar{\theta} : S \dashrightarrow^{\ell} R$ the corresponding backward transition. Two transitions are said to be *coinitial* if they have the same source and *cofinal* if they have the same target. Two transitions are *composable* when the target of the first transition coincides with the source of the second transition. A finite sequence of pairwise composable transitions is called a *path*. We use ϵ for the empty path and ω to range over paths, with $|\omega|$ denoting the length of ω, i.e., the number of transitions constituting ω. When ω is a forward path, we denote by $\bar{\omega}$ the corresponding backward path, where the order of the transitions is reversed, and by $\mathtt{time}(\omega)$ the duration of ω, i.e., the sum of the labels of its delay transitions. The notions of source, target, coinitiality, cofinality, and composability naturally extend to paths. We indicate with $\omega_1 \omega_2$ the composition of the two paths ω_1 and ω_2 when they are composable.

Before specifying when two transitions are concurrent [12], we need to present the notion of process context along with the set of causes – identified by action keys – that lead to a given communication key for actions.

A *process context* is a process with a hole • in it, generated by the grammar:

$$\mathcal{C} ::= \bullet \mid a[i].\mathcal{C} \mid (n)^{[i]}.\mathcal{C} \mid \langle n^i \rangle.\mathcal{C} \mid R + \mathcal{C} \mid \mathcal{C} + R \mid R \parallel_L \mathcal{C} \mid \mathcal{C} \parallel_L R$$

We write $\mathcal{C}[R]$ to denote the process obtained by replacing the hole in $\mathcal{C}$ with R. The *causal set* $\mathsf{cau}_a(R, i)$ of $R \in \mathbb{P}$ until $i \in \mathcal{K}$ is inductively defined as:

$$\mathsf{cau}_a(P, i) = \emptyset$$

$$\mathsf{cau}_a(a[j].R, i) = \begin{cases} \emptyset & \text{if } j = i \text{ or } i \notin \mathsf{keys}_a(R) \\ \{j\} \cup \mathsf{cau}_a(R, i) & \text{otherwise} \end{cases}$$

$$\mathsf{cau}_a(\delta(n, j).R, i) = \mathsf{cau}_a(R, i)$$

$$\mathsf{cau}_a(R + S, i) = \mathsf{cau}_a(R, i) \cup \mathsf{cau}_a(S, i)$$

$$\mathsf{cau}_a(R \parallel_L S, i) = \mathsf{cau}_a(R, i) \cup \mathsf{cau}_a(S, i)$$

If $i \in \mathsf{keys}_a(R)$, then $\mathsf{cau}_a(R, i)$ represents the set of keys in R that caused i, with $\mathsf{cau}_a(R, i) \subset \mathsf{keys}_a(R)$ as on the one hand $i \notin \mathsf{cau}_a(R, i)$ and on the other hand keys that are not causally related to i are not considered. A key j causes i if it appears syntactically before i in R; equivalently, i is inside the scope of j.

We are now in a position to define, for coinitial transitions, what we mean by concurrent transitions on the basis of the notion of conflicting transitions. As in previous works, the first condition below tells that a forward action transition is in conflict with a coinitial backward one whenever the latter tries to undo a cause of the key of the former, while the second one deems as conflictual two action transitions respectively generated by the two subprocesses of a choice.

The further conditions are specific to this timed setting. The third one views as conflictual two coinitial delay transitions, regardless of their directions. The fourth one considers as conflictual a forward action transition and a forward delay transition that are coinitial, whereas a similar situation cannot show up in the backward direction because, if a delay can be undone in all subprocesses, then no action can be undone (both cases will be illustrated in Example 1). The fifth one regards as conflictual a forward delay transition and a backward action transition that are coinitial and originated from the same subprocess. In the sixth one the action transition is forward and the delay transition is backward. Figure 2 illustrates the first and the fifth ones.

Definition 1 (conflicting and concurrent transitions). *Two coinitial transitions θ_1 and θ_2 from a process $R \in \mathbb{P}$ are* in conflict *if one of the following conditions holds, otherwise they are said to be* concurrent:

1. $\theta_1 : R \xrightarrow{a[i]}_a S_1$ and $\theta_2 : R \dashrightarrow^{b[j]}_a S_2$ with $j \in \mathsf{cau}_a(S_1, i)$.

2. $R = \mathcal{C}[P_1 + P_2]$ with θ_k deriving from $P_k \xrightarrow{a_k[i_k]}_a S_k$ for $k = 1, 2$.

3. $\theta_1 : R \xmapsto{(n)^i}_d S_1$ and $\theta_2 : R \xmapsto{(m)^j}_d S_2$.

4. $\theta_1 : R \xrightarrow{a[i]}_a S_1$ and $\theta_2 : R \xrightarrow{(m)^j}_d S_2$.

5. $R = \mathcal{C}[a[i].(n).P]$ with θ_1 deriving from $(n).P \xrightarrow{(m)^{[j]}}_d S_1$ and θ_2 deriving from $a[i].(n).P \dashrightarrow^{a[i]}_a S_2$.

Fig. 2. Examples of conflicting transitions: conditions 1 (left) and 5 (right)

6. $R = \mathcal{C}[\delta(n,i).a.P]$ with θ_1 deriving from $a.P \xrightarrow{a[j]}_a S_1$ and θ_2 deriving from $\delta(n,i).a.P \xdashrightarrow{(n)^{[i]}}_d S_2$. ∎

We prove causal reversibility by exploiting the technique of [25], according to which causal consistency stems from the *square property* – which amounts to concurrent transitions being confluent – *backward transitions independence* – which generalizes the concept of backward determinism used for reversible sequential languages [42] – and *past well foundedness* – which ensures that reachable processes have a finite past.

We start with the square property, which states that concurrent transitions can commute while conflicting ones cannot.

Lemma 1 (square property). *Let* $\theta_1 : R \xmapsto{\ell_1} S_1$ *and Let* $\theta_2 : R \xmapsto{\ell_2} S_2$ *be two coinitial transitions from a process* $R \in \mathbb{P}$. *If* θ_1 *and* θ_2 *are concurrent, then there exist two cofinal transitions* $\theta'_2 : S_1 \xmapsto{\ell_2} S$ *and* $\theta'_1 : S_2 \xmapsto{\ell_1} S$ *with* $S \in \mathbb{P}$. ∎

Unlike [25], backward transitions independence holds as long as at least one of the two coinitial backward transitions is not a delay transition.

Lemma 2 (backward transitions independence). *Let* $R \in \mathbb{P}$. *Then two coinitial backward transitions* $\theta_1 : R \xdashleftarrow{\ell_1} S_1$ *and* $\theta_2 : R \xdashleftarrow{\ell_2} S_2$ *are concurrent provided that at least one of them is not a delay transition.* ∎

For coinitial backward delay transitions, the novel *backward triangularity* property comes into play, which is exemplified by the backward delay transitions in the left part of Fig. 1.

Lemma 3 (backward triangularity). *Let* $R \in \mathbb{P}$. *Whenever* $R \xdashrightarrow{(n)^{[i]}}_d S_1$ *and* $R \xdashrightarrow{(m)^{[j]}}_d S_2$ *with* $m > n$, *then* $S_1 \xdashrightarrow{(m-n)^{[k]}}_d S_2$. ∎

As far as past well foundedness is concerned, under laziness and maximal progress we observe that the adoption of the dynamic delay prefix $\langle n^i \rangle$ in rules IDLING1, IDLING2, IDLING3, IDLING1•, IDLING2•, IDLING3• avoids the generation of backward self-loops, from which infinite sequence of backward transitions would be obtained.

Lemma 4 (past well foundedness). *Let* $R_0 \in \mathbb{P}$. *Then there is no infinite sequence of backward transitions such that* $R_i \xdashrightarrow{\ell_i} R_{i+1}$ *for all* $i \in \mathbb{N}$. ∎

Following [12,27], we also define a notion of *causal equivalence* over paths, which abstracts from the order of concurrent action transitions. In this way, paths obtained by swapping the order of their concurrent action transitions are identified with each other. Due to time determinism, the swap operation does not apply to delay transitions. Moreover, the composition of a transition with its inverse is identified with the empty path. Unlike other approaches, our causal equivalence has to deal with time additivity. More precisely, a path made out of forward (resp. backward) delay transitions followed by a path made out of backward (resp. forward) delay transitions returning to the origin is identified with the empty path provided that the two original paths have the same duration. This can be seen in Fig. 1 if we take for example the delay path on the left $\xrightarrow{\quad(1)^{[i]}\quad}_d \xrightarrow{\quad(1)^{[j]}\quad}_d \dashrightarrow_d^{(2)^{[i]}}$.

Definition 2 (causal equivalence). *Causal equivalence $\asymp$ is the smallest equivalence relation over paths that is closed under composition and satisfies the following:*

1. *$\theta_1 \theta_2' \asymp \theta_2 \theta_1'$ for every two coinitial concurrent action transitions $\theta_1 : R \xmapsto{a[i]} R_1$ and $\theta_2 : R \xmapsto{b[j]} R_2$ and every two cofinal action transitions $\theta_2' : R_1 \xmapsto{b[j]} S$ and $\theta_1' : R_2 \xmapsto{a[i]} S$ respectively composable with the previous ones.*
2. *$\theta\overline{\theta} \asymp \epsilon$ and $\overline{\theta}\theta \asymp \epsilon$ for every transition θ.*
3. *$\omega_1\overline{\omega_2} \asymp \epsilon$ and $\overline{\omega_2}\omega_1 \asymp \epsilon$ for every two coinitial and cofinal forward paths ω_1 and ω_2 with delay transitions only such that $\mathtt{time}(\omega_1) = \mathtt{time}(\omega_2)$.* ∎

The further property below, called *parabolic lemma* in [25], states that every path can be seen as a backward path followed by a forward path. As observed in [12], up to causal equivalence one can always reach for the maximum freedom of choice among transitions by going backward and only then going forward (not the other way around). Intuitively, one could depict computations as parabolas: the system first draws potential energy from its memory, by undoing all the executed actions, and then restarts.

In this timed setting the parabolic lemma has to be proven directly. Unlike [25], it does not stem from the square property and backward transitions independence as the latter does not hold for all coinitial backward transitions.

Lemma 5 (parabolic lemma). *For each path ω, there exist two forward paths ω_1 and ω_2 such that $\omega \asymp \overline{\omega_1}\omega_2$ and $|\omega_1| + |\omega_2| \leq |\omega|$.* ∎

Example 1. If rules IDLING1, IDLING2, IDLING3, IDLING1•, IDLING2•, IDLING3• did not respectively introduce and retract dynamic delay prefixes of the form $\langle n^i \rangle$, then the parabolic lemma would not hold.

Consider the process $R = a \cdot (n) \cdot \underline{0} \, \| \, _\emptyset (n) \cdot \underline{0}$. Under eagerness it can initially perform only $R \xrightarrow{a[i]}_a a[i] \cdot (n) \cdot \underline{0} \, \| \, _\emptyset (n) \cdot \underline{0} = S_1$. Under laziness it can also perform $R \xrightarrow{(n)^{[j]}}_d \langle n^j \rangle \cdot a \cdot (n) \cdot \underline{0} \, \| \, _\emptyset (n)^{[j]} \cdot \underline{0} = S_2$ because in R the execution of action a on the left can be postponed via IDLING2 by as many time units as there are in delay (n) on the right where DELAY1 applies, then TCOO is used.

If we keep going forward, we obtain $S_1 \xrightarrow{(n)^{[j]}}_d a[i] \cdot (n)^{[j]} \cdot \underline{0} \parallel_\emptyset (n)^{[j]} \cdot \underline{0} = S_1'$ while on the lazy side $S_2 \xrightarrow{a[i]}_a \langle n^j \rangle \cdot a[i] \cdot (n) \cdot \underline{0} \parallel_\emptyset (n)^{[j]} \cdot \underline{0} = S_2'$ followed by $S_2' \xrightarrow{(n)^{[k]}}_d \langle n^j \rangle \cdot a[i] \cdot (n)^{[k]} \cdot \underline{0} \parallel_\emptyset (n)^{[j]} \cdot \langle n^k \rangle \cdot \underline{0} = S_2''$ because in S_2' the subprocess $\underline{0}$ on the right can let via IDLING1 as many time units pass as there are in delay (n) on the left. Note that the square property does not hold because S_1' and S_2'' are different. Indeed, the two initial transitions of R are in conflict according to condition 4 of Definition 1; moreover, from S_1' delay $(n)^{[j]}$ can be undone, whereas action $a[i]$ cannot.

When going backward, by virtue of the presence of dynamic delays $\langle n^j \rangle$ and $\langle n^k \rangle$ all the transitions above are undone in the reverse order and the same states are traversed thanks to IDLING1$^\bullet$ and IDLING2$^\bullet$. However, if dynamic delays were not adopted by the aforementioned idling rules, so that on the lazy side we would end up in $a[i] \cdot (n)^{[k]} \cdot \underline{0} \parallel_\emptyset (n)^{[j]} \cdot \underline{0}$, then, observing that $(n)^{[k]}$ and $(n)^{[j]}$ have different keys and hence cannot be undone together via TCOO$^\bullet$, either $(n)^{[k]}$ is undone via IDLING1$^\bullet$ applied to the subprocess $\underline{0}$ on the right, or $(n)^{[j]}$ is undone via IDLING1$^\bullet$ applied to the subprocess $\underline{0}$ on the left. In the latter case, the new state $a[i] \cdot (n)^{[k]} \cdot \underline{0} \parallel_\emptyset (n) \cdot \underline{0}$ is encountered, from which it is only possible to redo $(n)^{[j]}$ via IDLING1 applied to the subprocess $\underline{0}$ on the left; note that $(n)^{[k]}$ cannot be undone because $(n) \cdot \underline{0}$ cannot let time pass backward.

The presence of this new state would violate the parabolic lemma. In particular, the path traversing R, S_2, S_2', S_2'', and the new state could not be causally equivalent to anyone composed of a backward path followed by a forward one. ∎

We conclude by obtaining a property called *causal consistency* in [25], which establishes that being coinitial and cofinal is necessary and sufficient in order for two paths to be causally equivalent, i.e., to contain concurrent action transitions in different orders (swap) or to be one the empty path and the other a transition followed by its reverse or a delay path followed by an identically lasting delay path in the reverse direction (cancelation).

Theorem 1 (causal consistency). *Let ω_1 and ω_2 be two paths. Then $\omega_1 \asymp \omega_2$ iff ω_1 and ω_2 are both coinitial and cofinal.* ∎

Theorem 1 shows that causal equivalence characterizes a space for admissible rollbacks that are (i) correct as they do not lead to states not reachable by some forward path and (ii) flexible enough to allow on the one hand undo operations to be rearranged with respect to the order in which the undone concurrent action transitions were originally performed and on the other hand time additivity to be taken into account. This implies that the states reached by any backward path could be reached by performing forward paths only. Therefore, we can conclude that RTPC meets causal reversibility.

Example 2. Following [29] we can define the timeout operator TIMEOUT(P, Q, t). It allows the process P to communicate with the environment within t time units. After this time has passed, and P has not communicated yet, the process Q takes control. The operator is rendered in RTPC as $\text{TIMEOUT}(P,Q,t) = P + (t)\,.\,\tau\,.\,Q$ under maximal progress.

Timeouts are usually employed in fault-tolerant systems to prevent some operations from blocking forever. As a matter of fact, the Erlang programming language provides a timeout facility on blocking receive. For example, let us consider the following snippet of Erlang code in which two actors (e.g., processes) execute in parallel:

```
1  process_A () ->              7  process_B (Pid) ->
2     receive                   8     timer:sleep(100),
3        X -> handleMsg()       9     Pid! Msg    end.
4     after 50 ->              10
5        handleTimeout()       11  PidA=spawn(?MODULE, process_A', []),
6     end end.                 12  spawn(?MODULE, process_B , [PidA]).
```

Process A (lines 1–6) awaits a message from the environment (e.g., from process B); if a message is received within 50 ms, then process A calls function handleMsg(), otherwise it calls function handleTimeout(). Process B (lines 7–9) sleeps for 100 ms and then sends a message to Pid, the identifier of process A.

The translation of the code for the two processes into RTPC is as follows:

$$A = \text{TIMEOUT}(a\,.\,P, Q, 50)$$
$$B = (100)\,.\,a\,.\,\underline{0}$$

where P encodes handleMsg() and Q encodes handleTimeout().

If we run the two processes in parallel (mimicking lines 11–12), we have the following forward execution under maximal progress:

$$A \parallel_{\{a\}} B \xrightarrow{\ (50)^{[i]}\ }_{\text{d}} (a\,.\,P + (50)^{[i]}\,.\,\tau\,.\,Q) \parallel_{\{a\}} ((50)^{[i]}\,.\,(50)\,.\,a\,.\,\underline{0})$$
$$\xrightarrow{\ \tau[j]\ }_{\text{a}} (a\,.\,P + (50)^{[i]}\,.\,\tau[j]\,.\,Q) \parallel_{\{a\}} ((50)^{[i]}\,.\,(50)\,.\,a\,.\,\underline{0})$$

at which point Q takes over. If process B wants to revert its behavior (e.g., going back by 50 ms), it cannot do it alone as it has to wait for process A to first undo $\tau[j]$ and then undo $(50)^{[i]}$ together. This is clearly a causally consistent backward computation as no new process is encountered along the way. ∎

4 Conclusions

In this paper we have studied the causal reversibility of timed process calculi. With respect to the reversible nondeterministic setting of [12,32,25], we have addressed a number of issues that are listed at the end of Sect. 1. With respect to the reversible timed setting of [8], which builds on TPL [17], we have considered not only laziness but also eagerness and, most importantly, like in temporal CCS [29] we have described time via numeric delays – instead of unitary delays – subject to time additivity, which results in a variation of the loop property and a restriction of backward transitions independence.

As future work, we plan to investigate suitable notions of bisimilarity for RTPC based on the approaches of [32,14,6]. Moreover, similar to [5], we would like to allow backward delays to be different from the corresponding forward delays. Finally, we are interested in moving from discrete time to dense time.

Acknowledgments. This work has been supported by the Italian MUR PRIN 2020 project *NiRvAna*, the French ANR project ANR-18-CE25-0007 *DCore*, and the INdAM-GNCS project CUP_E55F22000270001 *Proprietà Qualitative e Quantitative di Sistemi Reversibili*.

References

1. Aceto, L., Murphy, D.: Timing and causality in process algebra. Acta Informatica **33**, 317–350 (1996)
2. Baeten, J.C.M., Bergstra, J.A.: Real time process algebra. Formal Aspects Comput. **3**, 142–188 (1991)
3. Bennett, C.H.: Logical reversibility of computations. IBM J. Res. Dev. **17**, 525–532 (1973)
4. Bernardo, M., Corradini, F., Tesei, L.: Timed process calculi with deterministic or stochastic delays: commuting between durational and durationless actions. Theoret. Comput. Sci. **629**, 2–39 (2016)
5. Bernardo, M., Mezzina, C.A.: Bridging causal reversibility and time reversibility: a stochastic process algebraic approach. Logical Methods Comput. Sci. **19**(2:6), 1–27 (2023)
6. Bernardo, M., Rossi, S.: Reverse bisimilarity vs. forward bisimilarity. In: Proceedings of the 26th International Conference on Foundations of Software Science and Computation Structures (FOSSACS 2023). LNCS, vol. 13992, pp. 265–284. Springer (2023). https://doi.org/10.1007/978-3-031-30829-1_13
7. Bérut, A., Arakelyan, A., Petrosyan, A., Ciliberto, S., Dillenschneider, R., Lutz, E.: Experimental verification of Landauer's principle linking information and thermodynamics. Nature **483**, 187–189 (2012)
8. Bocchi, L., Lanese, I., Mezzina, C.A., Yuen, S.: The reversible temporal process language. In: Proceedings of the 42nd International Conference on Formal Techniques for Distributed Objects, Components, and Systems (FORTE 2022). LNCS, vol. 13273, pp. 31–49. Springer (2022). https://doi.org/10.1007/978-3-031-08679-3_3
9. Bolognesi, T., Lucidi, F.: LOTOS-like process algebras with urgent or timed interactions. In: Proceedings of the 4th International Conference on Formal Description Techniques for Distributed Systems and Communication Protocols (FORTE 1991). IFIP Transactions, vol. C-2, pp. 249–264 (1991)
10. Corradini, F.: Absolute versus relative time in process algebras. Inf. Comput. **156**, 122–172 (2000)
11. Corradini, F., Vogler, W., Jenner, L.: Comparing the worst-case efficiency of asynchronous systems with PAFAS. Acta Informatica **38**, 735–792 (2002)
12. Danos, V., Krivine, J.: Reversible communicating systems. In: Gardner, P., Yoshida, N. (eds.) CONCUR 2004. LNCS, vol. 3170, pp. 292–307. Springer, Heidelberg (2004). https://doi.org/10.1007/978-3-540-28644-8_19
13. Danos, V., Krivine, J.: Transactions in RCCS. In: Abadi, M., de Alfaro, L. (eds.) CONCUR 2005. LNCS, vol. 3653, pp. 398–412. Springer, Heidelberg (2005). https://doi.org/10.1007/11539452_31
14. De Nicola, R., Montanari, U., Vaandrager, F.: Back and forth bisimulations. In: Baeten, J.C.M., Klop, J.W. (eds.) CONCUR 1990. LNCS, vol. 458, pp. 152–165. Springer, Heidelberg (1990). https://doi.org/10.1007/BFb0039058

15. Frank, M.P.: Physical foundations of Landauer's principle. In: Kari, J., Ulidowski, I. (eds.) RC 2018. LNCS, vol. 11106, pp. 3–33. Springer, Cham (2018). https://doi.org/10.1007/978-3-319-99498-7_1

16. Giachino, E., Lanese, I., Mezzina, C.A.: Causal-consistent reversible debugging. In: Gnesi, S., Rensink, A. (eds.) FASE 2014. LNCS, vol. 8411, pp. 370–384. Springer, Heidelberg (2014). https://doi.org/10.1007/978-3-642-54804-8_26

17. Hennessy, M., Regan, T.: A process algebra for timed systems. Inf. Comput. **117**, 221–239 (1995)

18. Hoare, C.A.R.: Communicating Sequential Processes. Prentice Hall (1985)

19. Kelly, F.P.: Reversibility and Stochastic Networks. John Wiley & Sons (1979)

20. Krivine, J.: A verification technique for reversible process algebra. In: Glück, R., Yokoyama, T. (eds.) RC 2012. LNCS, vol. 7581, pp. 204–217. Springer, Heidelberg (2013). https://doi.org/10.1007/978-3-642-36315-3_17

21. Landauer, R.: Irreversibility and heat generated in the computing process. IBM J. Res. Dev. **5**, 183–191 (1961)

22. Lanese, I., Lienhardt, M., Mezzina, C.A., Schmitt, A., Stefani, J.-B.: Concurrent flexible reversibility. In: Felleisen, M., Gardner, P. (eds.) ESOP 2013. LNCS, vol. 7792, pp. 370–390. Springer, Heidelberg (2013). https://doi.org/10.1007/978-3-642-37036-6_21

23. Lanese, I., Medić, D., Mezzina, C.A.: Static versus dynamic reversibility in CCS. Acta Informatica **58**, 1–34 (2021)

24. Lanese, I., Nishida, N., Palacios, A., Vidal, G.: CauDEr: a causal-consistent reversible debugger for Erlang. In: Proceedings of the 14th International Symposium on Functional and Logic Programming (FLOPS 2018). LNCS, vol. 10818, pp. 247–263. Springer (2018). https://doi.org/10.1007/978-3-319-90686-7_16

25. Lanese, I., Phillips, I., Ulidowski, I.: An axiomatic approach to reversible computation. In: FoSSaCS 2020. LNCS, vol. 12077, pp. 442–461. Springer, Cham (2020). https://doi.org/10.1007/978-3-030-45231-5_23

26. Laursen, J.S., Ellekilde, L.P., Schultz, U.P.: Modelling reversible execution of robotic assembly. Robotica **36**, 625–654 (2018)

27. Lévy, J.J.: An algebraic interpretation of the $\lambda\beta K$-calculus; and an application of a labelled λ-calculus. Theoret. Comput. Sci. **2**, 97–114 (1976)

28. Milner, R.: Communication and Concurrency. Prentice Hall (1989)

29. Moller, F., Tofts, C.: A temporal calculus of communicating systems. In: Baeten, J.C.M., Klop, J.W. (eds.) CONCUR 1990. LNCS, vol. 458, pp. 401–415. Springer, Heidelberg (1990). https://doi.org/10.1007/BFb0039073

30. Nicollin, X., Sifakis, J.: The algebra of timed processes ATP: theory and application. Inf. Comput. **114**, 131–178 (1994)

31. Perumalla, K.S., Park, A.J.: Reverse computation for rollback-based fault tolerance in large parallel systems - evaluating the potential gains and systems effects. Clust. Comput. **17**, 303–313 (2014)

32. Phillips, I., Ulidowski, I.: Reversing algebraic process calculi. J. Logic Algebraic Program. **73**, 70–96 (2007)

33. Phillips, I., Ulidowski, I., Yuen, S.: A reversible process calculus and the modelling of the ERK signalling pathway. In: Glück, R., Yokoyama, T. (eds.) RC 2012. LNCS, vol. 7581, pp. 218–232. Springer, Heidelberg (2013). https://doi.org/10.1007/978-3-642-36315-3_18

34. Pinna, G.M.: Reversing steps in membrane systems computations. In: Gheorghe, M., Rozenberg, G., Salomaa, A., Zandron, C. (eds.) CMC 2017. LNCS, vol. 10725, pp. 245–261. Springer, Cham (2018). https://doi.org/10.1007/978-3-319-73359-3_16

35. Quemada, J., de Frutos, D., Azcorra, A.: TIC: a timed calculus. Formal Aspects Comput. **5**, 224–252 (1993)
36. Reed, G.M., Roscoe, A.W.: A timed model for communicating sequential processes. Theoret. Comput. Sci. **58**, 249–261 (1988)
37. Schordan, M., Oppelstrup, T., Jefferson, D.R., Barnes, P.D., Jr.: Generation of reversible C++ code for optimistic parallel discrete event simulation. N. Gener. Comput. **36**, 257–280 (2018)
38. Siljak, H., Psara, K., Philippou, A.: Distributed antenna selection for massive MIMO using reversing Petri nets. IEEE Wireless Commun. Lett. **8**, 1427–1430 (2019)
39. Vassor, M., Stefani, J.-B.: Checkpoint/rollback vs causally-consistent reversibility. In: Kari, J., Ulidowski, I. (eds.) RC 2018. LNCS, vol. 11106, pp. 286–303. Springer, Cham (2018). https://doi.org/10.1007/978-3-319-99498-7_20
40. de Vries, E., Koutavas, V., Hennessy, M.: Communicating transactions. In: Gastin, P., Laroussinie, F. (eds.) CONCUR 2010. LNCS, vol. 6269, pp. 569–583. Springer, Heidelberg (2010). https://doi.org/10.1007/978-3-642-15375-4_39
41. Yi, W.: CCS + time = an interleaving model for real time systems. In: Albert, J.L., Monien, B., Artalejo, M.R. (eds.) ICALP 1991. LNCS, vol. 510, pp. 217–228. Springer, Heidelberg (1991). https://doi.org/10.1007/3-540-54233-7_136
42. Yokoyama, T., Glück, R.: A reversible programming language and its invertible self-interpreter. In: Proceedings of the 13th ACM Workshop on Partial Evaluation and Semantics-based Program Manipulation (PEPM 2007), pp. 144–153. ACM Press (2007)

Automata with Timers

Véronique Bruyère[1], Guillermo A. Pérez[2], Gaëtan Staquet[1,2]([✉]),
and Frits W. Vaandrager[3]

[1] University of Mons, Mons, Belgium
{veronique.bruyere,gaetan.staquet}@umons.ac.be
[2] University of Antwerp – Flanders Make, Antwerp, Belgium
guillermo.perez@uantwerpen.be
[3] Radboud University, Nijmegen, The Netherlands
f.vaandrager@cs.ru.nl

Abstract. In this work, we study properties of deterministic finite-state automata with timers, a subclass of timed automata proposed by Vaandrager et al. as a candidate for an efficiently learnable timed model. We first study the complexity of the configuration reachability problem for such automata and establish that it is PSPACE-complete. Then, as simultaneous timeouts (we call these, races) can occur in timed runs of such automata, we study the problem of determining whether it is possible to modify the delays between the actions in a run, in a way to avoid such races. The absence of races is important for modelling purposes and to streamline learning of automata with timers. We provide an effective characterization of when an automaton is race-avoiding and establish that the related decision problem is in 3EXP and PSPACE-hard.

Keywords: Timed systems · model checking · reachability

1 Introduction

Timed automata were introduced by Alur & Dill [4] as finite-state automata equipped with real-valued clock variables for measuring the time between state transitions. These clock variables all increase at the same rate when time elapses, they can be reset along transitions, and be used in guards along transitions and in invariant predicates for states. Timed automata have become a framework of choice for modeling and analysis of real-time systems, equipped with a rich theory, supported by powerful tools, and with numerous applications [8].

Interestingly, whereas the values of clocks in a timed automaton *increase* over time, designers of real-time systems (e.g. embedded controllers and network protocols) typically use timers to enforce timing constraints, and the values of these timers *decrease* over time. If an application starts a timer with a certain

This work was supported by the Belgian FWO "SAILor" project (G030020N). Gaëtan Staquet is a research fellow (Aspirant) of the Belgian F.R.S.-FNRS. The research of Frits Vaandrager was supported by NWO TOP project 612.001.852 "Grey-box learning of Interfaces for Refactoring Legacy Software (GIRLS)".

value t, then this value decreases over time and after t time units—when the value has become 0—a timeout event occurs. It is straightforward to encode the behavior of timers using a timed automaton. Timed automata allow one to express a richer class of behaviors than what can be described using timers, and can for instance express that the time between two events is contained in an interval $[t - d, t + d]$. Moreover, timed automata can express constraints on the timing between arbitrary events, not just between start and timeout of timers.

However, the expressive power of timed automata entails certain problems. For instance, one can easily define timed automata models in which time stops at some point (timelocks) or an infinite number of discrete transitions occurs in a finite time (Zeno behavior). Thus timed automata may describe behavior that cannot be realized by any physical system. Also, learning [6,15] of timed automata models in a black-box setting turns out to be challenging [5,13,14]. For a learner who can only observe the external events of a system and their timing, it may be really difficult to infer the logical predicates (invariants and guards) that label the states and transitions of a timed automaton model of this system. As a result, all known learning algorithms for timed automata suffer from combinatorial explosions, which severely limits their practical usefulness.

For these reasons, it is interesting to consider variations of timed automata whose expressivity is restricted by using timers instead of clocks, as introduced by Dill in [11]. In an automaton with timers (AT), a transition may start a timer by setting it to a certain value. Whenever a timer reaches zero, it produces an observable timeout symbol that triggers a transition in the automaton. Dill also shows that the space of timer valuations can be abstracted into a finite number of so-called *regions*. However, the model we study here is slightly different, as, unlike Dill, we allow a timer to be stopped before reaching zero. We also study the regions of our AT and give an upper bound on their number.

Vaandrager et al. [18] provide a black-box active learning algorithm for automaton with a single timer, and evaluate it on a number of realistic applications, showing that it outperforms the timed automata based approaches of Aichernig et al. [2] and An et al. [5]. However, whereas [18] only support a single timer, the genetic programming approach of [2] is able to learn models with multiple clocks/timers. If we want to extend the learning algorithm of [18] to a setting with multiple timers, we need to deal with the issue of *races*, i.e., situations where multiple timers reach zero (and thus timeout) simultaneously. If a race occurs, then (despite the automaton being deterministic!) the automaton can process the simultaneous timeouts in various orders, leading to nondeterministic behavior. This means that during learning of an automaton with multiple timers, a learner needs to offer the inputs at specific times in order to avoid the occurrence of races. As long as there are no races, the behavior of the automaton will be deterministic, and a learner may determine, for each timeout, by which preceding input it was caused by slightly *wiggling* the timing of inputs and check whether the timing timeout changes in a corresponding manner.

Contribution. In this work, we take the one-timer definition from [18] and extend it to multiple timers while—to avoid overcomplicating the model—keeping the restriction that every transition can start or restart at most one timer. We first study the complexity of the configuration reachability problem for this model and establish that it is PSPACE-complete. Then, we turn our attention to the problem of determining whether it is possible to wiggle the delays between the inputs in a run, in a way to avoid races. The importance of the latter is twofold. First, automata with timers may not be an attractive modelling formalism in the presence of behaviors that do not align with those of the real-world systems they are meant to abstract. Second, the absence of races is a key property used in the learning algorithm for automata with a single timer. In this direction, we provide an effective characterization of when an automaton is race-avoiding and establish that the related decision problem is in 3EXP and PSPACE-hard. In a more pragmatic direction, while again leveraging our characterization, we show that with fixed input and timer sets, the problem is in PSPACE. Finally, we also give some simple yet sufficient conditions for an automaton to be race-avoiding. We refer to [9] for an extended version of our paper with all the proofs.

2   Preliminaries

An *automaton with timers* uses a finite set X of *timers*. Intuitively, a timer can be *started* to any integer value to become *active*. Subsequently, its value is decremented as time elapses (i.e., at the same fixed rate for all timers). When the value of a timer reaches 0, it *times out* and it is no longer active. Active timers can also be *stopped*, rendering them inactive, too. Such an automaton, along any transition, can stop a number of timers and update a *single* timer.

Some definitions are in order. We write $TO[X]$ for the set $\{to[x] \mid x \in X\}$ of *timeouts of X*. We denote by I a finite set of *inputs*, and by $\hat{I}$ the set $I \cup TO[X]$ of *actions*: either reading an input (an *input-action*), or processing a timeout (a *timeout-action*). Finally, $U = (X \times \mathbb{N}^{>0}) \cup \{\bot\}$ is the set of *updates*, where (x, c) means that timer x is started with value c, and $\bot$ stands for no timer update.

Definition 1 (Automaton with timers). *An automaton with timers (AT, for short) is a tuple $\mathcal{A} = (X, I, Q, q_0, \chi, \delta)$ where:*

- *X is a finite set of timers, I a finite set of inputs,*
- *Q is a finite set of states, with $q_0 \in Q$ the initial state,*
- *$\chi \colon Q \to \mathcal{P}(X)$, with $\chi(q_0) = \emptyset$, is a total function that assigns a finite set of active timers to each state,*
- *$\delta \colon Q \times \hat{I} \to Q \times U$ is a partial transition function that assigns a state and an update to each state-action pair, such that*
  - *$\delta(q, i)$ is defined iff either $i \in I$ or there is a timer $x \in \chi(q)$ with $i = to[x]$,*
  - *if $\delta(q, i) = (q', u)$ with $i = to[x]$ and $u = (y, c)$, then $x = y$ (when processing a timeout $to[x]$, only the timer x can be restarted).*

Moreover, any transition t of the form $\delta(q, i) = (q', u)$ must be such that

- *if $u = \bot$, then $\chi(q') \subseteq \chi(q)$ (all timers active in q' were already active in q in case of no timer update); moreover, if $i = to[x]$, then $x \notin \chi(q')$ (when the timer x times out and is not restarted, then x becomes inactive in q');*

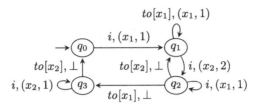

Fig. 1. An automaton with two timers x_1, x_2, such that $\chi(q_0) = \emptyset$, $\chi(q_1) = \{x_1\}$, $\chi(q_2) = \{x_1, x_2\}$, and $\chi(q_3) = \{x_2\}$.

- if $u = (x, c)$, then $x \in \chi(q')$ and $\chi(q') \setminus \{x\} \subseteq \chi(q)$ ((re)starting the timer x makes it active in q').

When a timer x is active in q and $i \neq to[x]$, we say that the transition t stops x if x is inactive in q', and that t discards x if t stops x or restarts x. We write $q \xrightarrow{i}_{u} q'$ if $\delta(q, i) = (q', u)$.

Example 1. An AT $\mathcal{A}$ is shown in Fig. 1 with set $X = \{x_1, x_2\}$ of timers and with set $I = \{i\}$ of inputs. In the initial state q_0, no timer is active, while x_1 is active in q_1 and q_2, and x_2 is active in q_2 and q_3. That is, $\chi(q_0) = \emptyset, \chi(q_1) = \{x_1\}, \chi(q_2) = \{x_1, x_2\}$, and $\chi(q_3) = \{x_2\}$. Timer updates are shown in the transitions. For instance, x_1 is started with value 1 when going from q_0 to q_1. The transition looping on q_2 discards x_1 and restarts it with value 1.

2.1 Timed Semantics

The semantics of an AT $\mathcal{A}$ is defined via an infinite-state labeled transition system that describes all possible configurations and transitions between them.

A *valuation* is a partial function $\kappa \colon X \to \mathbb{R}^{\geq 0}$ that assigns nonnegative real numbers to timers. For $Y \subseteq X$, we write $\mathsf{Val}(Y)$ for the set of all valuations κ such that $\mathrm{dom}(\kappa) = Y$.[1] A *configuration* of $\mathcal{A}$ is a pair (q, κ) where $q \in Q$ and $\kappa \in \mathsf{Val}(\chi(q))$. The *initial configuration* is the pair (q_0, κ_0) where κ_0 is the empty valuation since $\chi(q_0) = \emptyset$. If $\kappa \in \mathsf{Val}(Y)$ is a valuation in which all timers from Y have a value of at least $d \in \mathbb{R}^{\geq 0}$, then d units of time may elapse. We write $\kappa - d \in \mathsf{Val}(Y)$ for the valuation that satisfies $(\kappa - d)(x) = \kappa(x) - d$, for all $x \in Y$. The following rules specify the transitions between configurations $(q, \kappa), (q', \kappa')$.

$$\frac{\forall x \colon \kappa(x) \geq d}{(q, \kappa) \xrightarrow{d} (q, \kappa - d)} \tag{1}$$

$$\frac{q \xrightarrow{i}_{\perp} q', \quad i = to[x] \Rightarrow \kappa(x) = 0, \quad \forall y \in \chi(q') \colon \kappa'(y) = \kappa(y)}{(q, \kappa) \xrightarrow{i}_{\perp} (q', \kappa')} \tag{2}$$

---

[1] Notation $\mathrm{dom}(f)$ means the domain of the partial function f.

$$q \xrightarrow[(x,c)]{i} q', \quad i = to[x] \Rightarrow \kappa(x) = 0, \quad \forall y \in \chi(q') \colon \kappa'(y) = \begin{cases} c & \text{if } y = x \\ \kappa(y) & \text{otherwise} \end{cases}$$

$$(q, \kappa) \xrightarrow[(x,c)]{i} (q', \kappa') \tag{3}$$

Transitions of type (1) are called *delay transitions* (delay zero is allowed); those of type (2) and (3) are called *discrete transitions* (*timeout transitions* when $i = to[x]$ and *input transitions* otherwise). A *timed run* of $\mathcal{A}$ is a sequence of configurations such that delay and discrete transitions alternate, ending with a delay transition. The set *truns*($\mathcal{A}$) of timed runs is defined inductively as follows.

– The sequence $(q_0, \kappa_0) \xrightarrow{d} (q_0, \kappa_0 - d)$ is in *truns*($\mathcal{A}$).
– Suppose $\rho(q, \kappa)$ is a timed run ending with configuration (q, κ), then $\rho' = \rho(q, \kappa) \xrightarrow[u]{i} (q', \kappa') \xrightarrow{d} (q', \kappa' - d)$ is in *truns*($\mathcal{A}$).

A timed run is also written as $\rho = (q_0, \kappa_0) \, d_1 \, i_1/u_1 \, \ldots \, d_n \, i_n/u_n \, d_{n+1} \, (q, \kappa)$ such that only the initial configuration (q_0, κ_0) and the last configurations (q, κ) of ρ are given. The *untimed trace* of a timed run ρ, denoted *untime*(ρ), is the alternating sequence of states and actions from ρ, that is, *untime*(ρ) = $q_0 \, i_1 \, \ldots \, i_n \, q$ (we omit the valuations, the delays, and the updates).

Example 2. A sample timed run ρ of the AT of Example 1 is given below. Notice the transition with delay zero, indicating that two actions occur at the same time.

$$\rho = (q_0, \emptyset) \xrightarrow{1} (q_0, \emptyset) \xrightarrow[(x_1,1)]{i} (q_1, x_1 = 1) \xrightarrow{1} (q_1, x_1 = 0) \xrightarrow[(x_2,2)]{i} (q_2, x_1 = 0, x_2 = 2)$$

$$\xrightarrow{0} (q_2, x_1 = 0, x_2 = 2) \xrightarrow[\perp]{to[x_1]} (q_3, x_2 = 2) \xrightarrow{2} (q_3, x_2 = 0) \xrightarrow[\perp]{to[x_2]} (q_0, \emptyset) \xrightarrow{0.5} (q_0, \emptyset).$$

The untimed trace of ρ is *untime*(ρ) = $q_0 \, i \, q_1 \, i \, q_2 \, to[x_1] \, q_3 \, to[x_2] \, q_0$.

2.2   Blocks and Races

In this section, given an AT $\mathcal{A}$, we focus on its timed runs $\rho = (q_0, \kappa_0) \, d_1 \, i_1/u_1 \, \cdots \, d_n \, i_n/u_n \, d_{n+1} \, (q, \kappa)$ such that their first and last delays are non-zero and no timer times out in their last configuration, i.e., $d_1 > 0, d_{n+1} > 0$ and $\kappa(x) \neq 0$ for all $x \in \chi(q)$.[2] Such runs are called *padded*, and we denote by *ptruns*($\mathcal{A}$) the set of all padded timed runs of $\mathcal{A}$. To have a good intuition about padded timed runs, their decomposition into *blocks* is helpful and will be often used in the proofs. A block is composed of an input i that starts a timer x and of the succession of timeouts and restarts of x, that i induces inside a timed run. Let us formalize this notion. Consider a padded timed run $\rho = (q_0, \kappa_0) \, d_1 \, i_1/u_1 \, \ldots \, d_n \, i_n/u_n \, d_{n+1} \, (q, \kappa)$ of an AT. Let k, k' be such that $1 \leq k < k' \leq n$. We say that i_k *triggers* $i_{k'}$ if there is a timer x such that:

---

[2] The reason for this choice will be clarified at the end of this section.

- i_k (re)starts x, that is, $u_k = (x, c)$,
- $i_{k'}$ is the action $to[x]$, and
- there is no ℓ with $k < \ell < k'$ such that $i_\ell = to[x]$ or i_ℓ discards x.

Note that $i_{k'}$ may restart x or not, and if it does, x later times out or is discarded.

Definition 2 (Block). *Let* $\rho = (q_0, \kappa_0)\ d_1\ i_1/u_1\ \ldots\ d_n\ i_n/u_n\ d_{n+1}\ (q, \kappa)$ *be a padded timed run of an AT. A* block *of* ρ *is a pair* $B = (k_1 k_2 \ldots k_m, \gamma)$ *such that* $i_{k_1}, i_{k_2}, \ldots, i_{k_m}$ *is a maximal subsequence of actions of* ρ *such that* $i_{k_1} \in I$, i_{k_ℓ} *triggers* $i_{k_{\ell+1}}$ *for all* $1 \leq \ell < m$, *and* γ *is the* timer fate *of* B *defined as:*

$$\gamma = \begin{cases} \bot & \textit{if } i_{k_m} \textit{ does not restart any timer,} \\ \bullet & \textit{if } i_{k_m} \textit{ restarts a timer which is discarded by some } i_\ell, \textit{ with } k_m < \ell \leq n, \\ & \textit{when its value is zero,} \\ \times & \textit{otherwise.} \end{cases}$$

In the timer fate definition, consider the case where i_{k_m} restarts a timer x. For the purposes of Sect. 4.1, it is convenient to know whether x is later discarded or not, and in case it is discarded, whether this occurs when its value is zero ($\gamma = \bullet$). Hence, $\gamma = \times$ covers both situations where x is discarded with non-zero value, and x is still active in the last configuration (q, κ) of ρ. Notice that in the latter case, x has also non-zero value in (q, κ) as ρ is padded. When no confusion is possible, we denote a block by a sequence of inputs rather than the corresponding sequence of indices, that is, $B = (i_{k_1} i_{k_2} \ldots i_{k_m}, \gamma)$. In the sequel, we use notation $i \in B$ to denote an action i belonging to the sequence of B.

By definition of an AT, recall that the same timer x is restarted along a block B. Hence we also say that B is an *x-block*. Note also that the sequence of a block can be composed of a single input $i \in I$.

As this notion of blocks is not trivial but plays a great role in this paper, let us give several examples illustrating multiple situations.

Example 3. Consider the timed run ρ of Example 2 from the AT $\mathcal{A}$ depicted in Fig. 1. It has two blocks: an x_1-block $B_1 = (i\ to[x_1], \bot)$ and an x_2-block $B_2 = (i\ to[x_2], \bot)$, both represented in Fig. 2a.[3] In this visual representation of the blocks, time flows left to right and is represented by the thick horizontal line. A "gap" in that line indicates that the time is stopped, i.e., the delay between two consecutive actions is zero. We draw a vertical line for each action, and join together actions belonging to a block by a horizontal (non-thick) line.

Consider another timed run σ from $\mathcal{A}$:

$$\sigma = (q_0, \emptyset) \xrightarrow{1} (q_0, \emptyset) \xrightarrow[(x_1, 1)]{i} (q_1, x_1 = 1) \xrightarrow{1} (q_1, x_1 = 0) \xrightarrow[(x_1, 1)]{to[x_1]} (q_1, x_1 = 1)$$

$$\xrightarrow{0} (q_1, x_1 = 1) \xrightarrow[(x_2, 2)]{i} (q_2, x_1 = 1, x_2 = 2) \xrightarrow{1} (q_2, x_1 = 0, x_2 = 1)$$

$$\xrightarrow[\bot]{to[x_1]} (q_3, x_2 = 1) \xrightarrow{1} (q_3, x_2 = 0) \xrightarrow[\bot]{to[x_2]} (q_0, \emptyset) \xrightarrow{0.5} (q_0, \emptyset).$$

This timed run has also two blocks represented in Fig. 2b, such that $B_1 = (i\ to[x_1]\ to[x_1], \bot)$ with x_1 timing out twice.

---

[3] When using the action indices in the blocks, we have $B_1 = (1\ 3, \bot)$ and $B_2 = (2\ 4, \bot)$.

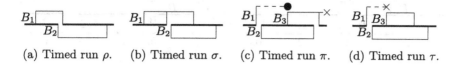

(a) Timed run ρ.   (b) Timed run σ.   (c) Timed run π.   (d) Timed run τ.

Fig. 2. Block representations of four timed runs.

We conclude this example with two other timed runs, π and τ, such that some of their blocks have a timer fate $\gamma \neq \perp$. Let π and τ be the timed runs:

$$\pi = (q_0, \emptyset) \xrightarrow{1} (q_0, \emptyset) \xrightarrow[(x_1,1)]{i} (q_1, x_1 = 1) \xrightarrow{0} (q_1, x_1 = 1) \xrightarrow[(x_2,2)]{i} (q_2, x_1 = 1, x_2 = 2)$$

$$\xrightarrow{1} (q_2, x_1 = 0, x_2 = 1) \xrightarrow[(x_1,1)]{i} (q_2, x_1 = 1, x_2 = 1) \xrightarrow{1} (q_2, x_1 = 0, x_2 = 0)$$

$$\xrightarrow[\perp]{to[x_2]} (q_1, x_1 = 0) \xrightarrow{0} (q_1, x_1 = 0) \xrightarrow[(x_1,1)]{to[x_1]} (q_1, x_1 = 1) \xrightarrow{0.5} (q_1, x_1 = 0.5)$$

$$\tau = (q_0, \emptyset) \xrightarrow{1} (q_0, \emptyset) \xrightarrow[(x_1,1)]{i} (q_1, x_1 = 1) \xrightarrow{0} (q_1, x_1 = 1) \xrightarrow[(x_2,2)]{i} (q_2, x_1 = 1, x_2 = 2)$$

$$\xrightarrow{0.5} (q_2, x_1 = 0.5, x_2 = 1.5) \xrightarrow[(x_1,1)]{i} (q_2, x_1 = 1, x_2 = 1.5) \xrightarrow{1} (q_2, x_1 = 0, x_2 = 0.5)$$

$$\xrightarrow[\perp]{to[x_1]} (q_3, x_2 = 0.5) \xrightarrow{0.5} (q_3, x_2 = 0) \xrightarrow[\perp]{to[x_2]} (q_0, \emptyset) \xrightarrow{0.5} (q_0, \emptyset).$$

The run π has three blocks $B_1 = (i, \bullet)$ (x_1 is started by i and then discarded while its value is zero), $B_2 = (i\ to[x_2], \perp)$, and $B_3 = (i\ to[x_1], \times)$ (x_1 is again started in B_3 but π ends before x_1 reaches value zero). Those blocks are represented in Fig. 2c, where we visually represent the timer fate of B_1 (resp. B_3) by a dotted line finished by $\bullet$ (resp. $\times$). Finally, the run τ has its blocks depicted in Fig. 2d. This time, x_1 is discarded before reaching zero, i.e., $B_1 = (i, \times)$.

As illustrated by the previous example, blocks satisfy the following property.[4]

Lemma 1. *Let* $\rho = (q_0, \kappa_0)\ d_1\ i_1/u_1\ \dots\ d_n\ i_n/u_n\ d_{n+1}\ (q, \kappa)$ *be a padded timed run of an AT. Then, the sequences of the blocks of ρ form a partition of the set of indices $\{1, \dots, n\}$ of the actions of ρ.*

Along a timed run of an AT $\mathcal{A}$, it can happen that a timer times out at the same time that another action takes place. This leads to a sort of *nondeterminism*, as $\mathcal{A}$ can process those concurrent actions in any order. This situation appears in Example 3 each time a gap appears in the time lines of Fig. 2. We call these situations *races* that we formally define as follows.

Definition 3 (Race). *Let* B, B' *be two blocks of a padded timed run ρ with timer fates γ and γ'. We say that B and B' participate in a race if:*

---

[4] Recall that the sequence of a block can be composed of a single action.

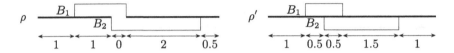

Fig. 3. Modifying the delays in order to remove a race.

- *either there exist actions $i \in B$ and $i' \in B'$ such that the sum of the delays between i and i' in ρ is equal to zero, i.e., no time elapses between them,*
- *or there exists an action $i \in B$ that is the first action along ρ to discard the timer started by the last action $i' \in B'$ and $\gamma' = \bullet$, i.e., the timer of B' (re)started by i' reaches value zero when i discards it.*

We also say that the actions i and i' participate in this race.

The first case of the race definition appears in Fig. 2a, while the second case appears in Fig. 2c (see the race in which blocks B_1 and B_3 participate). The nondeterminism is highlighted in Figs. 2a and b where two actions (i and $to[x]$) occur at the same time but are processed in a different order in each figure. Unfortunately, imposing a particular way of resolving races (i.e. imposing a particular action order) may seem arbitrary when modelling real-world systems. It is therefore desirable for the set of sequences of actions along timed runs to be independent to the resolution of races.

Definition 4 (Race-avoiding). *An AT $\mathcal{A}$ is race-avoiding iff for all padded timed runs $\rho \in ptruns(\mathcal{A})$ with races, there exists some $\rho' \in ptruns(\mathcal{A})$ with no races such that $untime(\rho') = untime(\rho)$.*

Example 4. Let us come back to the timed run ρ of Example 2 that contains a race (see Fig. 2a). By moving the second occurrence of action i slightly earlier in ρ, we obtain the timed run ρ':

$$\rho' = (q_0, \emptyset) \xrightarrow{1} (q_0, \emptyset) \xrightarrow[(x_1, 1)]{i} (q_1, x_1 = 1) \xrightarrow{0.5} (q_1, x_1 = 0.5) \xrightarrow[(x_2, 2)]{i} (q_2, x_1 = 0.5, x_2 = 2)$$

$$\xrightarrow{0.5} (q_2, x_1 = 0, x_2 = 1.5) \xrightarrow[\perp]{to[x_1]} (q_3, x_2 = 1.5) \xrightarrow{1.5} (q_3, x_2 = 0) \xrightarrow[\perp]{to[x_2]} (q_0, \emptyset) \xrightarrow{1} (q_0, \emptyset).$$

Notice that $untime(\rho') = q_0 \, i \, q_1 \, i \, q_2 \, to[x_1] \, q_3 \, to[x_2] \, q_0 = untime(\rho')$. Moreover, ρ' contains no races as indicated in Fig. 3.

Notice that several blocks could participate in the same race. The notion of block has been defined for padded timed runs only, as we do not want to consider runs that end *abruptly* during a race (some pending timeouts may not be processed at the end of the run, for instance). Moreover, it is always possible for the first delay to be positive as no timer is active in the initial state. Finally, non-zero delays at the start and the end of the runs allow to move blocks as introduced in Example 4 and further detailed in Sect. 4.1.

In Sect. 4, we study whether it is decidable that an AT is race-avoiding, and how to eliminate races in a race-avoiding AT while keeping the same traces. Before, we study the (classical) reachability problem in Sect. 3.

3   Reachability

The *reachability problem* asks, given an AT $\mathcal{A}$ and a state q, whether there exists a timed run $\rho \in \mathit{truns}(\mathcal{A})$ from the initial configuration to some configuration (q, κ). In this section, we argue that this problem is PSPACE-complete.

Theorem 1. *The reachability problem for ATs is* PSPACE-*complete.*

For hardness, we reduce from the acceptance problem for linear-bounded Turing machines (LBTM, for short), as done for timed automata, see e.g. [1]. In short, given an LBTM $\mathcal{M}$ and a word w of length n, we construct an AT that uses n timers x_i, $1 \leq i \leq n$, such that the timer x_i encodes the value of the i-th cell of the tape of $\mathcal{M}$. We also rely on a timer x that is always (re)started at one, and is used to synchronize the x_i timers and the simulation of $\mathcal{M}$. The simulation is split into *phases*: The AT first seeks the symbol on the current cell i of the tape (which can be derived from the moment at which the timer x_i times out, using the number of times x timed out since the beginning of the phase). Then, the AT simulates a transition of $\mathcal{M}$ by restarting x_i, reflecting the new value of the i-th cell. Finally, the AT can reach a designated state iff $\mathcal{M}$ is in an accepting state. Therefore, the reachability problem is PSPACE-hard.

For membership, we follow the classical argument used to establish that the reachability problem for timed automata is in PSPACE: We first define *region automata* for ATs (which are a simplification of region automata for timed automata) and observe that reachability in an AT reduces to reachability in the corresponding region automaton. The region automaton is of size exponential in the number of timers and polynomial in the number of states of the AT. Hence, the reachability problem for ATs is in PSPACE via standard arguments.

We define region automata for ATs much like they are defined for timed automata [3,4,7]. Let $\mathcal{A} = (X, I, Q, q_0, \chi, \delta)$ be an AT. For a timer $x \in X$, c_x denotes the largest constant to which x is updated in $\mathcal{A}$. Let $C = \max_{x \in X} c_x$. Two valuations κ and κ' are said *timer-equivalent*, noted $\kappa \cong \kappa'$, iff $\mathrm{dom}(\kappa) = \mathrm{dom}(\kappa')$ and the following hold for all $x_1, x_2 \in \mathrm{dom}(\kappa)$: *(i)* $\lfloor \kappa(x_1) \rfloor = \lfloor \kappa'(x_1) \rfloor$, *(ii)* $\mathrm{frac}(\kappa(x_1)) = 0$ iff $\mathrm{frac}(\kappa'(x_1)) = 0$, *(iii)* $\mathrm{frac}(\kappa(x_1)) \leq \mathrm{frac}(\kappa(x_2))$ iff $\mathrm{frac}(\kappa'(x_1)) \leq \mathrm{frac}(\kappa'(x_2))$. A *timer region* for $\mathcal{A}$ is an equivalence class of timer valuations induced by $\cong$. We lift the relation to configurations: $(q, \kappa) \cong (q', \kappa')$ iff $\kappa \cong \kappa'$ and $q = q'$. Finally, $[\![(q, \kappa)]\!]_{\cong}$ denotes the equivalence class of (q, κ).

We are now able to define a finite automaton called the *region automaton* of $\mathcal{A}$ and denoted $\mathcal{R}$. The alphabet of $\mathcal{R}$ is $\Sigma = \{\tau\} \cup \hat{I}$ where τ is a special symbol used in non-zero delay transitions. Formally, $\mathcal{R}$ is the finite automaton (Σ, S, s_0, Δ) where:

- $S = \{(q, \kappa) \mid q \in Q, \kappa \in \mathsf{Val}(\chi(q))\}_{/\cong}$, i.e., the quotient of the configurations by $\cong$, is the set of states,
- $s_0 = (q_0, [\![\kappa_0]\!]_{\cong})$ with κ_0 the empty valuation, is the initial state,
- the set of transitions $\Delta \subseteq S \times \Sigma \times S$ includes $([\![(q, \kappa)]\!]_{\cong}, \tau, [\![(q, \kappa')]\!]_{\cong})$ if $(q, \kappa) \xrightarrow{d} (q, \kappa')$ in $\mathcal{A}$ whenever $d > 0$, and $([\![(q, \kappa)]\!]_{\cong}, i, [\![(q', \kappa')]\!]_{\cong})$ if $(q, \kappa) \xrightarrow[u]{i} (q', \kappa')$ in $\mathcal{A}$.

It is easy to check that the timer-equivalence relation on configurations is a *(strong) time-abstracting bisimulation* [10,17]. That is, for all $(q_1, \kappa_1) \cong (q_2, \kappa_2)$ the following holds:

- if $(q_1, \kappa_1) \xrightarrow[u]{i} (q_1', \kappa_1')$, then there is $(q_2, \kappa_2) \xrightarrow[u]{i} (q_2', \kappa_2')$ with $(q_1', \kappa_1') \cong (q_2', \kappa_2')$,
- if $(q_1, \kappa_1) \xrightarrow{d_1} (q_1, \kappa_1')$, then there exists $(q_2, \kappa_2) \xrightarrow{d_2} (q_2, \kappa_2')$ where $d_1, d_2 > 0$ may differ such that $(q_1, \kappa_1') \cong (q_2, \kappa_2')$, and
- the above also holds if (q_1, κ_1) and (q_2, κ_2) are swapped.

Using this property, we can prove the following about $\mathcal{R}$.

Lemma 2. *Let $\mathcal{A} = (X, I, Q, q_0, \chi, \delta)$ be an AT and $\mathcal{R}$ be its region automaton.*

1. *The size of $\mathcal{R}$ is linear in $|Q|$ and exponential in $|X|$. That is, $|S|$ is smaller than or equal to $|Q| \cdot |X|! \cdot 2^{|X|} \cdot (C+1)^{|X|}$.*
2. *There is a timed run ρ of $\mathcal{A}$ that begins in (q, κ) and ends in (q', κ') iff there is a run ρ' of $\mathcal{R}$ that begins in $[\![(q, \kappa)]\!]_\cong$ and ends in $[\![(q', \kappa')]\!]_\cong$.*

Example 5. Let us consider the AT $\mathcal{A}$ of Fig. 1 and the timed run π given in Example 3. The corresponding run π' in the region automaton $\mathcal{R}$ is

$$(q_0, [\![\emptyset]\!]_\cong) \xrightarrow{\tau} (q_0, [\![\emptyset]\!]_\cong) \xrightarrow{i} (q_1, [\![x_1 = 1]\!]_\cong) \xrightarrow{i} (q_2, [\![x_1 = 1, x_2 = 2]\!]_\cong)$$

$$\xrightarrow{\tau} (q_2, [\![x_1 = 0, x_2 = 1]\!]_\cong) \xrightarrow{i} (q_2, [\![x_1 = 1, x_2 = 1]\!]_\cong) \xrightarrow{\tau} (q_2, [\![x_1 = 0, x_2 = 0]\!]_\cong)$$

$$\xrightarrow{to[x_2]} (q_1, [\![x_1 = 0]\!]_\cong) \xrightarrow{to[x_1]} (q_1, [\![x_1 = 1]\!]_\cong) \xrightarrow{\tau} (q_1, [\![0 < x_1 < 1]\!]_\cong).$$

Notice that the transitions with delay zero of π do not appear in π'.

4   Race-Avoiding ATs

In this section, we study whether an AT $\mathcal{A}$ is race-avoiding, i.e., whether for any padded timed run ρ of $\mathcal{A}$ with races, there exists another run ρ' with no races such that $untime(\rho) = untime(\rho')$. We are able to prove the next theorem.

Theorem 2. *Deciding whether an AT is race-avoiding is PSPACE-hard and in 3EXP. It is in PSPACE if the sets of actions I and of timers X are fixed.*

Our approach is, given $\rho \in ptruns(\mathcal{A})$, to study how to slightly move blocks along the time line of ρ in a way to get another $\rho' \in ptruns(\mathcal{A})$ where the races are eliminated while keeping the actions in the same order as in ρ. We call this action *wiggling*. Let us first give an example and then formalize this notion.

Example 6. We consider again the AT of Fig. 1. We have seen in Example 4 and Fig. 3 that the block B_2 of ρ can be slightly moved to the left to obtain the timed run ρ' with no race such that $untime(\rho) = untime(\rho')$. Figure 3 illustrates how to move B_2 by changing some of the delays.

In contrast, this is not possible for the timed run π of Example 3. Indeed looking at Fig. 2c, we see that it is impossible to move block B_2 to the left due to its race with B_1 (remember that we need to keep the same action order). It is also not possible to move it to the right due to its race with B_3. Similarly, it is impossible to move B_1 neither to the right (due to its race with B_2), nor to the left (otherwise its timer will time out instead of being discarded by B_3). Finally, one can also check that block B_3 cannot be moved.

Given a padded timed run $\rho = (q_0, \kappa_0)\ d_1\ i_1/u_1\ \ldots\ d_n\ i_n/u_n\ d_{n+1}(q, \kappa) \in ptruns(\mathcal{A})$ and a block $B = (k_1 \ldots k_m, \gamma)$ of ρ participating in a race, we say that we can *wiggle* B if for some ϵ, we can move B to the left (by $\epsilon < 0$) or to the right (by $\epsilon > 0$), and obtain a run $\rho' \in ptruns(\mathcal{A})$ such that $untime(\rho) = untime(\rho')$ and B no longer participates in any race. More precisely, we have $\rho' = (q_0, \kappa_0)\ d_1'\ i_1/u_1\ \ldots\ d_n'\ i_n/u_n\ d_{n+1}'\ (q, \kappa')$ such that

- for all $i_{k_\ell} \in B$ with $k_\ell > 1$, if $i_{k_\ell-1} \notin B$ (the action before i_{k_ℓ} in ρ does not belong to B), then $d_{k_\ell}' = d_{k_\ell} + \epsilon$,
- if there exists $i_{k_\ell} \in B$ with $k_\ell = 1$ (the first action of B is the first action of ρ), then $d_1' = d_1 + \epsilon$,
- for all $i_{k_\ell} \in B$ with $k_\ell < n$, if $i_{k_\ell+1} \notin B$ (the action after i_{k_ℓ} in ρ does not belong to B), then $d_{k_\ell+1}' = d_{k_\ell+1} - \epsilon$,
- if there exists $i_{k_\ell} \in B$ with $k_\ell = n$ (the last action of B is the last action of ρ), then $d_{n+1}' = d_{n+1} - \epsilon$,
- for all other d_k', we have $d_k' = d_k$.

As $\rho' \in ptruns(\mathcal{A})$ and $untime(\rho) = untime(\rho')$, we must have $d_k' \geq 0$ for all k and $d_1', d_{n+1}' > 0$. Observe that to wiggle B we move every action of B.

We say that we can wiggle ρ, or that ρ is *wigglable*, if it is possible to wiggle its blocks, *one block at a time*, to obtain $\rho' \in ptruns(\mathcal{A})$ with no races such $untime(\rho) = untime(\rho')$. Hence if all padded timed runs with races of an AT $\mathcal{A}$ are wigglable, then $\mathcal{A}$ is race-avoiding.

In the next sections, we first associate a graph with any $\rho \in ptruns(\mathcal{A})$ in a way to characterize when ρ is wigglable thanks to this graph. We then state the equivalence between the race-avoiding characteristic of an AT and the property that all $\rho \in ptruns(\mathcal{A})$ can be wiggled (Theorem 3). This allows us to provide logic formulas to determine whether an AT has an unwigglable run, and then to prove the upper bound of Theorem 2. We also discuss its lower bound. Finally, we discuss some sufficient hypotheses for a race-avoiding AT.

4.1   Wiggling a Run

In this section, given an AT $\mathcal{A}$ and a padded timed run $\rho \in ptruns(\mathcal{A})$, we study the conditions required to be able to wiggle ρ. For this purpose, we define the following graph G_ρ associated with ρ. When two blocks B and B' of ρ participate in a race, we write $B \prec B'$ if there exist actions $i \in B$ and $i' \in B'$ such that i, i' participate in this race and, according to Definition 3:

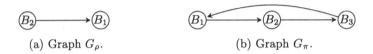

(a) Graph G_ρ.   (b) Graph G_π.

Fig. 4. Block graphs of the timed runs ρ and π of Example 3.

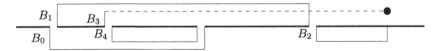

Fig. 5. Races of a padded timed run ρ with $B_\ell \prec B_{\ell+1 \bmod 5}$, $0 \le \ell \le 4$.

– either i occurs before i' along ρ and the total delay between i and i' is zero.
– or the timer of B' (re)started by i' reaches value zero when i discards it.

We define the *block graph* $G_\rho = (V, E)$ of ρ where V is the set of blocks of ρ and E has an edge (B, B') iff $B \prec B'$.

Example 7. Let $\mathcal{A}$ be the AT from Fig. 1, and ρ and π be the timed runs from Example 3, whose block decomposition is represented in Figs. 2a and 2c. For the run ρ, it holds that $B_2 \prec B_1$ leading to the block graph G_ρ depicted in Fig. 4a. For the run π, we get the block graph G_π depicted in Fig. 4b.

Notice that G_ρ is acyclic while G_π is cyclic. By the following proposition, this difference is enough to characterize that ρ can be wiggled and π cannot.

Proposition 1. *Let $\mathcal{A}$ be an AT and $\rho \in ptruns(\mathcal{A})$ be a padded timed run with races. Then, ρ can be wiggled iff G_ρ is acyclic.*

Intuitively, a block cannot be moved to the left (resp. right) if it has a predecessor (resp. successor) in the block graph, due to the races in which it participates. Hence, if a block has both a predecessor and a successor, it cannot be wiggled (see Fig. 2c and 4b for instance). Then, the blocks appearing in a cycle of the block graph cannot be wiggled. The other direction holds by observing that we can do a topological sort of the blocks if the graph is acyclic. We then wiggle the blocks, one by one, according to that sort.

The next corollary will be useful in the following sections. It is illustrated by Fig. 5 with the simple cycle $(B_0, B_1, B_2, B_3, B_4, B_0)$.

Corollary 1. *Let $\mathcal{A}$ be an AT and $\rho \in ptruns(\mathcal{A})$ be a padded timed run with races. Suppose that G_ρ is cyclic. Then there exists a cycle $\mathcal{C}$ in G_ρ such that*

– *any block of $\mathcal{C}$ participate in exactly two races described by this cycle,*
– *for any race described by $\mathcal{C}$, exactly two blocks of $\mathcal{C}$ participate in the race,*
– *the blocks $B = (k_1 \ldots k_m, \gamma)$ of $\mathcal{C}$ satisfy either $m \ge 2$, or $m = 1$ and $\gamma = \bullet$.*

From the definition of wiggling, we know that if all padded timed runs with races of an AT $\mathcal{A}$ are wigglable, then $\mathcal{A}$ is race-avoiding. The converse also holds as stated in the next theorem. By Proposition 1, this means that an AT is race-avoiding iff the block graph of all its padded timed run is acyclic.

Theorem 3. *An AT $\mathcal{A}$ is race-avoiding*

- *iff any padded timed run $\rho \in ptruns(\mathcal{A})$ with races can be wiggled,*
- *iff for any padded timed run $\rho \in ptruns(\mathcal{A})$, its graph G_ρ is acyclic.*

Let us sketch the missing proof. By modifying $\rho \in ptruns(\mathcal{A})$ to explicitly encode when a timer is discarded, one can show the races of ρ cannot be avoided if the block graph of ρ is cyclic as follows. Given two actions i, i' of this modified run, it is possible to define the *relative elapsed time* between i and i', noted reltime(i, i'), from the sum d of all delays between i and i': if i occurs before i', then reltime$(i, i') = d$, otherwise reltime$(i, i') = -d$. Lifting this to a sequence of actions from ρ is defined naturally. Then, one can observe that the relative elapsed time of a cyclic sequence of actions is zero, i.e., reltime$(i_1, i_2, \ldots, i_k, i_1) = 0$. Finally, from a cycle of G_ρ as described in Corollary 1, we extract a cyclic sequence of actions and prove, thanks to the concept of relative elapsed time, that any run ρ' such that $untime(\rho) = untime(\rho')$ must contain some races.

4.2   Existence of an Unwigglable Run

In this section, we give the intuition for the announced complexity bounds for the problem of deciding whether an AT $\mathcal{A}$ is race-avoiding (Theorem 2).

Let us begin with the 3EXP-membership. The crux of our approach is to use the characterization of the race-avoiding property given in Theorem 3, to work with a slight modification of the region automaton $\mathcal{R}$ of $\mathcal{A}$, and to construct a finite-state automaton whose language is the set of runs of $\mathcal{R}$ whose block graph is cyclic. Hence deciding whether $\mathcal{A}$ is race-avoiding amounts to deciding whether the language accepted by the latter automaton is empty. To do so, we construct a *monadic second-order* (MSO, for short; see [12,16] for an introduction) formula that is satisfied by words w labeling a run ρ of $\mathcal{R}$ iff the block graph of ρ is cyclic.

Our *modification* of $\mathcal{R}$ is best seen as additional annotations on the states and transitions of $\mathcal{R}$. We extend the alphabet Σ as follows: *(i)* we add a timer to each action $i \in \hat{I}$ to remember the updated timers *(ii)* we also use new symbols $di[x]$, $x \in X$, with the intent of explicitly encoding in $\mathcal{R}$ when the timer x is discarded while its value is zero. Therefore, the modified alphabet is $\Sigma = \{\tau\} \cup (\hat{I} \times \hat{X}) \cup \{di[x] \mid x \in X\}$ where $\hat{X} = X \cup \{\bot\}$. As a transition in $\mathcal{A}$ can discard more than one timer, we store the set D of discarded timers in the states of $\mathcal{R}$, as well as outgoing transitions labeled by $di[x]$, for all discarded timers x. For this, the states of $\mathcal{R}$ become $S = \{(q, [\kappa]_{\cong}, D) \mid q \in Q, \kappa \in \mathsf{Val}(\chi(q)), D \subseteq X\}$ and Δ is modified in the natural way so that D is updated as required. Note that the size of this modified $\mathcal{R}$ is only larger than what is stated in Lemma 2 by a factor of $2^{|X|}$.

Note that any x-block $(i_{k_1}, \ldots, i_{k_m}, \gamma)$ of a timed run ρ in $\mathcal{A}$ is translated into the sequence of symbols $(i'_{k_1}, \ldots, i'_{k_m}, \gamma')$ in the corresponding run ρ' of the modified $\mathcal{R}$ with an optional symbol γ' such that:

- $i'_{k_\ell} = (i_{k_\ell}, x)$, for $1 \leq \ell < m$,
- $i'_{k_m} = (i_{k_m}, \bot)$ if $\gamma = \bot$, and (i_{k_m}, x) otherwise,
- $\gamma' = di[x]$ if $\gamma = \bullet$, and γ' does not exist otherwise.

It follows that, instead of considering padded timed runs $\rho \in ptruns(\mathcal{A})$ and their block graph G_ρ, we work with their corresponding (padded) runs, blocks, and block graphs in the modified region automaton $\mathcal{R}$ of $\mathcal{A}$.

Example 8. The run π' of Example 5 becomes

$$(q_0, [\![\emptyset]\!]_\cong, \emptyset) \xrightarrow{\tau} (q_0, [\![\emptyset]\!]_\cong, \emptyset) \xrightarrow{(i,x_1)} (q_1, [\![x_1 = 1]\!]_\cong, \emptyset) \xrightarrow{(i,x_2)} (q_2, [\![x_1 = 1, x_2 = 2]\!]_\cong, \emptyset)$$

$$\xrightarrow{\tau} (q_2, [\![x_1 = 0, x_2 = 1]\!]_\cong, \emptyset) \xrightarrow{(i,x_1)} (q_2, [\![x_1 = 1, x_2 = 1]\!]_\cong, \{x_1\})$$

$$\xrightarrow{di[x_1]} (q_2, [\![x_1 = 1, x_2 = 1]\!]_\cong, \emptyset) \xrightarrow{\tau} (q_2, [\![x_1 = 0, x_2 = 0]\!]_\cong, \emptyset)$$

$$\xrightarrow{(to[x_2], \bot)} (q_1, [\![x_1 = 0]\!]_\cong, \emptyset) \xrightarrow{(to[x_1], x_1)} (q_1, [\![x_1 = 1]\!]_\cong, \emptyset) \xrightarrow{\tau} (q_1, [\![0 < x_1 < 1]\!]_\cong, \emptyset).$$

The transition with label $di[x_1]$ indicates that the timer x_1 is discarded in the original timed run while its value equals zero (see the race in which blocks B_1 and B_3 participate in Fig. 2c). The three blocks of π become $B'_1 = ((i, x_1), di[x_1])$, $B'_2 = ((i, x_2), (to[x_2], \bot))$, and $B'_3 = ((i, x_1), (to[x_1], x_1))$ in π'. The fact that in π, B_1 and B_2 participate in a race (with a zero-delay between their respective actions i and i), is translated in π' with the non existence of the τ-symbol between the symbols (i, x_1) and (i, x_2) in B'_1 and B'_2 respectively.

Lemma 3. *Let $\mathcal{A}$ be an AT and $\mathcal{R}$ be its modified region automaton. We can construct an MSO formula Φ of size linear in I and X such that a word labeling a run ρ of $\mathcal{R}$ satisfies Φ iff ρ is a padded run that cannot be wiggled. Moreover, the formula Φ, in prenex normal form, has three quantifier alternations.*

The formula Φ of this lemma describes the existence of a cycle $\mathcal{C}$ of blocks $B_0, B_1, \ldots, B_{k-1}$ such that $B_\ell \prec B_{\ell+1 \bmod k}$ for any $0 \leq \ell \leq k - 1$, as described in Corollary 1 (see Fig. 5). To do so, we consider the actions (i.e., symbols of the alphabet Σ of $\mathcal{R}$) participating in the races of $\mathcal{C}$: $i_0, i_1, \ldots, i_{k-1}$ and $i'_0, i'_1, \ldots, i'_{k-1}$ such that for all ℓ, i_ℓ, i'_ℓ belong to the same block, and $i'_\ell, i_{\ell+1 \bmod k}$ participate in a race. One can write MSO formulas expressing that two actions participate in a race (there is no τ transition between them), that two actions belong to the same block, and, finally, the existence of these two action sequences.

From the formula Φ of Lemma 3, by the Büchi-Elgot-Trakhtenbrot theorem, we can construct a finite-state automaton whose language is the set of all words satisfying Φ. Its size is triple-exponential. We then compute the intersection $\mathcal{N}$ of this automaton with $\mathcal{R}$—itself exponential in size. Finally, the language of $\mathcal{N}$ is empty iff each padded timed run of $\mathcal{A}$ can be wiggled, and emptiness can be checked in polynomial time with respect to the triple-exponential size of $\mathcal{N}$, thus showing the 3EXP-membership of Theorem 2. Notice that when we fix the sets of inputs I and of timers X, the formula Φ becomes of constant size. Constructing $\mathcal{N}$ and checking its emptiness can be done "on the fly", yielding a nondeterministic decision procedure which requires a polynomial space only. We thus obtain that, under fixed inputs and timers, deciding whether an AT is race-avoiding is in PSPACE.

The complexity lower bound of Theorem 2 follows from the PSPACE-hardness of the reachability problem for ATs (see the intuition given in Sect. 3). We can show that any run in the AT constructed from the given LBTM and word w can be wiggled. Once the designated state for the reachability reduction is reached, we add a widget that forces a run that cannot be wiggled. Therefore, as the only way of obtaining a run that cannot be wiggled is to reach a specific state (from the widget), the problem whether an AT is race-avoiding is PSPACE-hard. Notice that this hardness proof is no longer valid if we fix the sets I and X.

4.3 Sufficient Hypotheses

Let us discuss some sufficient hypotheses for an AT $\mathcal{A}$ to be race-avoiding.

1. If every state in $\mathcal{A}$ has at most one active timer, then $\mathcal{A}$ is race-avoiding. Up to renaming the timers, we actually have a single-timer AT in this case.
2. If we modify the notion of timed run by imposing non-zero delays everywhere in the run, then $\mathcal{A}$ is race-avoiding. Indeed, the only races that can appear are when a zero-valued timer is discarded, and it is impossible to form a cycle in the block graph with only this kind of races. Imposing a non-zero delay before a timeout is debateable. Nevertheless, imposing a non-zero delay before inputs only is not a sufficient hypothesis.
3. Let us fix a total order $<$ over the timers, and modify the semantics of an AT to enforce that, in a race, any action of an x-block is processed before an action of a y-block, if $x < y$ (x is preemptive over y). Then the AT is race-avoiding. Towards a contradiction, assume there are blocks $B_0, B_1, \ldots, B_{k-1}$ forming a cycle as described in Corollary 1, where each B_i is an x_i-block. By the order and the races, we get $x_0 \leq x_1 \leq \ldots \leq x_{k-1} \leq x_0$, i.e., we have a single timer (as in the first hypothesis). Hence, it is always possible to wiggle, which is a contradiction.

5 Conclusion and Future Work

In this paper, we studied automata with timers. We proved that the reachability problem for ATs is PSPACE-complete. Moreover, given a padded timed run in an AT, we defined a decomposition of its actions into blocks, and provided a way to remove races (concurrent actions) inside the run by wiggling blocks one by one. We also proved that this notion of wiggling is necessary and sufficient to decide whether an AT is race-avoiding. Finally, we showed that deciding whether an AT is race-avoiding is in 3EXP and PSPACE-hard.

For future work, it may be interesting to tighten the complexity bounds for the latter decision problem, both when fixing the sets I and X and when not. A second important direction, which we plan to pursue, is to work on a learning algorithm for ATs, as initiated in [18] with Mealy machines with one timer. This would allow us to construct ATs from real-world systems, such as network protocols, in order to verify that these systems behave as expected.

References

1. Aceto, L., Laroussinie, F.: Is your model checker on time? On the complexity of model checking for timed modal logics. J. Log. Algebraic Meth. Program. **52–53**, 7–51 (2002). https://doi.org/10.1016/S1567-8326(02)00022-X
2. Aichernig, B.K., Pferscher, A., Tappler, M.: From passive to active: learning timed automata efficiently. In: Lee, R., Jha, S., Mavridou, A., Giannakopoulou, D. (eds.) NFM 2020. LNCS, vol. 12229, pp. 1–19. Springer, Cham (2020). https://doi.org/10.1007/978-3-030-55754-6_1
3. Alur, R.: Timed automata. In: Halbwachs, N., Peled, D. (eds.) CAV 1999. LNCS, vol. 1633, pp. 8–22. Springer, Heidelberg (1999). https://doi.org/10.1007/3-540-48683-6_3
4. Alur, R., Dill, D.L.: A theory of timed automata. Theor. Comput. Sci. **126**(2), 183–235 (1994). https://doi.org/10.1016/0304-3975(94)90010-8
5. An, J., Chen, M., Zhan, B., Zhan, N., Zhang, M.: Learning One-Clock Timed Automata. In: TACAS 2020, Part I. LNCS, vol. 12078, pp. 444–462. Springer, Cham (2020). https://doi.org/10.1007/978-3-030-45190-5_25
6. Angluin, D.: Learning regular sets from queries and counterexamples. Inf. Comput. **75**(2), 87–106 (1987). https://doi.org/10.1016/0890-5401(87)90052-6
7. Baier, C., Katoen, J.: Principles of Model Checking. MIT Press (2008)
8. Bouyer, P., Fahrenberg, U., Larsen, K.G., Markey, N., Ouaknine, J., Worrell, J.: Model checking real-time systems. In: Handbook of Model Checking, pp. 1001–1046. Springer, Cham (2018). https://doi.org/10.1007/978-3-319-10575-8_29
9. Bruyère, V., Pérez, G.A., Staquet, G., Vaandrager, F.W.: Automata with timers. CoRR abs/2305.07451 (2023). https://doi.org/10.48550/arXiv.2305.07451
10. Clarke, E.M., Henzinger, T.A., Veith, H., Bloem, R. (eds.): Handbook of Model Checking. Springer, Heidelberg (2018). https://doi.org/10.1007/978-3-319-10575-8
11. Dill, D.L.: Timing assumptions and verification of finite-state concurrent systems. In: Sifakis, J. (ed.) CAV 1989. LNCS, vol. 407, pp. 197–212. Springer, Heidelberg (1990). https://doi.org/10.1007/3-540-52148-8_17
12. Grädel, E., Thomas, W., Wilke, T.: Automata, Logics, and Infinite Games: A Guide to Current Research, vol. 2500. Springer, Heidelberg (2003). https://doi.org/10.1007/3-540-36387-4
13. Grinchtein, O., Jonsson, B., Leucker, M.: Learning of event-recording automata. Theor. Comput. Sci. **411**(47), 4029–4054 (2010). https://doi.org/10.1016/j.tcs.2010.07.008
14. Grinchtein, O., Jonsson, B., Pettersson, P.: Inference of event-recording automata using timed decision trees. In: Baier, C., Hermanns, H. (eds.) CONCUR 2006. LNCS, vol. 4137, pp. 435–449. Springer, Heidelberg (2006). https://doi.org/10.1007/11817949_29
15. Howar, F., Steffen, B.: Active automata learning in practice. In: Bennaceur, A., Hähnle, R., Meinke, K. (eds.) Machine Learning for Dynamic Software Analysis: Potentials and Limits. LNCS, vol. 11026, pp. 123–148. Springer, Cham (2018). https://doi.org/10.1007/978-3-319-96562-8_5

16. Thomas, W.: Languages, automata, and logic. In: Rozenberg, G., Salomaa, A. (eds.) Handbook of Formal Languages, pp. 389–455. Springer, Heidelberg (1997). https://doi.org/10.1007/978-3-642-59126-6_7

17. Tripakis, S., Yovine, S.: Analysis of timed systems using time-abstracting bisimulations. Formal Meth. Syst. Des. **18**(1), 25–68 (2001). https://doi.org/10.1023/A:1008734703554

18. Vaandrager, F., Ebrahimi, M., Bloem, R.: Learning Mealy machines with one timer. Inf. Comput., 105013 (2023). https://doi.org/10.1016/j.ic.2023.105013

Layered Controller Synthesis for Dynamic Multi-agent Systems

Emily Clement[1]([⊠]), Nicolas Perrin-Gilbert[1]([⊠]),
and Philipp Schlehuber-Caissier[2]([⊠])

[1] Sorbonne Université, CNRS, Institut des Systèmes Intelligents et de Robotique,
ISIR, 75005 Paris, France
clement@sorbonne-universite.fr, perrin-gilbert@sorbonne-universite.fr
[2] EPITA Research Laboratory, Le Kremlin-Bicêtre, France
philipp@lrde.epita.fr

Abstract. In this paper we present a layered approach for multi-agent control problem, decomposed into three stages, each building upon the results of the previous one. First, a high-level plan for a coarse abstraction of the system is computed, relying on parametric timed automata augmented with stopwatches as they allow to efficiently model simplified dynamics of such systems. In the second stage, the high-level plan, based on SMT-formulation, mainly handles the combinatorial aspects of the problem, provides a more dynamically accurate solution. These stages are collectively referred to as the SWA-SMT solver. They are correct by construction but lack a crucial feature: they cannot be executed in real time. To overcome this, we use SWA-SMT solutions as the initial training dataset for our last stage, which aims at obtaining a neural network control policy. We use reinforcement learning to train the policy, and show that the initial dataset is crucial for the overall success of the method.

1 Introduction

Controlling a system involving multiple agents sharing a common task is a problem occurring in several domains such as mobile or industrial robotics. Concrete instances range from controlling swarms of drones, autonomous vehicles or warehouse robots. The problem is studied for specific instances but remains a difficult problem in general, especially in safety critical cases. The main complexity stems from the different types of decisions to take: such control problems often have a strong combinatorial side while the approach also has to deal with the physical reality of the agents, whose state typically evolves according to some differential equation, and limitations on the control inputs have to be taken into account. Finally, the controller has to be executed in real-time, which typically limits the applicability of formal methods due to their high complexity.

This work was partially funded by ANR project TickTac (ANR-18-CE40-0015).

L. Petrucci and J. Sproston (Eds.): FORMATS 2023, LNCS 14138, pp. 50–68, 2023.
https://doi.org/10.1007/978-3-031-42626-1_4

In this paper, we propose a layered approach for synthesizing control strategies for multi-agent dynamical systems, whose effectiveness we demonstrate on an example of centralized traffic guidance used for illustration throughout the paper.

The layered approach involves three stages, each one addressing a specific aspect of the control problem by building on the results of the previous stage. The first stage deals with the combinatorial side of the control problem: using a sufficiently coarse abstraction of the system dynamics, one can rely on timed automata augmented with stopwatches as a model. Efficient algorithms exist to explore such models allowing us to find a high-level plan that guarantees success in this abstract setting. The second stage takes the high-level plan as an input and refines it using a more realistic model of the system while maintaining a high degree of similarity between the refined and high-level solution. In our running example, we formulate this as an SMT problem, respecting the discrete version of the differential equation describing the system while also taking into account the input and state constraints. The complexity of this stage remains reasonable as the combinatorial aspects have already been solved. The final stage addresses the issue of real-time execution and generalization. To this end, we train a neural network policy via reinforcement learning. We use the two first stages to construct a dataset of successful episodes on many random instances of the problem, and exploit this dataset to guide the reinforcement learning towards good solutions. On our running example, we show that the initial dataset of solutions is crucial for the overall success: the reinforcement learning only succeeds if it has access to it.

The rest of the paper is structured as follows. In Sect. 2 we present our running example, Sect. 3 briefly discusses related work, and then we describe each stage of the approach in its own section along with the necessary technical background: the first stage using timed automata in Sect. 4, the second SMT-based stage in Sect. 5 and finally the synthesis of the actual controller based on reinforcement learning in Sect. 6. An extended version of this article is available [14].

2 Running Example: Centralized Traffic Control

Let us first present a multi-agent system used as running example (Fig. 1a) to illustrate our method throughout the article. In this example, each agent models a physical car on a road network. Each of the cars is given a fixed path to follow and it needs to attain its designated goal position from its initial position, while maintaining a security distance to the other cars. In such a setting the dynamics can be reduced to a second order ordinary differential equation with lower and upper bounds on the first and second derivative (corresponding to the speed and acceleration of the car).

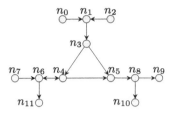

(a) An abstract 2-D representation of the traffic.

(b) Three different paths p_0, p_1, p_2.

Fig. 1. An abstract representation of our running example, arrows indicate which direction can be taken.

2.1 Multi-agent Traffic

We model the traffic as a network of sections on which a fixed number of cars have to navigate. Cars drive along their *paths* which consist of a list of sections. Cars cannot overtake or cross each other on the same section. A minimum security distance must be maintained at all time.

To define a **section**, denoted s, we specify its beginning node, n_b, its end node, n_e, and its length L. We can therefore write a section $s := s_{[n_b, n_e], L}$. To specify its direction ($\rightarrow$ or $\leftarrow$), we augment a section s with a direction $d \in \{\rightarrow, \leftarrow\}$ into a **directed section**, denoted $\boldsymbol{s}$, or $(s, \boldsymbol{d})$. The notion of beginning and end nodes of a section is extended to directed sections, reversing the two nodes if $\boldsymbol{d} = \leftarrow$. A directed section $\boldsymbol{s}'$ is a **successor** (*resp.* **predecessor**) of the directed section $\boldsymbol{s}$ if $n_e = n_b'$ (*resp.* $n_e' = n_b$). The sections $\boldsymbol{s}$ and $\boldsymbol{s}'$ are said to be **neighbours** if $\boldsymbol{s}$ is either a **successor** or **predecessor** of $\boldsymbol{s}'$.

A **path** p is defined as a finite list of directed sections: $p = (\boldsymbol{s}_k)_{0 \leq k \leq m}$ such that for all $k \in [0, m-1]$, $\boldsymbol{s}_{k+1}$ is a successor of $\boldsymbol{s}_k$. The end (*resp.* beginning) node of a path is the end (*resp.* beginning) node of its last (*resp.* first) directed section. By abuse of notation, we denote $\boldsymbol{s} \in p$ if there exists an index k such that $\boldsymbol{s} = \boldsymbol{s}_k$.

In Fig. 1b, 3 paths are described: directed sections $(s_{[n_4, n_6], L}, \leftarrow)$ and $(s_{[n_4, n_5], L}, \rightarrow)$ are neighbours, but $(s_{[n_4, n_6], L}, \rightarrow)$ and $(s_{[n_4, n_5], L}, \rightarrow)$ are not.

A **car** is defined as a tuple of an index i and a path p. A **car traffic**, denoted $\mathcal{C}$, is a set of cars. The set of sections (*resp.* directed sections) of the cars of a car traffic is denoted $\mathcal{S}$ (*resp.* $\boldsymbol{\mathcal{S}}$). A section s is an **intersection** if there exist two different paths p, p' and two directions $\boldsymbol{d}, \boldsymbol{d}' \in \{\rightarrow, \leftarrow\}$ such that $(s, \boldsymbol{d}) \in p, (s, \boldsymbol{d}') \in p'$.

Let us illustrate again with our example of Fig. 1 with a car traffic composed of three cars $(i, p_i)_{i=0,1,2}$. Intersections here are $s_{[n_1, n_3], L}$, $s_{[n_4, n_6], L}$ and $s_{[n_5, n_8], L}$.

Since the path of each car is fixed, we only need to keep track of its speed and its progress along its path.

2.2 Collision Avoidance Problem

Given a security distance ε, the initial positions of all cars, bounds on their speed, acceleration and deceleration, the goal is to find trajectories for all cars, which can be interpreted as a **centralized strategy**, that respect the three following rules.

Let $\mathrm{sect}(c,t)$ (*resp.* $\mathrm{sect}_d(c,t)$) denote the current section (*resp.* directed section) of car c at time t and $p_s(c,t)$ its current relative position within s.

1. **Same directed section:** for all cars $c_i, c_j \in \mathcal{C}$, $c_i \neq c_j$, for all $t \geq 0$, if $\mathrm{sect}_d(c,t) = \mathrm{sect}_d(c',t) = s$ then: $|p_s(c_i,t) - p_s(c_j,t)| \geq \varepsilon$
2. **Neighbouring sections:** If there exists a section s' such that there exists two cars $c_i = (i, [\cdots, (s', d'_i), \cdots]) \in \mathcal{C}$, and $c_j = (j, [\cdots, (s, d_j), (s', d'_j), (s'', d''_j), \cdots]) \in \mathcal{C}$ sharing the section s', then:
   - If $d'_i = d'_j$, then for all t, such that $\mathrm{sect}_d(c_i,t) = (s', d'_i)$, $\mathrm{sect}_d(c_j,t) = (s'', d''_j)$, we have $L' - p_{(s',d'_i)}(c_i,t) + p_{(s'',d''_j)}(c_j,t) \geq \varepsilon$.
   - If $d'_i \neq d'_j$, then for all t, such that $\mathrm{sect}_d(c_i,t) = (s', d'_i)$, $\mathrm{sect}_d(c_j,t) = (s, d_j)$, we have $L' - p_{(s',d'_i)}(c_i,t) + L - p_{(s,d_i)}(c_j,t) \geq \varepsilon$.
3. **Same section, opposite direction:** for all section $s \in \mathcal{S}$, for all $t \geq 0$ and for each pair of cars $c_i, c_j \in \mathcal{C}$: $\neg(\mathrm{sect}_d(c_i,t) = (s, \rightarrow) \wedge \mathrm{sect}_d(c_j,t) = (s, \leftarrow))$

2.3 Running Example

Let us consider three possible paths, illustrated in Fig. 1. All sections have the same security distance ε and the same length, $L = 30$, except for those from n_3 to n_5 and n_3 to n_4 that have length $30\sqrt{2}$. The cars are defined as $(i, p_0)_{i=1,2,3}$, $(i, p_1)_{i=4,5,6}$ and $(i, p_2)_{i=7,8,9}$. They all have different initial and goal positions, starting with a security distance 2ε between them as shown in Fig. 2. For instance, the initial position of car 2 is 2ε to the right of n_0 in direction of n_1. Its goal position is $L - 2\varepsilon$ to the right of n_6. All other cars are setup similarly. Let us precise that, to make the implementation of the car traffic more convenient, we created additional nodes dedicated to the initial and goal positions of each car, omitted here for clarity. Therefore in our actual implementation, the section from n_0 to n_1 is subdivided with nodes n'_0 and n''_0 representing the actual initial positions of car 2 and 3.

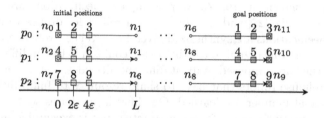

Fig. 2. Initial and goal position of cars

In the next sections, we present our method and apply it to this problem with several levels of abstraction. Firstly, in Sect. 4, we conceive a high-level plan relying on timed automata, assuming that the speed of cars is discretized to two values, a nominal value v and 0, and that cars can switch between these speeds instantly.

We also assume that all vehicles must respect the same security distance on all sections (extending to different speed or security distance between sections is trivial). Secondly, in Sect. 5, we refine this abstract model by allowing for arbitrarily many speed levels between v and 0 and also by respecting the maximal values for acceleration and deceleration. In Sect. 6, there are discrete time steps, but the neural network policy outputs continuous values for the acceleration/deceleration.

3   Related Work

There exists a rich literature on multi-agent systems, including path planning or controller synthesis. Providing a general overview over these topics is beyond the scope of this paper, however we give a brief overview of the ones that best match our objective. In our model, decisions are taken by a centralized control agent (the reference trajectories) with perfect knowledge and then executed by all executing agents (the cars). For a good survey of topics related to multi-agent systems we refer to [16].

Path planning, collision avoidance and controller synthesis for multi-agent systems in general as well as centralized traffic control allow for a rich variety of useful abstraction which in turn leads to a large spectrum of techniques and concepts that can be applied. Approaches can be differentiated into different categories: fully discretized approaches largely ignoring the underlying dynamics of the system fall into the category of multi-agent path finding. Here the problem boils down to a graph search on (very) large graphs, see [32,33]. Multi-agent motion planning in contrast takes into account the underlying the dynamics (possibly even uncertainty) and works over continuous domains as done in [13]. We are positioned in between these approaches: we consider the dynamics of the system, however the road system is fixed, so the planning is over a finite domain.

Another way to distinguish approaches is the complexity of the specification. If the target is known and the only goal is to avoid collision, less formal approaches ensuring safety and success in practice without a proof can provide good results as shown in [10,17]. More complex specifications are taken into account by works like [27] and [11]. In [27], controllers for drones verifying temporal logic specifications are synthesized given low-level controllers guaranteeing to bring them from one region to another exist; collision between different drones is ignored as they are supposed to fly at different altitudes. In [11] controllers for a fleet of warehouse robots that have to share resources to fulfill different task in a near optimal manner are learned. Our final layer shares some characteristics of [10]: it does not provide formal guarantees but is executable in real-time. With [11] we share the idea of a layered approach however to achieve different goals. In their work one controller is learned for resource distribution and another for path-planning. Our approach in contrast uses layers to refine plans with different levels of abstractions. In [28], temporal logic task specifications are translated into real-valued functions that can be used as reward signals to guide reinforcement learning.

Finally, there also exist many works tackling explicitly collision avoidance in traffic scenarios like [15,22–24,29]. The works of [22–24] rely on discretization and overapproximation, then proving collision freeness for a given set controllers and maneuvers in an offline manner. In [15] only intersections are treated but not the problem of sharing a section while driving in the same direction. [29] avoids collision by finding an optimal scheduling for the traffic lights, which is however only applicable in a very restricted scenario.

4   High Level Planning

Let us present the first level of our method, based on Timed Automata (TA), a well established tool to model real-time systems with timing constraints using clocks. Besides time, these clocks can also be used to model other quantities if they behave somewhat similarly to time in an abstract sense. In our running example, we assign to each car a clock that tracks its progress along its path. This basic framework is not expressive enough to obtain a useful model and we need to use several extensions. We augment the TA with stopwatches to represent the agent at standstill or driving at nominal speed. We rely on channels to ensure the collision avoidance and relative order between cars. To obtain reachability in minimal time, we dedicate a clock to represent global time (therefore never stopped nor reset), which is used as a parameter that does not appear in the constraints.

4.1   Timed Automata, Stopwatches and Channels

In this section we recall standard TA semantics as well as the needed extensions.

Definition 1 ([3]). *A Timed Automaton (TA) $\mathcal{A}$ can be defined by the tuple $(Q, \ell_0, \mathcal{X}, Inv, \Sigma, T)$, where Q is a finite set of locations, ℓ_0 is the initial location, $\mathcal{X}$ is a finite set of clocks, Σ a finite alphabet, $Inv : Q \to \mathcal{G}(\mathcal{X})$ is the function of invariants of locations and $T \subseteq Q \times \mathcal{G}(\mathcal{X}) \times \Sigma \times 2^{\mathcal{X}} \times Q$ a set of transitions.*
There are two types of transitions with the following semantics:

- *Time elapsing move: $(\ell, v) \xrightarrow{\delta} (\ell, v')$: elapses some amount of time δ by setting $v' = v + \delta$ and is only allowed if $v \models Inv(\ell)$ and $v' \models Inv(\ell)$*
- *Discrete transition: $(\ell, v) \to (\ell', v')$ indicates a discrete transition. This is only possible if (1) $v \models Inv(\ell)$ and $v' \models Inv(\ell')$ and (2) there exists a transition $t := (v, g, a, r, \ell') \in T$ such that $v \models Inv(\ell)$, $v \models g$, $v' = v[r \leftarrow 0]$ and $v' \models Inv(\ell')$. We say that t is labelled by a.*

Here, $v + \delta$ denotes the valuation v_δ such that for any clock x in the set of clocks, denoted $\mathcal{X}$, $v_\delta(x) = v(x) + \delta$ and $v\,[r \leftarrow 0]$ the valuation v_r such that for $v_r(x) = 0$ if $x \in r$ and $v(x)$ otherwise. $\mathcal{G}\,(\mathcal{X})$ defines the set of clock-constraints by a conjunction of simple (in-) equalities: $\wedge_i x \bowtie c_i$ for some clock $x \in \mathcal{X}$, some constant $c_i \in \mathbb{N}$ and $\bowtie \in \{\leq, <, =, >, \geq\}$. We denote $v \models g$ to express that a valuation v satisfies the constraint of $g \in \mathcal{G}\,(\mathcal{X})$.

Location based Stopwatch Timed Automata (SWA), presented in [2], are an extension of TA where clocks can be "frozen" on locations. More formally, it is a tuple $\mathcal{A} = (Q, \ell_0, \mathcal{X}, Inv, \Sigma, \mathcal{S}, T)$ with $Q, \ell_0, \mathcal{X}, Inv, \Sigma, T$ have the same definition as in Definition 1 and $\mathcal{S} : Q \rightarrow 2^{\mathcal{X}}$ is a function assigning to a location ℓ the set of stopped clocks at ℓ. The definition for discrete transitions is the same as in Definition 1, however the time-elapsing transition changes. $(\ell, v) \xrightarrow{\delta} (\ell, v')$: (1) elapses some amount of time δ by setting $v'(x) = v(x)$ if $x \in \mathcal{S}(\ell)$, $v(x) + \delta$ otherwise

Reachability of SWA is undecidable in general however, as shown in [20], there exist decidable fragments like **Initialized Stopwatch Timed Automata** (ISWA) for which deciding reachability remains in PSPACE as for TA.

Definition 2 ([20]). *Initialized Stopwatch Timed Automata a SWA $\mathcal{A}$ is a (ISWA) if for any transition $t = (\ell, g, a, r, \ell')$, if $(x \in \mathcal{S}(\ell) \wedge x \notin \mathcal{S}(\ell'))$ or $(x \notin \mathcal{S}(\ell) \wedge x \in \mathcal{S}(\ell'))$, then $x \in r$.*

That is a clock is only started or stopped if it is also reset. We will show in Sect. 4.2 that our TA abstraction of the running example falls into this category.

Definition 3 ([12]). *Channel systems are finite automata augmented with a finite number of channels. They can be thought of as FIFO (First In First Out) queues for symbols used for asynchronous communication. During a transition, we can either (1) Leave the channels untouched (2) Push a symbol into a channel $\mathfrak{c}$, denoted $\ell \xrightarrow{\mathfrak{c}!a} \ell'$ indicating that the symbol a is appended to $\mathfrak{c}$. This is always possible if channels are unbounded, i.e. can contain an unbounded number of symbols. (3) Peek and pop a symbol from a channel $\mathfrak{c}$, denoted $\ell \xrightarrow{\mathfrak{c}?a} \ell'$. This action looks at the head of $\mathfrak{c}$. If it contains the symbol a, it is removed from $\mathfrak{c}$ when taking the transition, otherwise the transition is deactivated.*

Bounded channel systems, that is channel systems in which channels can only contain a fixed number of symbols, are decidable. They can be translated into a finite automaton (with exponentially many locations in both the number of different symbols and the maximal length of the channel), which can then form a synchronized product with the other automata.

As a high-level abstraction, we model our example as a parallel composition of ISWA communicating via strong synchronization augmented by channels.

4.2   Timed Automata Representation of Our Running Example

To model our car traffic with systems of Timed Automata, we suppose that each car begins/ends at the beginning/end node of a section and that it stops instantly. Let us describe the automata we generate to model our system with a simple example[1].

For each car A, the clock x_A represents its progress along its path. For each directed section $s' = (s'_{[n_i,n_j],L}, d)$ of its path, A performs three steps corresponding to three locations in the TA: **(1)** waiting within the section s' (location $w_{s'}$) after entering in s' (action $\text{sync}_{s'}(x_A)$); here the associated clock is stopped, **(2)** driving in the section (location $d_{s'}$), **(3)** arriving at the end of the section (location $a_{s'}$) after having traveled a distance of L (*resp.* letting L time unit elapses). We represent theses steps in Fig. 3, in which L_0 denotes the accumulated distance to arrive at the end of section s. The timed automaton of car A, is the concatenation of "sub-automata" of each directed section along the path. If s' has no successor (*resp.* predecessor), a_s (*resp.* $d_{s'}$) is the goal (*resp.* initial) location of the automaton.

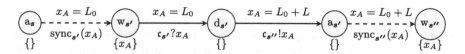

Fig. 3. The sub-automaton of our car Timed Automaton

If a section s is indeed an intersection, then multiple copies of its sub-automaton will be present in the automata of the corresponding cars. In order to ensure that a trace in this abstract model allows for collision avoidance in the real-world, we need to synchronize the different copies. To this end we create the intersection automaton shown in Fig. 4 for two cars sharing a section in direction $\rightarrow$.

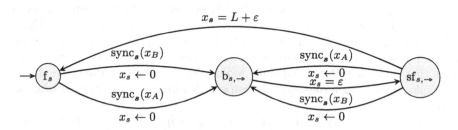

Fig. 4. The intersection automaton of s where A and B can drive in direction $\rightarrow$.

The three states correspond to: **free** (f_s): any car can enter in any direction; **blocked** ($b_{s,\rightarrow}$): no car can enter; **semi-free** ($sf_{s,\leftarrow}$): an additional car can enter in $\rightarrow$ direction. Together with the car automaton it ensures that at least

---

[1] The full construction is detailed in appendix A of the extended version [14].

ε time units pass before two cars can enter the same section in the same direction, respecting the security distance in an abstract fashion. Similarly, two cars entering the section in opposite direction must be separated by at least $L + \varepsilon$ time units, allowing the first car to cross the section safely before letting the second car in. Note that all guards only involve equality testing, which means we could additionally reset the clock to the same value, making our SWA effectively ISWA.

This ensures the safety distance, however not the relative order between the cars: to prevent cars from reversing their order in $w_{s'}$, cars have to announce themselves on the successor section by pushing their token on the corresponding channel $c_{s''}$ before entering $a_{s'}$. By doing so, the transition from waiting to driving is only activated if the relative order is respected.

4.3   Computing the Optimal Strategy for Reachability

Several mature tools handling timed automata able to answer reachability problems like IMITATOR [4], Uppaal [7,8] Tchecker [21] exist. However, at the time of our experiments, none of them supported all the features we needed: channels, stopwatches and time optimality.

What would be difficult for a general approach is to detect that a state cannot lead to a solution faster than the best one found so far, and it would typically lead to unnecessarily large computation times. This is what motivated us to propose a specific algorithm for time optimal reachability dedicated to our context.

A Time Optimal Reachability Algorithm. Our goal is to obtain a time optimal trace witnessing reachability and use it later to construct our control algorithm. We propose a Depth First Search (DFS) forward exploration that uses the properties of our systems of ISWA, synchronized with channels. As we do not use the full expressiveness of parameters, as defined in Parametric Timed Automata [6,25] and [5] (in our model, they never appear in any guards nor are they reset) we can compare the obtained traces and store the current best trace that minimizes the global time. Moreover, we can prune the states during the exploration using a conservative heuristic, leading to significant performance gains.

Here, we give a very brief overview of its principle of our algorithm[2]. States consist of the configuration (location, zone representation via Difference Bounded Matrix (DBM)) and the channels' configuration. We extend the subset relation for zones, denoted $\preceq$, to bounded channels: let s, s' be two states with respective zone z, z', $s \sqsubseteq s'$ iff they have the same location, the same channel configuration and $z \preceq z'$ holds. This gives a partial order on states. As all our guards consist in checking equality, we can compute the successors by letting time elapse in all locations, until a clock matches the equality constraints of the future transition.

---

[2] full description is presented in the appendix B of the extended version [14].

Finally, we use the conservative heuristic to detect if the current state implies a necessarily larger global time, in which case it is discarded.

5   Ensuring Feasibility of High-Level Plans

Our first layer guarantees correctness in the abstract setting, but is in general not physically realistic/realizable. This gap between the physical reality and the high-level plan has to be closed, or at least bounded, in order to obtain an actually feasible plan. We extract *important* events and their relative order, which represent the *combinatorial* part of the problem, and retain it for the refined solution. We so to speak build upon the high level plan to obtain a more realistic sequence of inputs which still guarantees correctness.

In our running example, the high-level plan is represented by the time optimal SWA-trace. Recall that the control input, the current speed of the car, is represented by the derivative of the clock associated to it. In particular this entails that the car can only be stopped (derivative equals 0) and the car drives at nominal speed (derivative equals 1) and there is no time-delay between them corresponding to infinite acceleration, a hardly realistic assumption.

To provide a more realistic model, we rely on satisfiability modulo theories (SMT). The SMT framework provides great flexibility and expressiveness resulting from the wide range of theories and functionalities disposable: Quantifiers, Theory of reals, Minimization of an objective function, arrays and functions etc.

For our running example, using these advanced functionalities comes at a very high cost and we therefore avoid them. We rely on a discretization to allow for a good trade-off between model accuracy and the complexity of the resulting problem. Moreover, instead of minimizing the global time using the built-in minimization functionalities of z3, it has proven to be more effective to perform a linear search, solving the problem for some given maximal global time repeatedly.

From SWA traces to piecewise linear control laws

The SMT instance for traffic control is composed of one set of constraints directly derived from the hybrid system and a second set of constraints representing the high-level plan. We model the traffic system as each car having a piecewise constant speed and discretize time into N steps of equal duration, that we denote δt. We create a variable representing the speed of the ith car during the kth time step, denoted $\tilde{v}_i(k)$, and denote $\tilde{x}_i(k)$ the position, in its path, of the car i at the beginning of the kth timestep. Without loss of generality, we suppose that $\delta t = 1$.

We derive two constraints to guarantee physical realizability under a bounded error. The position is the integral over the velocities, a simple sum as the velocities are piecewise constant: $\tilde{x}_i(k) = \sum_{l=0}^{k-1} \tilde{v}_i(l)$. Secondly we need to bound acceleration and velocity:

$$\forall i, \ \forall k \in [0 \cdots N - 2], \ \tilde{v}_i(k) - d_{\max} \leq \tilde{v}_i(k + 1) \leq \tilde{v}_i(k) + a_{\max}$$
$$\forall i, \ \forall k \in [0 \cdots N - 1], \ 0 \leq \tilde{v}_i(k) \leq v_{\max}$$

where $d_{\max}$ (*resp.* $a_{\max}$) is the maximal deceleration (*resp.* acceleration) and $v_{\max}$ is the maximal speed of the car ensuring a smaller gap between the actual capabilities of the car and the ones implied by the resulting reference trajectory.

To ensure coherence between the abstract solution represented by the SWA trace and the refined solution represented by the piecewise constant speed, as well as to reduce the search space of the SMT variables, we extract several conditions. Let us denote by $\tilde{p}_{i,s}^0$ (*resp.* $\tilde{p}_{i,s}^1$) the position at which the ith car **enters** (*resp.* **leaves**) some section s, which is obviously only defined if the total trajectory of the ith car passes through section s.

Relative Event Order. We want to ensure that *important* events happen in the same chronological order as given by the SWA trace. *Important* events, in our running example, are the moments when cars enter or leave a section. We impose the constraints for each pair of car and event. Suppose car i enters (*resp.* leaves) the section s before car j enters (*resp.* leaves) section s', this can be imposed by:

$$\forall k \in [0 \cdots N - 2], \forall e \in \{0, 1\}, \tilde{x}_i(k) < \tilde{p}_{i,s}^e \implies \tilde{x}_j(k) < \tilde{p}_{j,s'}^e$$

Safety Distance. Whenever a car uses an *intersection*, we need to ensure that it respects a security distance, denoted ε, from the other cars, even if the two cars are not currently sharing a section. Suppose c_i enters section s before c_j, then for any $k \in [0 \cdots N - 2]$:

$$(\tilde{p}_{i,s}^0 \leq \tilde{x}_i(k) \leq \tilde{p}_{i,s}^1 \wedge \tilde{p}_{j,s}^0 \leq \tilde{x}_j(k) \leq \tilde{p}_{j,s}^1) \implies ((\tilde{x}_i(k) - \tilde{p}_{i,s}^0) - (\tilde{x}_j(k) - \tilde{p}_{j,s}^0) > \varepsilon)$$

Approximate Timing. To further restrict the search space for the SMT problem and to increase the similarity between the abstract and refined solution, we do not only keep the relative order between *important* events, but we also impose that they happen at approximately the same global time.

To do this, we introduce a parameter p, which limits the difference between the global time at which an *important* event happens in the high-level plan and the refined plan. This permits a trade-off between the similarity of the high-level, the refined plan and the danger of the SMT instance becoming unsatisfiable (smaller value for p implies higher similarity however the high-level plan may be infeasible for the more realistic model rendering the SMT instance unsatisfiable).

More formally, consider the important event of c_i entering s at the global time t_0. To ensure that the event will actually happen at most p time-units later, we impose: $\tilde{x}_i(t_0 + p) \geq \tilde{p}_{i,s}^0$, since the duration of each step equals 1 (w.l.o.g.).

Interpreting the Solution. If a satisfying solution for the SMT instance is found, we can readily extract the refined plan from it. All information necessary are the speed values for each time-step and car, *i.e.* the value for all the $\tilde{v}_i(k)$.

6   Reinforcement Learning to Get Real-Time Policies

Our global approach is divided into 3 stages, and in the previous sections we have presented the 2 first stages, which correspond to distinct levels of abstraction of the multi-agent system we want to control. The solver presented in the two first stages in Sect. 4 and 5 are collectively called SMT-SWA solver. Given initial conditions of the system, these two stages enable us to get trajectories for all agents that solve the problem, but not in real-time, so if new initial conditions are faced at a high frequency, and if a high responsiveness is required, then the approach is not practical. For the third stage of our layered approach, which we present in this section, we create a dataset of SWA-SMT solutions on a large number of random instances of the problem, and use this dataset as the initial experience replay buffer of a reinforcement learning (RL) algorithm. Thereby we will first obtain a policy that imitates and slightly generalizes the SWA-SMT solutions, and will then progressively improve. At the end of the learning process, we get a neural network policy that can react in real-time to new conditions and can control the multi-agent system with a high success rate. We could also try to directly solve the multi-agent control problem with RL, with an initially empty experience replay buffer, but with our running example we show that for complex problems, the SWA-SMT solutions are crucial: without the initial dataset, the RL algorithm fails to find any solution to the problem, while with the initial dataset, the RL algorithm quickly matches and then outperforms the success rate of the SWA-SMT approach. In fact, RL algorithms are efficient at progressively improving control policies based on a dense reward signal, but problems with both continuous and combinatorial aspects may result in rewards that are very difficult to find. Multi-agent systems often have these properties, and the associated hard exploration problems are well known failure cases for standard reinforcement learning algorithms [9]. We believe that in this context, a layered approach as the one presented in this paper can be particularly efficient. Using high level abstractions and formal verification, we ignore most of the continuous aspects of the problem, but solve its the most combinatorial and discrete parts, and get traces that can be refined into acceptable solutions. We then build a dataset that can be exploited by reinforcement learning to quickly get good policies, and then iteratively improve them.

To apply reinforcement learning, we cast the problem as a Markov Decision Process (MDP) with a state space S, an action space A, an initial state distribution $p(s_0 \in S)$, a reward function $r(s_t \in S, a_t \in A, s_{t+1} \in S)$ and transition dynamics $p(s_{t+1} \in S | s_t \in S, a_t \in A)$. Since the running example we consider is deterministic, we more specifically use a deterministic transition function: $s_{t+1} = \texttt{step}(s_t, a_t)$. In this MDP, valid SWA-SMT trace should be directly interpretable as high reward episodes. See Appendix A for a detailed description of the elements of the MDP for our running example.

Using the initial state distribution, we define random instances of the problem, and run the SWA-SMT solver to get valid solutions, i.e. traces. We then transform each trace into an episode of the MDP. To do so, we first retrieve the sequence of states and actions (see Appendix A for details), then we compute the reward for all transitions of the episode, and we terminate the episode if a terminal state is reached (which happens only at the end because we only consider successful traces). The episodes we get correspond exactly to episodes of the MDP previously defined (again, see Appendix A for details). We should discard episodes exceeding the maximum number of transitions (85), but we have set this number conservatively so that the time optimal SWA-SMT solutions are always shorter than the limit.

For our running example, we used the SWA-SMT solver on random initial states to generate 2749 successful episodes (with reward ≥ 2000, see Appendix A) resulting in a total number of 176913 transitions. About 15% of the random initial conditions were solved by the SWA-SMT solver and led to successful traces.[3]

For the reinforcement learning, we select off-policy algorithms [31] that use a replay buffer to store experience (episode transitions). During training, random batches of transitions are sampled from the buffer, and gradients of loss functions computed on these batches are used to iteratively update the parameters of neural networks (typically the policy network or actor and the value network or critic). New episodes are continuously run with the trained policy to fill the buffer. We compare two approaches, one in which an RL algorithm is trained from scratch (with an initially empty replay buffer), and one in which an RL algorithm starts with its replay buffer filled with the 176913 transitions collected from the SWA-SMT solutions. More specifically, to perform RL form scratch, we first use TD3 [19], a popular off-policy reinforcement learning algorithm, whereas TD3BC [18] is used to perform RL with the replay buffer. TD3BC is TD3 with a slight modification: in the actor loss, a regularization term of behavioral cloning is added, helping the RL algorithm to handle and imitate expert training data that does not come from the trained policy. Originally designed for offline RL (*i.e.* RL on purely offline data, without running episodes), TD3BC can also be seen as a variant of TD3 that is able to start with a non-empty replay buffer initialized with expert data. We use exactly the same hyperparameters for TD3 and TD3BC (see Appendix B), and for the additional behavioral cloning regularization term in TD3BC, we use the default parameter $\alpha = 2.5$ (cf. [18]). Figure 5 shows the results we obtained with a training of 3 million steps on 5 random seeds for each method[4]. We define successful episodes as episodes with a cumulated reward greater than 2000, which only happens when each car reaches its final destination. We observe that the first approach (TD3 from scratch) never learns to solve the problem. On the other hand, after 250k steps (one step is one discrete

---

[3] Generating a successful SWA-SMT trace takes on average about 15sec on a Intel i5-1235u with 16 GB of RAM. Note that there is a high variance in this runtime ranging from under a second to several minutes. A timeout was set to 900 s.

[4] Using the *xpag* RL library [30], with a single Intel Core i7 CPU, 32 GB of RAM, and a single NVIDIA Quadro P3000 GPU, the training took between 40 and 50 min per million steps.

time step in an episode play with the neural network policy being trained), the second approach (TD3BC) already reaches the same success rate as the SWA-SMT solver (about 15%), and then it continues to improve during the 3 million steps of training. In the end, we obtain neural network policies with a success rate of approximately 35% in average, which is more than twice the success rate of the SWA-SMT solver. So we not only obtain policies that can be executed in real-time, we also obtain policies that find solutions more consistently.

However, while the SWA-SMT solutions are optimal by construction (*i.e.* they achieve success with the minimum number of steps), there is no such guarantee with the neural network policies trained via reinforcement learning. Figure 6 shows an episode played by a neural network policy trained with TD3BC. A full video of this episode and a few others is hosted at perso.eleves.ens-rennes.fr/people/Emily.Clement/Implementation/multi-agent.h tml The tool we implemented in open-source and can be found at gitlab.com/Millly/robotic-synthesis.

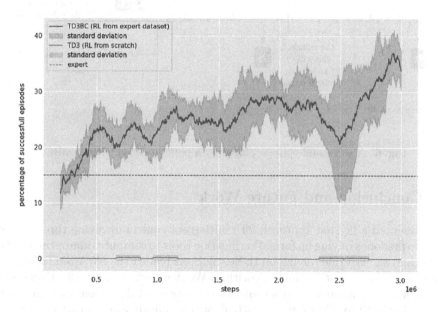

Fig. 5. Percentage of successful episodes during training.

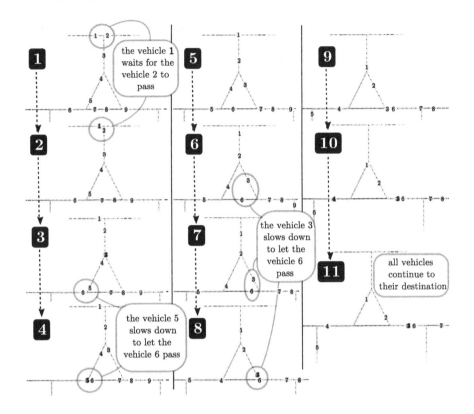

Fig. 6. A successful episode played by a policy trained with TD3BC.

7 Conclusion and Future Work

We presented a layered approach for multi-agent control involving three stages, the two first ones relying on formal verification tools to compute time optimal solutions, and the last one relying on these solutions (called the SWA-SMT data) to guide a reinforcement learning algorithm. We demonstrated the effectiveness of the approach by applying it to a centralized traffic control problem, showing that, thanks to the SWA-SMT data, the RL algorithm quickly learns to solve the problem and progressively improves to obtain higher success rates. Our results demonstrate the potential of combining layered approaches with RL for multi-agent control. The high-level abstraction in the first stage places emphasis on the combinatorial elements of the problem, leading to high-level plans which are then refined into solutions addressing the actual continuous dynamics of the agents. While it is difficult to construct these solutions in real-time, a rich enough dataset of such solutions can be used to efficiently guide the reinforcement learning, thus eliminating the need for the RL algorithm to tackle the difficult task of exploring the combinatorial aspects of the multi-agent control problem. Ultimately, we obtain a neural network policy capable of controlling the multi-agent system in real-time. In future

work, we would like to implement our proposed algorithm for time optimal reachability in ISWA with bounded channels in the open-source tool TChecker [21], and
apply our layered approach to decentralized multi-agent systems.

A   Markov Decision Process for the Running Example

The Markov Decision Process is defined by its state space S, action space A,
initial state distribution $p(s_0 \in S)$, reward function $r(s_t \in S, a_t \in A, s_{t+1} \in S)$
and deterministic transition function $s_{t+1} = \texttt{step}(s_t, a_t)$.

   We describe here all the elements of the MDP defined for our running example:

- **The state space ($\mathbb{R}^{720}$).** The environment contains 3 paths, which are
  unions of sections, and as detailed in Sect. 2, we have imposed a maximum
  number of 3 cars per path, so there are at most 9 cars, to which we can
  attribute a unique identifier (we use $\{-1, 0, 1\}^2$). The state is entirely defined
  by the speed and position of each car. We could thus use vectors of size 18 to
  represent states, but instead we chose a sparser representation with a better
  structure. To remain coherent, we use the same road network presented in
  Sect. 2 which is composed of 24 section (since every car has a dedicated initial
  and goal node subdividing the sections containing initial and goal positions).
  On this road network, three different paths are defined, and each section being
  shared by at most 2 paths. At any given time any section may contain at most
  6 cars by construction. For each section, we define a list of 6 tuples, all equal
  to $(0, 0, (0, 0), 0)$ if no car is currently inside the section. However if there
  are cars in the section, say 2 cars for example, then the first two tuples have
  this structure:

  (position with the section, normalized velocity, car identifier, 1)

  We represent states as a concatenation of the values of all these tuples for
  all the 24 sections, which amounts to a vector of size 720. It is a sparse
  representation, but its advantage is that it makes it easy to find cars close to
  each other, as they are either in the same section or in neighbor sections.
- **The action space ($\mathbb{R}^9$) and transition dynamics.** Given an ordering
  of the 9 cars, an action is simply a vector of 9 accelerations. If a_i is the
  acceleration for the car i, and if at the current time step its position within
  its path is p_i, and its speed is v_i, then at the next time step its position will
  be $p_i + v_i$, and its speed will be $v_i + a_i$. This defines the transition dynamics
  of the MDP. The components of an action corresponding to cars that are not
  present in the state are simply ignored. Remark: actions can be computed
  straightforwardly from a sequence of states as they are equal to the difference
  between consecutive speeds for each car.
- **The reward.** When all cars have reached their destination, i.e. crossed the
  end of their path, a reward of 2000 is given, and the episode is terminated.
  Besides, when there is either a collision (a violation of the safety distance
  between two cars) or two car facing each other in opposite directions in the

same section, a negative reward (-100) is given and the episode is terminated. Finally, at each time step, two positive rewards are given, one proportional to the average velocity of the cars (to encourage cars to go fast), and one proportional to the (clamped) minimum distance between all cars (to encourage cars to stay far from each other). We set the maximum number of time step per episode to 85, and adjust these rewards so that an episode cannot reach a cumulated reward of 2000 unless it is truly successful and gets the final $+2000$ reward.

- **The initial state distribution.** We define an arbitrary initial state distribution in which each of the 9 cars has an 80% chance of being present. The speed of each car is defined randomly, and positions are also defined randomly (within roughly the first two third of each path). Safety distances are ensured, so that the inital states are not in collision, however speeds may be such that there will a collision after the first time step, so there is no guarantee of feasibility.

B   Hyperparameters of the RL Algorithms

For TD3:

- Actor network architecture: multi-layer perceptron (MLP) [1] with 3 hidden layers of size 256 and rectified linear unit (ReLU) activation functions.
- Actor optimizer: ADAM [26], actor learning rate: 10^{-3}
- Critic network architecture: MLP with 3 hidden layers of size 256 and ReLU activation functions.
- Critic optimizer: ADAM, critic learning rate: 10^{-3}
- Discount factor: 0.99
- Soft update coefficient (τ): 0.05

For TD3BC:

- Actor network architecture: MLP with 3 hidden layers of size 256 and ReLU activation functions.
- Actor optimizer: ADAM, actor learning rate: 10^{-3}
- Critic network architecture: MLP with 3 hidden layers of size 256 and ReLU activation functions.
- Critic optimizer: ADAM, critic learning rate: 10^{-3}
- Discount factor: 0.99
- Soft update coefficient (τ): 0.05
- α: 2.5

References

1. Almeida, L.B.: Multilayer perceptrons. In: Handbook of Neural Computation, pp. C1.2:1–C1.2:30 (1997)

2. Alur, R., et al.: The algorithmic analysis of hybrid systems. Theoret. Comput. Sci. **138**(1), 3–34 (1995). ISSN 0304-3975. https://doi.org/10.1016/0304-3975(94)00202-T. https://www.sciencedirect.com/science/article/pii/030439759400202T. Accessed 03 Oct 2023

3. Alur, R., Dill, D.L.: A theory of timed automata. Theoret. Comput. Sci. **126**(2), 183–235 (1994). ISSN 0304-3975. https://doi.org/10.1016/0304-3975(94)90010-8. https://www.sciencedirect.com/science/article/pii/0304397594900108

4. André, É.: IMITATOR 3: synthesis of timing parameters beyond decidability. In: Silva, A., Leino, K.R.M. (eds.) CAV 2021. LNCS, vol. 12759, pp. 552–565. Springer, Cham (2021). https://doi.org/10.1007/978-3-030-81685-8_26

5. André, É.: What's decidable about parametric timed automata? Int. J. Softw. Tools Technol. Transf. **21**(2), 203–219 (2019)

6. André, É., Lime, D., Roux, O.H.: Decision problems for parametric timed automata. In: Ogata, K., Lawford, M., Liu, S. (eds.) ICFEM 2016. LNCS, vol. 10009, pp. 400–416. Springer, Cham (2016). https://doi.org/10.1007/978-3-319-47846-3_25

7. Behrmann, G., et al.: UPPAAL 4.0. In: 3rd International Conference on the Quantitative Evaluation of Systems, QEST 2006, Riverside, California, USA, September 2006, pp. 125–126. IEEE Computer Society (2006). https://doi.org/10.1109/QEST.2006.59

8. Behrmann, G., Cougnard, A., David, A., Fleury, E., Larsen, K.G., Lime, D.: UPPAAL-Tiga: time for playing games! In: Damm, W., Hermanns, H. (eds.) CAV 2007. LNCS, vol. 4590, pp. 121–125. Springer, Heidelberg (2007). https://doi.org/10.1007/978-3-540-73368-3_14

9. Bellemare, M., et al.: Unifying count-based exploration and intrinsic motivation. In: Advances in Neural Information Processing Systems. vol. 29 (2016). https://proceedings.neurips.cc/paper_files/paper/2016/file/afda332245e2af431fb7b672a68b659d-Paper.pdf

10. van den Berg, J.P., Lin, M.C., Manocha, D.: Reciprocal velocity obstacles for real-time multi-agent navigation. In: 2008 IEEE International Conference on Robotics and Automation, ICRA 2008, Pasadena, USA, pp. 1928–1935 (2008). https://doi.org/10.1109/ROBOT.2008.4543489

11. Bøgh, S., et al.: Distributed fleet management in noisy environments via model-predictive control. In: Proceedings of the International Conference on Automated Planning and Scheduling, vol. 32, pp. 565–573 (2022)

12. Brand, D., Zafiropulo, P.: On communicating finite-state machines. J. ACM **30**(2), 323–342 (1983). https://doi.org/10.1145/322374.322380

13. Chen, J., et al.: Scalable and safe multi-agent motion planning with nonlinear dynamics and bounded disturbances. In: Proceedings of the AAAI Conference on Artificial Intelligence, vol. 35, pp. 11237–11245 (2021)

14. Clement, E., Perrin-Gilbert, N., Schlehuber-Caissier, P.: Layered controller synthesis for dynamic multi-agent systems (2023). arXiv:2307.06758 [cs.AI]

15. Colombo, A., Del Vecchio, D.: Efficient algorithms for collision avoidance at intersections. In: Dang, T., Mitchell, I.M. (eds.) Hybrid Systems: Computation and Control, HSCC 2012, Beijing, China, pp. 145–154 (2012). https://doi.org/10.1145/2185632.2185656

16. Dorri, A., Kanhere, S.S., Jurdak, R.: Multi-agent systems: a survey. IEEE Access **6**, 28573–28593 (2018)

17. Fiorini, P., Shiller, Z.: Motion planning in dynamic environments using velocity obstacles. Int. J. Robot. Res. **17**(7), 760–772 (1998). https://doi.org/10.1177/027836499801700706

18. Fujimoto, S., Gu, S.S.: A minimalist approach to offline reinforcement learning. In: Advances in Neural Information Processing Systems, vol. 34, pp. 20132–20145 (2021)

19. Fujimoto, S., Hoof, H., Meger, D.: Addressing function approximation error in actor-critic methods. In: International Conference on Machine Learning, pp. 1587–1596. PMLR (2018)

20. Henzinger, T.A., et al.: What's decidable about hybrid automata? J. Comput. Syst. Sci. **57**(1), 94–124 (1998). https://doi.org/10.1006/jcss.1998.1581

21. Herbreteau, F., Point, G.: The TChecker tool and librairies. https://github.com/ticktac-project/tchecker

22. Hilscher, M., Linker, S., Olderog, E.-R.: Proving safety of traffic manoeuvres on country roads. In: Liu, Z., Woodcock, J., Zhu, H. (eds.) Theories of Programming and Formal Methods. LNCS, vol. 8051, pp. 196–212. Springer, Heidelberg (2013). https://doi.org/10.1007/978-3-642-39698-4_12

23. Hilscher, M., Schwammberger, M.: An abstract model for proving safety of autonomous urban traffic. In: Sampaio, A., Wang, F. (eds.) ICTAC 2016. LNCS, vol. 9965, pp. 274–292. Springer, Cham (2016). https://doi.org/10.1007/978-3-319-46750-4_16

24. Hilscher, M., Linker, S., Olderog, E.-R., Ravn, A.P.: An abstract model for proving safety of multi-lane traffic manoeuvres. In: Qin, S., Qiu, Z. (eds.) ICFEM 2011. LNCS, vol. 6991, pp. 404–419. Springer, Heidelberg (2011). https://doi.org/10.1007/978-3-642-24559-6_28

25. Hune, T., et al.: Linear parametric model checking of timed automata. J. Logic Algebraic Program. **52**, 183–220 (2002)

26. Kingma, D.P., Ba, J.: Adam: a method for stochastic optimization. In: ICLR (Poster) (2015). http://dblp.uni-trier.de/db/conf/iclr/iclr2015.html#KingmaB14

27. Kress-Gazit, H., Fainekos, G.E., Pappas, G.J.: Where's Waldo? Sensor-based temporal logic motion planning. In: 2007 IEEE International Conference on Robotics and Automation, ICRA 2007, 10–14 April 2007, Roma, Italy, pp. 3116–3121. IEEE (2007). https://doi.org/10.1109/ROBOT.2007.363946

28. Li, X., Ma, Y., Belta, C.: A policy search method for temporal logic specified reinforcement learning tasks. In: 2018 Annual American Control Conference (ACC), pp. 240–245. IEEE (2018)

29. Loos, S.M., Platzer, A.: Safe intersections: at the crossing of hybrid systems and verification. In: 14th International IEEE Conference on Intelligent Transportation Systems, ITSC 2011, Washington, DC, USA, pp. 1181–1186. IEEE (2011). https://doi.org/10.1109/ITSC.2011.6083138

30. Perrin-Gilbert, N.: xpag: a modular reinforcement learning library with JAX agents (2022). https://github.com/perrin-isir/xpag

31. Precup, D., Sutton, R.S., Dasgupta, S.: Off-policy temporal difference learning with function approximation. In: ICML, pp. 417–424 (2001)

32. Queffelec, A.: Connected multi-agent path finding: how robots get away with texting and driving. Ph.D. thesis. University of Rennes, France (2021). https://tel.archives-ouvertes.fr/tel-03517091

33. Stern, R.: Multi-agent path finding-an overview. In: Artificial Intelligence: 5th RAAI Summer School, Tutorial Lectures, Dolgoprudny, Russia, 4–7 July 2019, pp. 96–115 (2019)

On the Susceptibility of QDI Circuits to Transient Faults

Raghda El Shehaby[1] , Matthias Függer[2(✉)] , and Andreas Steininger[1]

[1] TU Wien, Institute of Computer Engineering, Vienna, Austria
[2] CNRS & LMF, ENS Paris-Saclay, Université Paris-Saclay & Inria,
Gif-sur-Yvette, France
mfuegger@lmf.cnrs.fr

Abstract. By design, quasi delay-insensitive (QDI) circuits exhibit higher resilience against timing variations as compared to their synchronous counterparts. Since computation in QDI circuits is event-based rather than clock-triggered, spurious events due to transient faults such as radiation-induced glitches, a priori are of higher concern in QDI circuits. In this work we propose a formal framework with the goal to gain a deeper understanding on how susceptible QDI circuits are to transient faults. We introduce a worst-case model for transients in circuits. We then prove an equivalence of faults within this framework and use this result to provably exhaustively check a widely used QDI circuit, a linear Muller pipeline, for its susceptibility to produce non-stable output signals.

Keywords: transient faults · QDI circuits · automatic evaluation

1 Introduction

A transient fault in a circuit is a temporarily incorrect value at a circuit's signal, e.g., induced by radiation. It is well known that synchronous (i.e., clocked) circuits exhibit a natural resilience against transient faults through masking. Specifically, the relevant effects are electrical masking (short fault pulses are filtered by low-pass behavior of subsequent gates and interconnect), logical masking (depending on other input levels, the logic level of the faulty input may be irrelevant for the gate output) and temporal masking (the flip-flop samples its data input at the active clock edges while ignoring faults that happen between these). However, synchronous circuits have little resilience against (fault) effects that impact the timing. By contrast, asynchronous (i.e., self-timed, handshake-based) and in particular quasi delay-insensitive (QDI) [1] circuits exhibit large, ideally unlimited, tolerance against timing variations by construction. This is

This research was partially supported by the project ENROL (grant I 3485-N31) of the Austrian Science Fund (FWF), the Doctoral College on Resilient Embedded Systems (DC-RES), the ANR project DREAMY (ANR-21-CE48-0003), and the French government's excellence scholarships for research visits.

L. Petrucci and J. Sproston (Eds.): FORMATS 2023, LNCS 14138, pp. 69–85, 2023.
https://doi.org/10.1007/978-3-031-42626-1_5

due to their event-driven operation principle. Unfortunately, this very event driven operation makes them prone to transient faults. While electrical masking and logical masking mitigate fault effects like in the synchronous case, it is not obvious whether considerable temporal masking occurs. Previous works have shown that asynchronous pipelines, e.g., have data accepting windows during which they are susceptible to fault pulses. The size of these windows depends on several parameters, most notably the mode of pipeline operation (bubble-limited/balanced/token-limited). For unbalanced operation these windows may reach considerable size, making the circuit clearly more susceptible to faults than in the synchronous case with its instantaneous sampling. That is why several mitigation methods [2] aim at minimizing the data accepting windows. In any case there is some effect equivalent to temporal masking, and most often it is constituted by Muller C-elements (MCEs): During the *combinational* mode of operation (matching inputs), the MCE ignores fault pulses on any input and not even a pulse at the output can flip its state. In *storage* mode (non-matching inputs), however, the MCE's state can be easily flipped by a fault pulse at one of the inputs or at the output (directly at the keeper). So apparently, the share of time during which an MCE is in combinational mode determines the masking provided by it. In a reasonably complex practical setting, however, this insight is hard to map to a general prediction of the whole circuit.

Given an asynchronous circuit, a natural question thus is at which signals and at which times the circuit is susceptible to a transient fault. In this paper we present an approach to efficiently and provably exhaustively answer this question.

Organization. We discuss related work in Sect. 2 and introduce our circuit model in Sect. 3. In Sect. 4 we start with basic consistency results of the model, followed by our main technical result: the definition of value regions in executions along with a proof of the equivalence of glitches within those regions (Theorem 2). Based on this result we then present our tool for sensitivity-window exploration (Sect. 4.4) and apply it to a widely used QDI circuit for illustration. We conclude in Sect. 5.

2   Related Work

Transient Faults in Asynchronous Circuits. Several studies have explored the effects of transient faults on asynchronous circuits. Detection and mitigation techniques with some form of redundancy have been proposed alongside.

The authors in [3] perform a thorough analysis of single-event transient (SET) effects, among other types of faults, in QDI circuits. The fault's impact is first presented at the gate level, then on communication channels, translating the fault to a deadlock. They also discuss other possible errors (synchronization failure, token generation, and token consumption). An efficient failure detection method for QDI circuits is presented in [4]. The method brings the circuit to a fail-safe state in the presence of hard and soft errors. The authors investigate the probability for a glitch to propagate through a state-holding element in asynchronous circuits. In [5], the authors propose a formal method to model the behavior of QDI circuits in the presence of transient faults. They use symbolic simulation to provide an exhaustive list of possible effects and analyze which of these cases are theoretically reachable. Their model, however, does not support delay parameters, which potentially reduces the set of reachable states, further improving the resistance of a design against single-event upsets (SEUs). They also discuss in [6] the Muller C-element fault sensitivity and specify a global sensitivity criterion to SETs for asynchronous circuits. The work provides a behavioral analysis of QDI circuits in the presence of faults. With the help of signal transition graphs (STGs), the authors in [2] informally analyze SEUs due to glitches on QDI network-on-chip links. Several mitigation techniques are proposed with a focus on reducing the latch's sensitive window to a glitch. Some of these techniques are tested and compared against other proposed variations in [7,8], and [9]. The assessment there is based on extensive fault injection simulations into different QDI buffer styles, in order to identify the main culprits of the circuit. The authors provide a quantitative analysis to determine the windows of vulnerability to SETs and the impact of certain parameter choices on the resilience of the circuit. However, the analysis is done based on a regular timing grid, which causes linear complexity in time and in resolution, and cannot exclude the potential of overlooking relevant windows between the grid points.

Hazards in PRSs. QDI circuits can be modeled on different levels. The Production Rule Set (PRS), introduced by Martin [1], is a widely-used low-level representation that can be directly translated to a CMOS transistor implementation. PRSs do not normally support hazards, and by guaranteeing *stability* and *non-interference* characteristics [10], a PRS execution is assumed to be hazard-free. The authors consider an SEU as flipping of a variable's value and model it in so called transition graphs to identify deadlock or abnormal behavior. [11] extends the semantics of PRSs in order to be able to address hazards as circuit failures, but it is limited to checking the hazard-freedom property of a circuit.

These papers are focused on the *possibility* of failure and are restricted to precedence of events, without explicitly considering timing. Our work enables further propagation of what we define as a glitch in order to check whether it has reached the final outputs of a circuit and, based on actual timing information, *quantify* this proportion of failure.

3   Model

Following the work by Martin [1], we model a circuit as a set of production rules. We extend the model by delays and propagation of non-Boolean values. We start with definitions of signal values and production rules in our context.

Signal and Signal Values. Signals are from a finite alphabet S. Signals have values that may change over time. We extend the values a signal may attain from the classical Boolean values $\mathbf{B} = \{0, 1\}$ to the three-valued set $\mathbf{B_X} = \{0, X, 1\}$, where X is a potentially non-binary value. Examples for non-binary values are glitches, oscillations, and metastable values. A signal that has value X may, however, be 0 or 1.

We will make use of logical operations like $\wedge$ and $\neg$ on the extended domain $\mathbf{B_X}$. If not stated otherwise, we resort to the semantics of the 3-valued Kleene logic, introduced by Goto for these operations; see [12]. In short, using the classical algebraic interpretation of Boolean formulas on $\{0, 1\} \subset \mathbf{R_0^+}$ where, $\neg a \equiv 1 - a$, $a \wedge b \equiv \min(a, b)$, and $a \vee b \equiv \max(a, b)$, one obtains the Kleene semantics by the correspondence $X \equiv 1/2$. For example, one obtains, $1 \wedge X = X$ and $1 \vee X = 1$.

Production Rules. A production rule is a guarded Boolean action with delay. It is of the form

$$G \rightarrow s = 1 \; [d] \quad \text{or} \quad G \rightarrow s = 0 \; [d] \; , \tag{1}$$

where the guard G is a logical predicate on signals, s is a signal, and $d \in (0, \infty)$ is the propagation delay. Intuitively, a production rule with guard G, action $s = b$, where $b \in \{0, 1\}$, and delay d sets signal s's value to b upon predicate G being true for d time.

Circuit. A circuit is specified by:

- Finite, disjoint sets of input, local, and output signals, denoted by $\mathcal{I}$, $\mathcal{L}$, and $\mathcal{O}$.
- Initial values for all local and output signals. We write $s(0)$ for the initial value of signal $s \in \mathcal{L} \cup \mathcal{O}$.
- A set of production rules R whose guards are predicates on the circuit's signals and whose actions involve only local and output signals. We require that (i) for each signal s, there is at most one production rule that sets s to 1, and at most one that sets s to 0, and (ii) guards of production rules that set a signal s are mutually exclusive for all signal values from $\mathbf{B}$.

Similarly to Martin [1] we use production rules to model gates: actions that set a value to 1 correspond to the pull-up stack of a gate and actions that set a value to 0 to the pull-down stack. Any meaningful circuit will further have the properties that any local and output signal appears in a production rule that sets it to 0 and one that sets it to 1; if not, the signal will remain at its initial value for all times. Further, as already demanded in the last bullet above, the guards of these opposing production rules will not both evaluate to true for any choice of signal values; if not, the pull-up and pull-down stacks of this gate will drive the gate's output at the same time.

Signal Trace. A signal trace for signal $s \in S$ is a function $v_s : \mathbf{R}_0^+ \rightarrow \mathbf{B}_X$ mapping the time t to the value of s at time t. By slight abuse of notation, we write $s(t)$ for $v_s(t)$. We restrict signal traces to contain only finitely many value-changes in each finite time interval.

Execution. It remains to define how a circuit, with a given input, switches signal values. For that purpose fix a circuit, input signal traces for all its inputs I, and a time $T > 0$ until which the execution is to be generated.

Intuitively an *execution induced by the circuit and the input signal traces* is inductively generated via applying the production rules to the current signal values. If a guard of a production rule is true, its action is scheduled to take place after the rule's delay.

Care has to be taken to handle instability of guards. If a guard that results in a scheduled action on a signal, but whose action has not yet been applied, becomes false, we remove the scheduled action and instead set the signal to X after a small delay $\varepsilon > 0$. An ε smaller than the rule's delay accounts for the fact that non-binary outputs can propagate faster than full-swing transitions. The signal's value X is then propagated accordingly throughout the circuit. Indeed we will let $\varepsilon \rightarrow 0$ in later sections to account for the worst case behavior of gates.

Formally, the *execution prefix until time T, induced by the circuit and the input signal traces*, is a signal trace prefix until time T for each local and output signal obtained as follows:

1. Initially, all signals are set to their initial values as specified by the circuit. Further, the current time $t = 0$, and the set of scheduled actions is empty.
2. Handle unstable guards:
   - For each production rule whose action $s = b$, with $b \in \mathbf{B}$, currently being scheduled: if the rule's guard evaluates to 0 or X, and $s(t) \neq b$ (we say the guard is unstable), then remove the event from the scheduled events and set $s = \text{X}$. *(generate-X)*
3. Apply actions:
   - For each action $s = v$, with $v \in \mathbf{B}_X$, scheduled for time t, set $s(t) = v$ and remove the action from the scheduled actions.
4. Schedule actions:
   - For each production rule: if its guard evaluates to 1, schedule the rule's action $s = b$ to take place after the rule's delay d, i.e., at time $t + d$ (unless $s(t) = b$ already).
   - For each production rule: if its guard evaluates to X and the rule's action is $s = b$ with $s(t) \neq b$, schedule the action $s = \text{X}$ for time $t + \varepsilon$ (unless $s(t) = \text{X}$ already). *(propagate-X)*
5. Advance time t to the nearest future time at which an action is scheduled or an input signal switches value. If $t \geq T$, return the local and output signal traces until time T; otherwise, continue with step 2.

One observes that an execution prefix until time $T' > T$ is an extension of an execution prefix until time T: for each local and output signal s, the signal values in both prefixes are identical within $[0, T]$. We may thus speak of the execution as the limit of execution prefixes until times $T \rightarrow \infty$.

3.1 Example

As an example let us consider the circuit with input signal i, no local signals, and output signal o. As initial value we choose $o(0) = 1$. The circuit comprises of a single inverter with input i, output o, and delay 1.0, i.e., the circuit's production rules are:

$$i \rightarrow o = 0 \ [1.0] \tag{2}$$
$$\neg i \rightarrow o = 1 \ [1.0] \ . \tag{3}$$

We consider three input traces: (a) Initially $i(0) = 0$, then i transitions to 1 at time 1 where it remains. (b) Prefix like (a), but the input transitions back to 0 at time 1.5. (c) Like (b), but with value X during times $[1, 1.5)$.

The execution prefixes until time $T = 4$ induced by the above circuit and the input signal traces (a), (b), and (c) are depicted in Fig. 1.

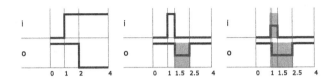

Fig. 1. Execution prefixes until time $T = 4$ of an inverter with input i and output o. Signal value X is depicted as a value of 0.5 and marked red. The propagation delay ε for signal value X is set to 0.1. Left: input signal trace (a). Middle: input signal trace (b). Right: input signal trace (c).

In the example, input traces (a) and (b) result in the guard of rule (2) becoming true at time 1. Accordingly, an action to set $o = 0$ is scheduled for time $1 + d = 2$. While in input trace (a), the guard remains true until time 2, and thus o is set to 0 at time 2, in input trace (b), the guard is falsified at time 1.5, resulting in the action being canceled and o is set to X at time 1.5 (generate-X in the algorithm).

For input trace (b), we have that the guard of rule (3) becomes true at time 1.5. Accordingly the action $o = 1$ is scheduled for time $1.5 + d = 2.5$. Since the guard remains true until time 2.5, the action is applied resulting in $o(2.5) = 1$.

Finally, input trace (c) demonstrates the algorithmic rule propagate-X in step 5: the X value at the input is propagated with propagation delay $\varepsilon = 0.1$ to the output. Resetting the output to 1 at time 2.5 occurs as for input trace (b).

4   Results

4.1   Well-Defined Executions

We start with a basic result on the consistency of an execution as defined by the algorithm.

Lemma 1. *Any signal trace of an execution has at most finitely many value-changes within a finite time interval; it is thus a well-defined signal trace.*

Proof. Assume by contradiction that a signal trace has infinitely many value-changes within a finite interval $[t, t'] \subset \mathbf{R}$. By consistency of prefixes of executions, this implies that the algorithm returns an execution with infinitely many value-changes when setting $T = t'$.

In the algorithm, at any point in time τ there is at most one action per non-input signal in the set of scheduled actions and at most bounded many actions per input signal until time T. Observing that there is a minimum propagation delay $d_{\min} > 0$ for signal values 0, 1, and X, any newly scheduled action must occur at earliest at time $\tau + d_{\min}$. Thus, only bounded many actions occur within $[\tau, \tau + d_{\min}]$. The statement follows.   □

4.2   A Transient-Fault Insertion Tool

To study the effect of short transient faults on the behavior of circuits we extend the algorithm from Sect. 3 to allow the insertion of external events: signal transitions from a set of *external events* are applied at the end of step 3. Step 5 is changed to include external events when updating time t to the time of the next event. A transient fault then corresponds to two subsequent signal transitions of the same signal in the set of external events in our model. This is less general than transient faults in physical implementations, where a transient fault, e.g., induced by an additional charge due to a particle hit, can lead to a single early transition by happening just before a valid signal transition. The assumption, however, is conservative in the sense that we assume that such a charge is small enough to lead to a pulse, i.e., double transition, potentially violating a gate's stability condition: in fact we will later in Sect. 4.3 assume that transient faults are not necessarily full-swing binary pulses and have value X in our model.

We have implemented the algorithm in Python and shall discuss results for a widely-used QDI circuit component, a linear pipeline, in the following.

Linear Pipeline. To study the susceptibility of QDI circuits to transient faults, we used the tool to insert short pulses (glitches) at different times. As a proto-typical QDI circuit, we used the linear 3-stage Muller pipeline shown in Fig. 2.

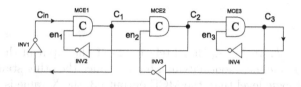

Fig. 2. Linear Muller pipeline with 3 stages. The delays are set to 1 (INV2, INV3), 5 (C gate), 4 (source delay = INV1), and 4 (sink delay = INV4).

Delays have been uniformly set to 1 for the two pipeline inverters INV2 and INV3, to 5 for all Muller C-elements (MCE1 to MCE3), and 4 for the leftmost inverter INV1 and the rightmost inverter INV4, which model the source and sink of the pipeline, respectively. Figure 3 shows an execution prefix until time $T = 32$ in absence of transient faults, generated by our tool. Figures 4 and 5 show execution prefixes of the same circuit until time $T = 32$ when a glitch of width 0.1 is inserted at the same signal, c2, at different points in time: the intervals during which a signal has value X are marked in red. One observes that the behavior is different in presence of the glitch, as detailed in the following.

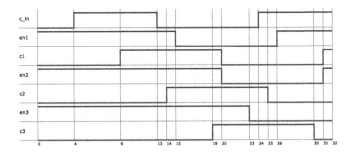

Fig. 3. Execution prefix of linear 3-stage pipeline until time $T = 32$.

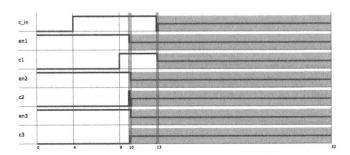

Fig. 4. Execution prefix of linear 3-stage pipeline until time $T = 32$ with glitch of width 0.1 inserted at time 10 at signal c2.

Non-masked Glitch. In Fig. 4, the glitch occurs at the input of the MCE while it is in storage mode, i.e., non-matching inputs. Since the other stable input en3 is at a different logic level than the MCE output c3, the X value is generated at the latter signal, and subsequently propagates through the circuit.

Masked Glitch. By contrast, the glitch in Fig. 5 occurs at the MCE input while in combinational mode, i.e., matching inputs. The glitch is masked at the output c3, but the X value appears for a short period of time at en1 (since an inverter propagates its input value). During this time span, the X value appeared and disappeared while the other MCE was also in combinational mode, hence was prevented from propagating the unstable value further in the circuit.

Susceptibility to Transient Faults. The two different behaviors raise the question of when a QDI circuit like the linear pipeline can mask glitches successfully, and when it is susceptible to them. To address that, we relate susceptibility to the occurrence of glitches at signals of particular interest (typically the output signals to the environment). We call these signals of interest the *monitored signals*. For example, in the linear pipeline, signals c1 and c3 are the outputs to the environment represented by the source on the left and the sink on the right.

In general, let C be a circuit, and i an input signal trace. Let $M \subseteq \mathcal{L} \cup \mathcal{O}$ be the set of monitored signals. Then, (C, i) is *susceptible to a glitch (of width w) at signal $s \in \mathcal{I} \cup \mathcal{L} \cup \mathcal{O}$ at time t*, if there exists a signal $m \in M$ and a time t' such that in the execution, induced by the circuit C and the input signal traces i and with a glitch (of width w) at signal s and time t, it is $m(t') = \mathrm{X}$.

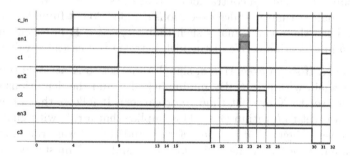

Fig. 5. Execution prefix of linear 3-stage pipeline until time $T = 32$ with glitch of width 0.1 inserted at time 22 at signal c2.

Revisiting the example of the linear pipeline, and letting $M = \{c1, c3\}$ be the set of monitored signals, the pipeline with its input is susceptible to a glitch (of width 0.1) at signal c2 at time 10, but not at time 22 (see Figs. 4 and 5).

This directly leads to the question of the sensitivity windows, i.e., the times when a circuit with an input is susceptible and when not. Related, if combined with a probability measure on faults occurring at these times, one may ask how likely a transient fault is to cause a glitch at a monitored signal. We address both questions in the following.

4.3   Equivalence of Transient Faults

While the previous tool allows one to sample the susceptibility at particular times, such an approach has several drawbacks: (i) it is time consuming to generate such sweeps and (ii) small susceptible windows may be overlooked.

In the following we present an alternative approach that relies on showing the equivalence between certain transient faults. We begin the analysis with a definition. We say *signal s has a pulse at time t of width* $w > 0$ if s changes value at time t, remains constant within time $[t, t + w)$, and changes value at time $t + w$. A *v-pulse*, with $v \in \mathbf{B}_X$, is a pulse that has value v during $[t, t+w)$. We speak of a *transient fault* as an X-pulse that has width of at most some predefined small $\gamma > 0$.

We are now ready to show a monotonicity property of the value X in executions: If transient faults are added to a circuit's execution, the resulting execution differs from the original one at most by turning Boolean values into X. For example, a transient fault may not result in a later 0–1 transition.

Theorem 1 (Monotonicity of X). *Let C be a circuit and i be input traces. Let e be the execution induced by circuit C and input traces i, and e' the execution induced by circuit C and input i in presence of transient faults. Then for all signals s and times t, if $s(t) \in \mathbf{B}$ in e', then $s(t)$ is identical in e and e'.*

Proof. Assume, by means of contradiction, that the statement does not hold and let t be the smallest time at which executions e and e' do not fulfill the theorem's statement. Then there is a signal s such that $s(t) = b \in \mathbf{B}$ in execution e' and $s(t) = v \neq b$ in execution e. We distinguish between two cases for value v:

Case $v = $ X. If so, in execution e, signal s was set to X at some time $\tau \leq t$, and not set again within $[\tau, t]$. By minimality of t, and the definitions of e and e', s was also set to X in e' at time τ (or earlier). It follows that in execution e', signal s was set to b within $(\tau, t]$. This implies that a rule with guard G and action $s = b$ was triggered at a time before t, and thus G was true in execution e'. By minimality of t and the definitions of e and e', G must have been also true in e, resulting in the same action being scheduled also in e; a contradiction to the assumption that $v = $ X.

Case $v = \neg b$. If so, s was set via two different rules in e and e' and not set to another value until time t. This implies that mutually exclusive guards have evaluated to 1 in e and e' before time t; a contradiction to the minimality of t in combination with the theorem's statement.

The theorem's statement follows in both cases.   □

We next define time intervals that play a central role in a circuit's behavior in presence of transient faults.

Given a circuit C and an execution e of C, the *set of value switching times*, $V_C(e)$, is the set of times $\tau_0 = 0, \tau_1, \dots$ at which a signal in execution e switches value. A *value region of execution* e is an interval $[t, t') \subset \mathbf{R}$, where t, t' are consecutive value switching times of execution e. A *postfix of a value region* $[t, t')$ is a (potentially empty) interval $[t'', t') \subseteq [t, t')$.

Theorem 2. *Let C be a circuit, i be input traces, $\gamma > 0$ the width of a transient fault, and $\varepsilon > 0$ the propagation delay of value X. Let e be the execution induced by circuit C and input traces i.*

Then, for a signal s of the circuit, and a value region R of execution e, the set $\Sigma_s(R)$ of times $t \in R$ such that (C, i) is susceptible to a transient fault (of width γ) at signal s at time $t \in R$ converges to a postfix of R as $\varepsilon \to 0$ and $\gamma \to 0$.

This means that every value region can be split into two intervals per signal: the left part of the region that contains the times at which the circuit is not susceptible, and the right part where it is susceptible to faults. Either part/interval can be empty.

Proof. In the following fix C, i, γ, ε, execution e, signal s, and value region R of execution e. We first show a monotonicity property within a value region.

Lemma 2. *Let $R = [t, t')$ be a value region of execution e and s a signal. Further, let e_1 and e_2 be executions of C with the same input traces as e, but with e_1 additionally having transient faults within R at s up to some time $\tau_1 \in R$ and e_2 having at least one transient at a time $\tau_2 \in R$ at s, where $\tau_1 \leq \tau_2 \leq t' - |C|\varepsilon - \gamma$.*

Then for all value regions R' of execution e and all signals s', if s' has value X at some time within R' in execution e_1, then it does so at some time within R' in execution e_2.

Proof. Within the same value region, both transient faults cause the same signals to become X, given that τ_1, τ_2 are sufficiently far from the value region's boundary t' to allow for propagation of X with delay ε (at most $|C|\varepsilon$ time): this follows from the fact that the circuit's signal values and set of scheduled actions are identical at the start of the first transient in e_1 and in e_2.

Further, a signal with value X remains so unless it is set again to a Boolean value by a production rule. This can only happen by its guard becoming true right after a transient fault. Since, $\tau_1 \leq \tau_2$, and both times are in the same value region, any event scheduled (and not canceled) after the transient fault at τ_2 must also be scheduled (and not canceled) after the transient faults that occur until time τ_1: signals have the same Boolean values and remain stable for a longer time in e_1 than in e_2.

The argument is inductively repeated for each subsequent value region of execution e. □

We are now in the position to show the section's main result.

Proof (Proof of Theorem 2). Letting $\varepsilon \to 0$ and $\gamma \to 0$, we have from Lemma 2 that if a transient fault at a signal s at a time $\tau_1 \in R$ that causes X at a signal s' then a transient fault at a signal s at a time $\tau_2 \in R$, where $\tau_1 \leq \tau_2$, also causes s' to become X at some point in time. The theorem's statement then follows from the definition of a postfix of R. □

4.4   Automated Computation of Susceptible Regions

Theorem 2 directly leads to an algorithm that marks all sensitivity windows, i.e., susceptible times, within an execution prefix: for each non-output signal s, and for each value region R, it finds per bisection of repeatedly inserting transient faults the boundary of non-susceptible times (on the left within R) and susceptible times (on the right within R). The algorithm's time complexity is determined by one bisection per region (with precision $\varepsilon > 0$), i.e., $\sum_R \log \frac{|R|}{\varepsilon}$, as opposed to a naive search that injects a fault every $\varepsilon > 0$ with a complexity inversely proportional to ε. Moreover, the naive algorithm may miss susceptibility windows smaller than ε, while our algorithm provably finds all such windows.

To test the algorithm's use on typical circuit instances we have implemented it in Python [13]: given a circuit, input traces, the set of monitored signals, as well as a time T until which an execution prefix is to be generated, it outputs a figure with all susceptible windows highlighted in blue as well as the percentage of the length of the susceptible windows in the execution prefix (by default excluding the monitored signals, but with the possibility to include them). This value corresponds to the probability of a transient fault causing an X value at a monitored signal, i.e., *the probability to fail* $P(\text{fail})$, given a uniform distribution of a single transient on all times in the execution prefix and on all signals that are not monitored signals (by default; alternatively on all signals). Clearly, though, the uniform distribution can be easily replaced by a more involved distribution. Towards this direction, the tool also outputs the probability per signal. This allows one to compute a weighted average, e.g., depending on driver strength or shielding at certain signals. Figure 6 shows the tool's output for the previous example of the 3-stage linear pipeline with sensitivity windows marked in blue.

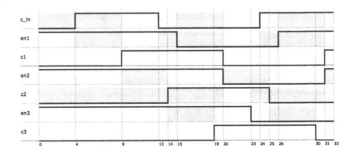

Fig. 6. Execution prefix of linear 3-stage pipeline until time $T = 32$ with sensitivity windows marked in blue. Monitored signals are c1 and c3. Here, $P(\text{fail}) = 0.54375$. (Color figure online)

A fault occurring at any point of the blue sensitivity windows will drive one (or more) of the circuit's monitored signals to X. A fault hitting any other region (excluding the monitored signals) will be masked and will not reach the monitored signals of the circuits. Observe that in this example all sensitivity windows are trivial postfixes of regions: a region is either fully non-susceptible or susceptible; in general this does not necessarily hold.

4.5   Comparison of Fault-Tolerance Depending on Speed

We next illustrate the use of our tool for a linear pipeline, where we vary the source and sink latencies. Inverter delays are symmetric and normalized to 1 and Muller C-element latencies are set to 5 inverter delays. The results are shown in Fig. 7, with cuts in Figs. 8 and 9. The length of the execution prefix has been chosen sufficiently high, to account for a sufficiently long time for $P(\text{fail})$ to be dominated by the periodic operation of the circuit rather than the initial transient phase: $T = 500$ in the overview plot and $T = 1000$ in the detailed sweeps.

Figure 7 shows an overview of the behavior of the circuit under a stable environment, be it fast or slow, and how the circuit reacts when there is an unbalance between the speeds of source and sink. The z-axis displays the probability of an X value presence at any of the monitored signals. The x and y-axes represent the speeds (latencies) of sink and source, respectively, in time units. The pattern of the plot is best visualized when having the latter axis inverted. The diagonal of the frame where both sink and source latencies are equal to 1 (fast) to where they are both 25 (slow) represents the stable/balanced environment, i.e., the source provides *tokens* with the same speed as the sink provides the *acknowledgment*. The figure indicates that $P(\text{fail})$ is high when the environment is stable and fast, and decreases as it gets stable and slow. When the environment is balanced, the MCEs in the circuit are not waiting for either the *data* or the *ack* signals; both are supplied within short intervals of time from each other. Since the waiting phases are those where the MCE operates in the vulnerable storage mode (inputs mismatching), one observes that reducing the waiting period decreases $P(\text{fail})$.

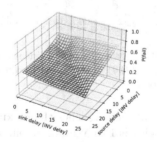

Fig. 7. Influence of source and sink speed on $P(\text{fail})$. Linear 3-stage pipeline with delays as follows: 1 (`INV`), 5 (`MCE`), varying source and sink delays. $T = 500$.

The environment imbalance is divided further into 2 modes of operation. On the right side (for relatively low source delay) of the figure, the circuit is operating in *bubble-limited* mode, where the sink's response to the source's new tokens is slow. On the left half of the figure, the sink's activity is faster than the source's, driving it in *token-limited* mode.

The vulnerability of the bubble-limited mode can be seen more clearly in Fig. 9; this is where the system is most prone to failure. The probability $P(\text{fail})$

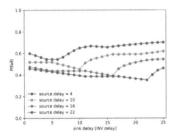

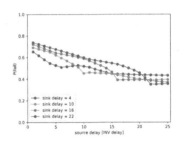

Fig. 8. Influence of sink speed on $P(\text{fail})$. Linear 3-stage pipeline with delays: 1 (INV), 5 (MCE), 4 different source delays, varying sink delay. $T = 1000$.

Fig. 9. Influence of source speed on $P(\text{fail})$. Linear 3-stage pipeline with delays: 1 (INV), 5 (MCE), 4 different sink delays, varying source delay. $T = 1000$.

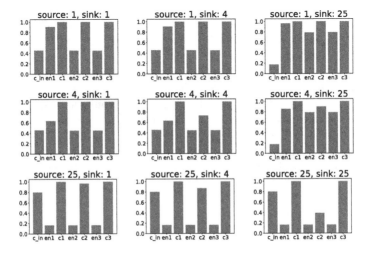

Fig. 10. Circuit fault probability per signal of the linear 3-stage pipeline with varying source and sink delays. Delays: 1 (INV), 5 (MCE), and 3 different source and sink delays indicated in the figure. $T = 1000$.

varies from around 60–80%, where it reaches the maximum when the sink delay is equal to 22 while source delay is 1 (maximum imbalance). Similarly, the token-limited mode falls near the sink latency of 1 in Fig. 8, varying from around 40–60%. The latter figures show several cross-sections of the 3D-plot from Fig. 7. In addition to mapping the token-limited and the bubble-limited areas to these 2 graphs, we can also spot the points belonging to the *balanced environment* diagonal in the frame in Fig. 7. These points are where the abrupt changes of behavior of each line occur, and consequently we can pinpoint where one region of the mode of operation ends and the other starts.

Finally, Fig. 10 shows the fault probabilities per signal of the linear pipeline as reported by our tool for varying source and sink delays (fast, normal, and slow). It allows us to give a more detailed interpretation of our observations in Fig. 8. The probabilities for the monitored signals c1 and c3 are always 1.0 as by definition of the fault probabilities.

Interestingly, c2 has a high fault probability, too. For fast sink this can be explained as follows: MCE3 spends most of the time in the vulnerable storage mode, waiting for a transition on c2. As soon as one occurs, it triggers a transition on c3 which, after the short sink delay, puts MCE3 back to storage mode. This only leaves a very short time window where MCE3 is masking faults at c2. The enable signals, in turn, are only vulnerable during those short windows, thus showing low fault probability, especially when the source delay is high, see subplot "source:25, sink:1".

Recall that we have chosen a relatively large switching delay for the MCE, and our pessimistic model assumes the MCE to be vulnerable during the whole switching duration. This explains why in general $P(\text{fail})$ increases for faster operation speed: the proportion of the sensitive MCE switching phase increases. This can be most directly observed for the balanced cases.

For the other imbalanced extreme with "source:1, sink:25" we observe high fault probability for the enable signals. This is not surprising, since now the MCEs spend most of the time waiting for transitions on these signals. A fault probability of 1.0 for c1 and c3 is also unsurprising, due to our definitions, as mentioned already. Quite unexpected, on the first glance, is the fact that c2 again shows high fault probability, even though we can assume good masking by MCE3 for that input. The reason here is that, via INV2, faults from c2 directly propagate to en1 which is known to have low protection by masking. As a result, we see a generally high fault probability in this mode.

5 Conclusion

We have shown that the regular operation of circuits can be decomposed into time windows within which faults are equivalent in that their effect (as perceived at some selected monitoring signals) remains the same. These time windows are bounded by an arbitrary bound on the left and a regular signal transition on the right. Consequently, for determining the effect of transient faults on a circuit, a single bisection between each pair of neighboring signal transitions is sufficient to determine all sensitivity windows.

The approach has two advantages over standard sweeping approaches to find sensitive regions: (i) it provably finds all sensitivity windows, no matter how small they are. Sweeping by contrast always leaves the possibility open that a small window may exist between two samples. (ii) It outperforms sweeping in that a small grid of samples is not necessary: many (large) windows require only a single sample via our method, and at most a bisection.

Based on this result we have developed a Python-based tool that, starting from a production-rule based circuit description, systematically explores its resilient and its vulnerable windows (along with the respective fault effects). The relative size of the windows is then used to predict the proportion of (random) faults that will be effective, and thus, given a fault rate, the failure rate. Since our approach allows identifying the windows individually, it is possible to attach weights to the diverse nodes to account for different susceptibility (drive strength, e.g.) in the overall prediction. We have illustrated the function of our tool on a typical QDI circuit example which showed that the tool is efficient and allows for fast analysis.

While we focused on a proof-of-concept with smaller circuits, a next step is to run our method on larger circuits. Another extension of our approach is to determine the constituent parameters for the window sizes. Since we determine all windows individually in our automated process, backtracking to the origins of the relevant signal transitions is possible. With that information we can determine in detail how individual parameters like circuit delays or pipeline load influence resilience and hence elaborate targeted optimizations. Finally, work on improving the performance of the implementation is planned: the proposed algorithm is easily parallelizable since windows can be determined independently and hence concurrently.

References

1. Martin, A.J.: Compiling communicating processes into delay-insensitive VLSI circuits. Distrib. Comput. **1**(4), 226–234 (1986)
2. Bainbridge, W.J., Salisbury, S.J.: Glitch sensitivity and defense of quasi delay-insensitive network-on-chip links. In: 2009 15th IEEE Symposium on Asynchronous Circuits and Systems, pp. 35–44. IEEE (2009)
3. LaFrieda, C., Manohar, R.: Fault detection and isolation techniques for quasi delay-insensitive circuits. In: International Conference on Dependable Systems and Networks, pp. 41–50. IEEE (2004)
4. Peng, S., Manohar, R.: Efficient failure detection in pipelined asynchronous circuits. In: 20th IEEE International Symposium on Defect and Fault Tolerance in VLSI Systems (DFT 2005), pp. 484–493. IEEE (2005)
5. Monnet, Y., Renaudin, M., Leveugle, R.: Formal analysis of quasi delay insensitive circuits behavior in the presence of SEUs. In: 13th IEEE International On-Line Testing Symposium (IOLTS 2007), pp. 113–120. IEEE (2007)
6. Monnet, Y., Renaudin, M., Leveugle, R.: Asynchronous circuits transient faults sensitivity evaluation. In: Proceedings of the 42nd Annual Design Automation Conference, pp. 863–868 (2005)
7. Huemer, F., Najvirt, R., Steininger, A.: Identification and confinement of fault sensitivity windows in QDI logic. In: Proceedings. Austrochip Workshop on Microelectronics 2020. IEEE (2020)
8. Behal, P., Huemer, F., Najvirt, R., Steininger, A., Tabassam, Z.: Towards explaining the fault sensitivity of different QDI pipeline styles. In: 2021 27th IEEE International Symposium on Asynchronous Circuits and Systems (ASYNC), pp. 25–33. IEEE (2021)
9. Tabassam, Z., Steininger, A.: SET hardened derivatives of QDI buffer template. In: 2022 IEEE International Symposium on Defect and Fault Tolerance in VLSI and Nanotechnology Systems (DFT), pp. 1–6. IEEE (2022)
10. Jang, W., Martin, A.J.: SEU-tolerant QDI circuits [quasi delay-insensitive asynchronous circuits]. In: 11th IEEE International Symposium on Asynchronous Circuits and Systems, pp. 156–165. IEEE (2005)
11. Katelman, M., Keller, S., Meseguer, J.: Rewriting semantics of production rule sets. J. Logic Algebr. Program. **81**(7–8), 929–956 (2012)

12. Brzozowski, J.A., Ésik, Z., Iland, Y.: Algebras for hazard detection. In: Proceedings 31st IEEE International Symposium on Multiple-Valued Logic, pp. 3–12. IEEE (2001)
13. Shehaby, R.E., Függer, M., Steininger, A.: Sensitivity analyzer for asynchronous logic (SeAL) (2023). https://github.com/mfuegger/SeAL

Maximum Satisfiability of Mission-Time Linear Temporal Logic

Gokul Hariharan[✉] , Phillip H. Jones , Kristin Yvonne Rozier ,
and Tichakorn Wongpiromsarn

Iowa State University, Ames, IA 50010, USA
{gokul,phjones,kyrozier,nok}@iastate.edu

Abstract. Mission-time Linear Temporal Logic (MLTL) is a variant
of Linear Temporal Logic (LTL) with finite interval bounds on temporal operators, and is a popular formal specification language for safety-
critical cyber-physical systems. Given a set of specifications, the maximum satisfiability problem (MaxSAT) asks to find the maximum number
of simultaneously satisfiable specifications. MaxSAT is useful for system
designing complex systems, e.g., system design and feature prioritization. Considering the significant advances in MaxSAT for Boolean logic,
we develop translations from MLTL to Boolean logic to solve the MLTL
MaxSAT problem. Given an MLTL formula φ of length $|\varphi|$ with maxi-
mum interval length m, our first (recursive) translator runs in $\mathcal{O}(m^{|\varphi|})$
time. Our second, improved (iterative) translator runs in $\mathcal{O}(|\varphi|^2 m^2)$ time.
Performance tests of satisfiability checks on MaxSAT instances illustrate
that these Boolean translations perform significantly better than the
best satisfiability checking approaches reported recently in the literature on real and random instances. Furthermore, the second translator
is embarrassingly parallelizable to a factor of $|\varphi|m$. We contribute to (1)
an easy-to-implement translation from MLTL to Boolean logic that runs
in $\mathcal{O}(m^{|\varphi|})$ time, and (2) an efficient translation that runs in $\mathcal{O}(|\varphi|^2 m^2)$
time, and prove their correctness and runtime. Lastly, (3) we consider
examples of using Boolean MaxSAT solvers to solve the MLTL MaxSAT
problem.

1 Introduction

Mission-time LTL (MLTL) is a variant of LTL with integer-bounded temporal
operators [22,24,32]. Whereas LTL specifications reason over an infinite computation [5], MLTL specifications reason over a finite computation. The latter is
better suited to cyber-physical systems that inherently have a finite computation
(e.g., due to battery life). Furthermore, the finite bounds in MLTL specifications
open avenues for efficient implementation in resource-constrained hardware like

Artifacts for reproducibility appear as a long-term archive at Zenodo, https://
zenodo.org/record/8118303, and with current updates at Github https://github.com/
gokulhari/MLTLMaxSAT-FORMATS. Funded in part by NSF:CPS Award #2038903.

L. Petrucci and J. Sproston (Eds.): FORMATS 2023, LNCS 14138, pp. 86–104, 2023.
https://doi.org/10.1007/978-3-031-42626-1_6

drones, UAVs, and robots [22]. Indeed, MLTL is used in specifications for flight missions, robotics, NASA drone aircraft, and other applications in the industry [4, 18, 21, 25, 29, 31, 33].

Extensive use of MLTL in safety-critical cyber-physical systems necessitates solving related problems in system specifications, such as satisfiability, realizability, and resolving conflicting objectives. MLTL satisfiability was extensively considered by Li et al. [24] and was motivated to aid debugging runtime verification specifications. Solving for the maximum requirements that satisfy a system simultaneously (MaxSAT for MLTL) is a related problem for resolving conflicting objectives. Safety-critical cyber-physical systems are often subject to multiple regulatory requirements, and therefore MaxSAT for MLTL is important for system design, feature prioritization, and cost analysis. Whereas most specifications in runtime verification are satisfiable (a specification has a bug if it can not be satisfied), the MaxSAT problem is more relevant to sets of formulas that are simultaneously unsatisfiable (due to conflicting objectives). We find that the best methods for satisfiability checking by Li et al. [24] do not show scalable performance for sets of formulas that are simultaneously unsatisfiable (Sect. 5). Therefore, although their approach [24] is suitable for specification debugging, better approaches are necessary to solve the MLTL MaxSAT problem.

We advocate translations from MLTL to Boolean logic to improve the performance of satisfiability checks for unsatisfiable formulas, and to solve the MLTL MaxSAT problem. Boolean SAT solvers have made unprecedented advancement in the last decade [3, 8–10, 15, 27]. Most solvers also report the (nonminimal) unsatisfiable core for unsatisfiable formulas. What is the best possible time complexity of a translator from MLTL to Boolean logic? Li et al. [24] show that the MLTL satisfiability problem is NEXP-Complete, i.e., the best translation to Boolean logic is at least exponential in time. We ask how fast this translation can be accomplished in practice. We will first review available translators from MLTL to other logics investigated by Li et al. [24], and then answer this question. Note that MLTL satisfiability for a fragment of formulas that have intervals starting at 0 is PSPACE-Complete [24].

Let m denote the maximum interval length of an MLTL formula φ of length $|\varphi|$. Li et al. [24] provide translations to LTL and LTLf, which run in $\mathcal{O}(m^{|\varphi|})$ time, and a translation to first-order logic (which we will call the SMT translation) that runs in $\mathcal{O}(|\varphi|)$ time. Li et al. [24] found that the SMT translation is the only scalable approach for the satisfiability checking of long formulas. We confirm that this approach works well, but the Boolean translation performs better (Sect. 5). Moreover, a Boolean translation can solve MLTL MaxSAT instances using off-the-shelf Boolean MaxSAT solvers.

First, we consider an extension from Li et al.'s [24] MLTL to LTL translation to make an MLTL to Boolean translator (Sect. 3). This approach takes the same runtime as the LTL translation, $\mathcal{O}(m^{|\varphi|})$. Next, we propose a more efficient translation to Boolean logic to improve the overall performance for sets of unsatisfiable formulas as in MLTL MaxSAT instances. Our efficient translation to Boolean logic runs in $\mathcal{O}(m|\varphi|)^2$ time (Sect. 4). Furthermore, the algorithm is embarrassingly parallelizable to a factor of $|\varphi|m$. Even without parallelizing the implementation of this algorithm, the total runtime (translation + satisfiability check) is better than the best approaches considered by Li et al. [24] (Sect. 5).

Although an $O(m|\varphi|)^2$ runtime algorithm will outperform an $\mathcal{O}(m^{|\varphi|})$ algorithm, both translations run in exponential time when the interval length is exponential in the formula length, e.g., $m = 2^{|\varphi|}$. This is expected as MLTL satisfiability is NEXP-Complete [24]. However, exponentially long interval lengths are unlikely in most practical situations. For example, the largest interval length considered by Li et al. [24] for a formula of length 100 is 10^5 (for extreme situations), which is much less than $2^{|\varphi|}$ $(= 2^{100} \sim 10^{30})$. Moreover, as MLTL is used in applications like robots and drones, the maximum interval length is at most the mission-time (an a priori known constant), and is generally smaller than the mission-time for efficient implementation in resource-constrained hardware. If the interval ranges were as large as 2^{100}, one would consider using alternative logic like LTL or a timescale-based logic for specifications [14,20,23].

The summary of contributions is as follows:

1. (Section 3) We develop a translation from MLTL to Boolean logic that runs in $\mathcal{O}(m^{|\varphi|})$ time (which we will call the "slow" translation) and prove its correctness and runtime.
2. (Section 4) We contribute to an efficient translation that runs in $\mathcal{O}(m|\varphi|)^2$ time (the "fast" translation) and prove its correctness and runtime.
3. (Section 5) We benchmark satisfiability using our approaches with the best approaches of Li et al. [24] on real instances from the NASA Air Traffic Controller specifications [13,16], as well as random MaxSAT instances.
4. (Section 6) We present preliminary results of solving MLTL MaxSAT problems using off-the-shelf Boolean MaxSAT solvers.

2   Preliminaries

MLTL is interpreted over a finite trace [32]. We formally define a trace, the MLTL syntax, and semantics.

Definition 1 *(Finite Computation/Trace). A finite computation/trace, denoted by π, is a finite sequence of sets of atomic propositions, and the ith set is denoted by $\pi[i]$. The trace length is denoted by $|\pi|$.*

Given a trace $\pi = \pi[0]\pi[1],\dots,\pi[N]$, where $N = |\pi| - 1$, we let π_i, where $i \in \{0, 1, \dots, N\}$, denote the suffix of π starting at the ith set, i.e., $\pi_i = \pi[i]\pi[i+1],\dots,\pi[N]$. We note that $\pi_0 = \pi$.

Definition 2 *(MLTL Syntax). A formula φ in MLTL is recursively defined over the set of atomic propositions $\mathcal{AP}$ as:*

$$\varphi := \text{true} \mid p \in \mathcal{AP} \mid \neg\varphi \mid \varphi_1 \wedge \varphi_2 \mid \varphi_1 \mathcal{U}_{[lb,ub]}\varphi_2, \tag{1}$$

where φ_1 and φ_2 are MLTL formulas, and lb and ub are finite natural numbers such that $0 \le lb \le ub$.

One can derive the abstract syntax tree (AST) of an MLTL formula φ using its syntax (Eq. (1)). The number of nodes in the AST gives the length of the formula and is denoted as $|\varphi|$. The height of the AST is between $\log(|\varphi|)$ and $|\varphi|$. The number of leaves (atomic propositions) is bounded by the number of nodes in the tree [12]. The set of atomic propositions in a formula φ is denoted as $alp(\varphi)$.

Definition 3 *(MLTL Semantics). The semantics of MLTL is recursively defined over a trace π starting at a position i as follows:*

- $\pi_i \models$ true,
- *for any $p \in \mathcal{AP}$, $\pi_i \models p$ iff $p \in \pi[i]$,*
- $\pi_i \models \neg\varphi$ iff $\pi_i \not\models \varphi$,
- $\pi_i \models \varphi_1 \wedge \varphi_2$ iff $\pi_i \models \varphi_1$ and $\pi_i \models \varphi_2$,
- $\pi_i \models \varphi_1 \mathcal{U}_{[lb,ub]}\varphi_2$ iff $|\pi| \geq (i + lb)$ and $\exists j \in [i + lb, i + ub]$ and $\pi_j \models \varphi_2$ and $\forall k \in [i + lb, i + ub]$, $k < j$, $\pi_k \models \varphi_1$.

Other useful operators can be derived from the semantics as in LTL: $\Diamond_{[lb,ub]}\varphi :=$ true $\mathcal{U}_{[lb,ub]}\varphi$ and $\Box_{[lb,ub]}\varphi := \neg\Diamond_{[lb,ub]}(\neg\varphi)$. The next operator is expressed as $\Box_{[1,1]}\varphi$.

Definition 4 *(MLTL Satisfiability). An MLTL formula φ is satisfiable if a finite computation π exists, such that $\pi_0 \models \varphi$.*

Definition 5 *(MLTL MaxSAT). Given a set of MLTL formulas A, find the subset $B \subseteq A$ of the largest cardinality such that $\bigwedge_{a \in B} a$ is satisfiable.*

In our notation, $\bigwedge_{a \in B} a$ denotes a formula by taking a conjunction of all formulas in B. We abbreviate Boolean satisfiability as SAT, MLTL satisfiability as MLTL-SAT, and LTL satisfiability as LTL-SAT. Li et al. [24] showed that the following function $f : \Phi \to \Psi$, where Φ and Ψ are the sets of MLTL and LTL formulas respectively, translates an MLTL formula to an equisatisfiable LTL formula (we simplified the until operator case):

$$f(\varphi) := \begin{cases} \text{true} & \text{if } \varphi = \text{true,} \\ p & \text{if } \varphi = p, \text{ for some } p \in \mathcal{AP}, \\ \neg f(\varphi_1) & \text{if } \varphi = \neg\varphi_1, \\ f(\varphi_1) \wedge f(\varphi_2) & \text{if } \varphi = \varphi_1 \wedge \varphi_2, \\ f(\varphi_2) & \text{if } \varphi = \varphi_1\mathcal{U}_{[lb,ub]}\varphi_2 \text{ and } (ub = 0), \\ X^{lb} f(\varphi_1\mathcal{U}_{[0,ub-lb]}\varphi_2) & \text{if } \varphi = \varphi_1\mathcal{U}_{[lb,ub]}\varphi_2 \text{ and } (lb > 0), \\ f(\varphi_2) \vee (f(\varphi_1) \wedge X\, f(\varphi_1\mathcal{U}_{[0,ub-1]}\varphi_2)) & \text{if } \varphi = \varphi_1\mathcal{U}_{[lb,ub]}\varphi_2 \text{ and } (lb = 0), \end{cases} \quad (2)$$

where X^i represents that X is repeated i times. The runtime of this translation is evident from the number of recursive calls to the function f in the case of the Until operator in Eq. (2). The number of recursive calls is $\mathcal{O}(ub - lb + 1)$. Let m be the maximum interval length in an MLTL formula φ, then the runtime of this translation is bounded by $m^{|\varphi|}$. A formula reaches this upper bound if it has all nodes as the Until operator, with all intervals as the maximum interval length.

Li et al. [24] also translate to first-order logic that can be conveniently encapsulated as an SMT formula. The first-order translation introduces an uninterpreted function for each $p \in \mathcal{AP}$, $f_p : \mathbb{N} \to \{\text{true}, \text{false}\}$, where $\mathbb{N}$ is the set of natural numbers. The function f_p is such that $f_p(k)$ is true if $p \in \pi[k]$, where π is the satisfying trace (see [7] for more information on uninterpreted functions). For an MLTL formula φ, the equisatisfiable SMT encapsulation is $\exists len.\ \text{fol}(\varphi, 0, len)$, where $\text{fol}(\varphi, k, len)$ was recursively defined as [24]

- $\text{fol}(\text{true}, k, len) = (len > k)$ and $\text{fol}(\text{false}, k, len) = \text{false}$,
- $\text{fol}(p, k, len) = (len > k) \wedge f_p(k)$,
- $\text{fol}(\varphi \wedge \xi, k, len) = (len > k) \wedge \text{fol}(\varphi, k, len) \wedge \text{fol}(\xi, k, len)$,
- $\text{fol}(\varphi \mathcal{U}_{[a,b]} \xi, k, len) = (len > k) \wedge (\exists i.((a + k) \leq i \leq (b + k)) \wedge (\text{fol}(\xi, k, len - i) \wedge (\forall j ((a + k) \leq j \leq i)) \Rightarrow \text{fol}(\varphi, k, len - j))$.

The runtime of this translation is bounded by $|\varphi|$, as the function visits every node once in the AST of the formula. Moreover, this runtime is independent of the interval length, unlike the LTL translation in Eq. (2). Interval dependence is mitigated in the runtime using first-order quantifiers at the cost of interpreting quantifiers during satisfiability checking.

3   The Slow (recursive) Translation to Boolean Logic

The LTL translation of Li et al. [24] almost immediately gives a method to translate to Boolean logic. Let $\mathbb{N}$ be the set of natural numbers, Φ be the set of MLTL formulas, and Φ_B be the set of Boolean formulas on an extended set of atomic propositions $\mathcal{AP}_{Ex} = \{p^i \mid i \in \mathbb{N} \text{ and } p \in \mathcal{AP}\}$. Consider the following recursive function, $f : \Phi \times \mathbb{N} \to \Phi_B$,

$$f(\varphi, i) := \begin{cases} \text{true} & \text{if } \varphi = \text{true}, \\ p^i & \text{if } \varphi = p, \text{ for some } p \in \mathcal{AP}, \\ \neg f(\varphi_1, i) & \text{if } \varphi = \neg \varphi_1, \\ f(\varphi_1, i) \wedge f(\varphi_2, i) & \text{if } \varphi = \varphi_1 \wedge \varphi_2, \\ f(\varphi_2, i) & \text{if } \varphi = \varphi_1 \mathcal{U}_{[lb,ub]} \varphi_2 \text{ and } (ub = 0), \\ f(\varphi_1 \mathcal{U}_{[0,ub-lb]} \varphi_2), i + lb) & \text{if } \varphi = \varphi_1 \mathcal{U}_{[lb,ub]} \varphi_2 \text{ and } (lb > 0), \\ f(\varphi_2, i) \vee (f(\varphi_1, i) \wedge f(\varphi_1 \mathcal{U}_{[0,ub-1]} \varphi_2), i + 1) & \text{if } \varphi = \varphi_1 \mathcal{U}_{[lb,ub]} \varphi_2 \text{ and } (lb = 0). \end{cases} \quad (3)$$

Lemma 1. *An MLTL formula φ is satisfiable iff the Boolean formula $f(\varphi, 0)$ is satisfiable, i.e., (φ is MLTL-SAT) $\Leftrightarrow$ ($f(\varphi, 0)$ is SAT).*

Proof Sketch. Let $\mathcal{G} = \{g \mid g : \mathcal{AP}_{Ex} \to \{\top, \bot\}\}$ denote the set of functions that evaluate the extended atomic propositions to a Boolean value (true/false), and Φ_B be the set of Boolean formulas. Lastly, let $Eval : \Phi_B \times \mathcal{G} \to \{\bot, \top\}$ take a Boolean formula $\varphi \in \Phi_B$, and a $g \in \mathcal{G}$, and return the evaluation of the Boolean formula, where the atomic propositions are assigned truth values according to g. We prove that:

$$(\exists \pi, \ s.t., \ \pi \models \varphi) \quad \Leftrightarrow \quad (\exists g \in \mathcal{G}, \ s.t., \ Eval(f(\varphi, 0), g) = \top). \quad (4)$$

Assume the left side of Eq. (4). For a given trace π, consider a $g \in \mathcal{G}$ defined by $g(p^i) = \top$ if $p \in \pi[i]$ and $g(p^i) = \bot$ otherwise. We prove that if $(\pi \models \varphi)$ holds, then $Eval(f(\varphi, 0), g) = \top$ by induction on the structure of φ. Similarly, assume the right side of Eq. (4), then we can construct a trace π, such that $p \in \pi[i]$ if $g(p^i) = \top$ for all $p \in alp(\varphi)$, such that $(\pi \models \varphi)$. The full proof is detailed in the Appendix and at http://temporallogic.org/research/MLTLMaxSAT/.

Lemma 2 *(Runtime and encoding length). Let m be the maximum interval length in an MLTL formula φ. Then, the runtime and encoding length of the slow Boolean translation (Eq. (3)) is $\mathcal{O}(m^{|\varphi|})$.*

Proof. Follows directly from the $\mathcal{O}(m)$ recursive calls to the same function in the until operator cases of Eq. (3). □

4   The Fast (iterative) Translation to Boolean Logic

Our ideas stemmed from the equivalence relationships used in the next normal form in the Black solver for LTL-SAT [17]. In addition, the proof to Lemma 1 gave insights into making an iterative version of Eq. (3) to remove redundant function calls. In the following, we first illustrate the main ideas of the algorithm using one example MLTL formula, and then generalize the idea formally.

4.1   Algorithm Overview

Consider a formula, $\square_{[a,b]}\square_{[c,d]}\square_{[e,f]}p$ and use slack atomic propositions $t_1, t_2 \in \mathcal{AP} \setminus alp(\varphi)$ to make the substitutions: $t_1 := \square_{[c,d]}\square_{[e,f]}p$ and $t_2 := \square_{[e,f]}p$. The formula can be expressed using the slack atomic proposition t_1 according to the MLTL semantics (Definition 3) as

$$f_{t_1}(a) \wedge f_{t_1}(a+1) \wedge \cdots \wedge f_{t_1}(b), \tag{5}$$

where $f_p : \mathbb{N} \to \{\text{true, false}\}$ is an uninterpreted function for an atomic proposition $p \in \mathcal{AP}$ (see [7,24]). Note that an uninterpreted function does not evaluate to an expression but is rather a data structure to represent an extended proposition with two attributes: its name and its extended index (the extended atomic proposition p^2, would have name "p", and index of 2, and is represented as $f_p(2)$). The SAT solver determines the value that the uninterpreted function returns; if the SAT solver finds a model, it will report assignments for these functions (e.g., $(f_p(2) = \text{true}) \equiv (p^2 = \text{true}).)$

Now the slack atomic propositions (with their extended set, i.e., $f_{t_1}(a) \ldots f_{t_1}(b)$ in Eq. (5)) are free variables that need to be defined. They are defined in the next step in terms of t_2 using the semantics of MLTL (Definition 3),

$$\begin{aligned}
f_{t_1}(a) &\leftrightarrow f_{t_2}(a+c) \wedge f_{t_2}(a+c+1) \wedge \cdots \wedge f_{t_2}(a+d), \\
f_{t_1}(a+1) &\leftrightarrow f_{t_2}(a+c+1) \wedge f_{t_2}(a+c+2) \wedge \cdots \wedge f_{t_2}(a+d+1), \\
&\ \vdots \\
f_{t_1}(b) &\leftrightarrow f_{t_2}(b+c) \wedge f_{t_2}(b+c) \wedge \cdots \wedge f_{t_2}(b+d).
\end{aligned} \tag{6}$$

Next, we define the slack variables corresponding to $f_{t_2}(i)$ in terms of the extended propositions of p (i.e., $f_p(i)$),

$$f_{t_2}(a+c) \leftrightarrow f_p(a+c+e) \wedge f_p(a+c+e+1) \wedge \cdots \wedge f_p(a+d+f),$$
$$f_{t_2}(a+c+1) \leftrightarrow f_p(a+c+e+1) \wedge f_p(a+c+e+2) \wedge \cdots \wedge f_p(a+d+f+1),$$
$$\vdots$$
$$f_{t_2}(b+d) \leftrightarrow f_p(b+d+e) \wedge f_p(b+d+e+1) \wedge \cdots \wedge f_p(b+d+f).$$
$$(7)$$

No new slack variables are introduced on the right-hand sides of Eq. (7). Each step expanded the operator based on the semantics (Definition 3), using slack variables. The bounds range from a until b on the left-hand sides of the equivalence relationships in Eq. (6), whereas on the right-hand sides, the bounds go from $a + c$ to $b + d$ ($f_{t_2}(a+c)$ and $f_{t_2}(b+d)$ in the first and last equivalence expressions of Eq. (6)). On proceeding to the next step in Eq. (7), the bounds on the left go from $a + c$ to $b + d$ and on the right from $a + c + e$ to $b + d + f$. Thus, on going down each step, we observe that the number of slack variables introduced are related to the accumulated bounds on the temporal operators of $\Box_{[a,b]}\Box_{[c,d]}\Box_{[e,f]}p$. Having provided an overview, we present the general algorithm and prove its correctness.

4.2   The Main Algorithm

Definition 6 *(Accumulated Bounds).* *The root node of a formula's AST has accumulated upper and lower bounds $\varphi.alb = \varphi.aub = 0$. For all other nodes, accumulated bounds are defined for children nodes as follows:*

- *If $\varphi = \neg\varphi_1$, then $\varphi_1.alb = \varphi.alb$ and $\varphi_1.aub = \varphi.aub$.*
- *If $\varphi = \varphi_1 \wedge \varphi_2$, then $\varphi_1.alb = \varphi.alb$, $\varphi_1.aub = \varphi.aub$, $\varphi_2.alb = \varphi.alb$, $\varphi_2.aub = \varphi.aub$.*
- *If $\varphi = \varphi_1 \mathcal{U}_{[lb,ub]}\varphi_2$, then $\varphi_1.alb = \varphi.alb + lb$, $\varphi_1.aub = \varphi.aub + ub - 1$, $\varphi_2.alb = \varphi.alb + lb$, $\varphi_2.aub = \varphi.aub + ub$.*

The accumulated bounds can be computed in $\mathcal{O}(|\varphi|)$ time by visiting each node once. We associate each subformula in a given MLTL formula φ with a unique slack variable denoted as $\varphi.t^i$, where i is the index of the extended atomic proposition corresponding to the atomic proposition $\varphi.t$. Furthermore, we define that $(t^i)^j := t^{i+j}$.

Definition 7 *(Associated Clauses).* *The associated clause of the root node of the AST of an MLTL formula φ is defined as follows:*

- *If $\varphi = \neg\varphi_1$, then the associated clause is $(\neg(\varphi_1.t^0))$,*
- *If $\varphi = \varphi_1 \wedge \varphi_2$, then the associated clause is $(\varphi_1.t^0 \wedge \varphi_2.t^0)$,*
- *If $\varphi = \varphi_1 \mathcal{U}_{[lb,ub]}\varphi_2$, then the associated clause is $f(\varphi_1.t^0 \ \mathcal{U}_{[lb,ub]} \ \varphi_2.t^0, 0)$.*

The associated clause for all other nodes is defined as follows:

Algorithm 1: Function initialize(φ_{AST})

Input: The AST of φ, φ_{AST}
Output: (V,Q)

```
1  Q = [] ;                                          // A queue
2  V = [] ;                                          // A vector of assertions
3  switch φ :                                        // Initialization begins
4  |   case p ∈ AP, true :
5  |   |   continue
6  |   case ¬φ₁ :
7  |   |   V.add(¬(φ₁.t⁰));                          // O(1)
8  |   case φ₁ ∧ φ₂ :
9  |   |   V.add(((φ₁.t⁰) ∧ (φ₂.t⁰)))                // O(1)
10 |   case φ₁𝒰[lb,ub]φ₂ :
11 |   |   temp = φ₂.tᵘᵇ;
12 |   |   for (i = ub − 1; i ≥ lb; i = i − 1) :
13 |   |   |   temp = φ₂.tⁱ ∨ (φ₁.tⁱ ∧ temp);
14 |   |   V.add(temp)                               // O(ub − lb + 1)
15 If v has children, add them to Q.
16 return (V,Q)
```

- If $\varphi = \neg\varphi_1$, then the associated clause is $\bigwedge_{j=[\varphi.alb,\varphi.aub]}(\varphi.t^j \Leftrightarrow \neg(\varphi_1.t^j))$,
- If $\varphi = \varphi_1 \wedge \varphi_2$, then the associated clause is $\bigwedge_{j=[\varphi.alb,\varphi.aub]}(\varphi.t^j \Leftrightarrow (\varphi_1.t^j \wedge \varphi_2.t^j))$,
- If $\varphi = \varphi_1\mathcal{U}_{[lb,ub]}\varphi_2$, then the associated clause is $\bigwedge_{j=[\varphi.alb,\varphi.aub]}(\varphi.t^j \Leftrightarrow f(\varphi_1.t^j\mathcal{U}_{[lb,ub]}\varphi_2.t^j,0))$.

Definition 8. *A slack variable is "defined" in an equivalence relation if it alone appears on the left-hand side of the equivalence expression, and if the right-hand side of the expression contains only new slack variables or extended atomic propositions $p^i \in \mathcal{AP}_{Ex}$, s.t., $p \in alp(\varphi)$.*

Lemma 3 *(Loop Invariance). Let φ be an MLTL formula. For the AST of φ, all the slack variables in the associated clause of the root node, and the right-hand sides of the equivalence relations in the associated clauses of other nodes are defined in the associated clause(s) of their children nodes.*

Proof. The operator at the root node is expressed in terms of slack variables of its immediate children, starting at index 0 (Definition 7).

- If the parent is a conjunction or negation, then the associated clause of the parent has the slack variables $\varphi_1.t^i$ and $\varphi_2.t^i$ for all $i \in [v.alb, v.aub]$. However, the accumulated upper and lower bounds do not change for the children nodes from Definition 6.

– If the parent is $\mathcal{U}_{[lb,ub]}$, the slack variables introduced are $\varphi_1.t^i$ and $\varphi_2.t^j$ for all $i \in [lb + alb, ub + aub - 1]$ and $j \in [lb + alb, ub + aub]$. From Definition 6, $[lb+alb, ub+aub-1] = [\varphi_1.alb, \varphi_1.aub]$ and $[lb+alb, ub+aub] = [\varphi_2.alb, \varphi_2.aub]$.

Hence from Definition 7, all the slack variables on the left-hand side of the parent node's associated clause are defined in the children nodes's associated clause.

Termination: If a child of a parent node is an atomic proposition, then no slack variables are introduced corresponding to that child.   □

Algorithm 2: Function main(φ_{AST})

Input: The AST of φ, φ_{AST}
Output: Vector of associated clauses (Definition 7) V

1 accumulatedBounds(φ)   // Assign alb and aub on each node of φ
      according to Definition 6, $\mathcal{O}(|\varphi|)$
2 (V,Q) = initialize(φ)   // Algorithm 1, $\mathcal{O}(ub - lb + 1)$
3 **while** *!Q.isEmpty()* :   // The main loop, $\mathcal{O}(|\varphi|)$
4 | v = Q.pop()
5 | **switch** v :
6 | | **case** $p \in \mathcal{AP}$, true :
7 | | | continue
8 | | **case** $\neg\varphi_1$:
9 | | | **foreach** $i \in [v.alb, v.aub]$:   // $\mathcal{O}(v.aub - v.alb + 1)$
10 | | | | V.add($v.t^i \Leftrightarrow \neg(\varphi_1.t^i)$);
11 | | **case** $\varphi_1 \wedge \varphi_2$:
12 | | | **foreach** $i \in [v.alb, v.aub]$:   // $\mathcal{O}(v.aub - v.alb + 1)$
13 | | | | V.add($v.t^i \Leftrightarrow ((\varphi_1.t^i) \wedge (\varphi_2.t^i))$)
14 | | **case** $\varphi_1\mathcal{U}_{[lb,ub]}\varphi_2$:
15 | | | **foreach** $j \in [v.alb, v.aub]$: // $\mathcal{O}(v.aub - v.alb + 1)(ub - lb + 1)$
16 | | | | temp = $\varphi_2.t^{ub+j}$
17 | | | | **for** $(i = ub - 1; i \geq lb; i = i - 1)$:
18 | | | | | temp = $\varphi_2.t^{i+j} \vee (\varphi_1.t^{i+j} \wedge \text{temp})$
19 | | | | V.add($v.t^j \Leftrightarrow$ temp)
20 | If v has children, add them to Q.
21 **return** V

Theorem 1. *Let V be the set of all associated clauses of an MLTL formula φ. Then, (φ is MLTL-SAT) $\Leftrightarrow$ (($\bigwedge_{v \in V} v$) is SAT).*

Proof. In Lemma 3, we showed that all the slack variables introduced are defined subsequently in the subexpression evaluations. To show that the conjunction of all elements in the set V is an equisatisfiable formula, it suffices to show that the slack variables are defined in accordance with the MLTL semantics (Definition 3). To see this, notice that Definition 7 uses the MLTL semantics (Definition 3). Hence proved.   □

Algorithms 1 and 2 give a breadth-first implementation to derive a vector of associated clauses according to Definition 7. Note that we implement the set in Theorem 1 as a vector. We describe the algorithms, and then analyze the runtime.

Description of Algorithm 1, initialize(φ_{AST}): The algorithm takes as input the AST of an MLTL formula φ (φ_{AST}), and returns a tuple (V,Q), where V is a vector of associated clauses, and Q is a queue to store nodes of φ_{AST}. This is the initialization step of Algorithm 2. Depending on the formula's root node type, an associated clause is inserted into V according to Definition 7. We use a slight abuse of notation to denote the node of the AST of a formula by the formula itself, e.g., in the switch statements in lines 3–14, φ, φ_1 and φ_2 denote the respective nodes of φ_{AST}.

Description of Algorithm 2, main(φ_{AST}): The algorithm takes as input the AST of an MLTL formula φ (φ_{AST}), and returns a vector of associated clauses of φ, V.

Lemma 4. *The worst case runtime and encoding length of Algorithm 2 is $\mathcal{O}(|\varphi|m)^2$, where m is the maximum interval length of the formula.*

Proof. The complexity is evaluated from line 15 in Algorithm 2 which has the worst-case runtime. To get an upper bound, we take the interval length $m = (ub - lb + 1)$ that is the maximum among all the temporal operators of φ. The accumulated interval bounds keep increasing with every visit to a temporal operator, as in m, $2m$, $3m$, and so on. Accounting for the additional factor of $m = (ub - lb + 1)$ (see line 15 of Algorithm 2), the total runtime is bounded by $m^2 + 2m^2 + 3m^2 \cdots |\varphi|m^2$ (as the maximum height of the AST is the formula length). This is bounded by $|\varphi|^2 m^2$.   □

Lemma 5. *Algorithm 2 is embarrassingly parallelizable to a factor of $|\varphi|m$.*

Proof. In each of lines 10, 13 and 19 of Algorithm 2, the for loop over the accumulated bounds $[v.alb, v.aub]$ are fully independent, and if embarrassingly parallelized will amount to an $\mathcal{O}(1)$ runtime (i.e., $\mathcal{O}(v.alb - v.aub + 1)(ub - lb + 1)$ becomes $\mathcal{O}(ub - lb + 1)$ when fully parallelized, in line 15 of Algorithm 2). Thus, when embarrassingly parallelized, the overall runtime is the maximum interval length, m, times the formula length, i.e., $\mathcal{O}(|\varphi|m)$.   □

Note that such an asymptotic runtime analysis is used to design parallel implementations of algorithms [19, Chapter 5]. We will consider specific parallel implementations in an extended version of this article.

5 Benchmarks

We benchmark MLTL-SAT using the Boolean translations in Sects. 3 and 4 against the translations considered by Li et al. [24]. We used two benchmark suites that we label as "Real instances", and "Random instances". **Real**

instances: LTL formulas of the NASA Air Traffic Controller [13,16] are assigned random intervals of maximum lengths 100, 1000, and 10000. Li et al., used a part of this data set (63 formulas with random intervals), whereas we consider the full set with 756 formulas. **Random instances:** While all the real instances were satisfiable formulas, MaxSAT instances are expected to be unsatisfiable. Our random formulas have a good mix of satisfiable and unsatisfiable instances (Table 1). The set is generated by taking the conjunction of 16 smaller formulas, each of length 10, with a normal distribution over operators $\neg$, $\vee$, $\wedge$, F, G, and U. Hence the overall length is 160 for each formula in this set. The formulas are generated over 4 atomic propositions, and the maximum random interval length is set to 100. A similar procedure is used to generate random MaxSAT instances in Boolean logic [1,11].

The final composition of the formulas is shown in Table 1. We do not use the random instances in Li et al. as they are again mostly satisfiable and may not yield the best perspective for MaxSAT instances (see Table 1; about 94% of formulas whose answers are known are satisfiable in Li et al.'s [24] random instances).

Table 1. Random formula composition.

Source	sat	unsat	unknown	timeout	total
Li et al. [24]	6404	438	1377	2222	10438
Our random formulas	38	62	0	0	100

All translations were implemented in C++, and they generate Boolean expressions in the SMT-LIB v2 format [6]. The SMT translation of Li et al. [24], was taken from their artifacts and fit into our C++ codes with minimal syntactic changes. Z3 was used as the SAT solver. In addition, we consider two SMV-based MLTL-SAT approaches that performed well in Li et al.'s benchmarks in [24]: klive and bmc. NuXmv (version 2.0.0) updated the command ncheck_ltlspec_klive to ncheck_ltlspec_ic3, and this was the only change we made to the commands used by Li et al. [24, Figure 1]. The SMV-translations are only considered on random formulas and not on the real formula set as the latter contained expressions such as the ternary operator that are not accommodated by the parsers of Li et al. [24]. Benchmarks were run on an isolated node with a single core and 128 GB memory on the NOVA supercomputer of Iowa State University. A timeout of 5 min was used, similar to the benchmarks presented for the Black solver for LTL [17] so that results presented here can be reproduced in a reasonable time frame (the 100 random instances took 17 h, and the 756 real instances took about 11 h with this timeout).

Figure 1a shows the translation time for the real NASA instances. Li et al.'s [24] SMT translation is labeled as SMT, and the slow (Sect. 3), and fast (Sect. 4) Boolean translations are labeled as Bool-slow and Bool-fast respectively. The symbols on the vertical dotted lines are used to distinguish curves corresponding to the different maximum interval lengths (m) of the random intervals; $\Diamond$, $\varhexagon$ and $\square$ correspond to $m = 10^2$, 10^3 and 10^4 respectively, and the vertical dotted lines at $x = 200$, 400, and 600 are used for Bool-slow, Bool-fast, and SMT respectively.

The separation between the diamond, pentagon and square in each of the vertical lines at $x = 200$, $x = 400$, and $x = 600$ gives the effect of increasing m for Bool-slow, Bool-fast, and SMT respectively. From the vertical dotted line at $x = 600$ in Fig. 1a, we see that Li et al.'s SMT translation has little effect on increasing m owing to its linear translation time. In contrast, the slow and fast translators (vertical dotted lines at 200 and 400, respectively) are affected

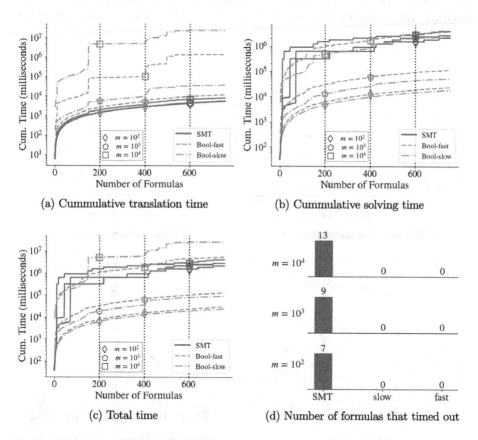

(a) Cummulative translation time

(b) Cummulative solving time

(c) Total time

(d) Number of formulas that timed out

Fig. 1. NASA Air Traffic Controller benchmarks [13,16] with random intervals. The cummulative (a) translation, (b) solving, and (c) total (translation + solving) times, and (d) the number of timeouts. SMT denotes the SMT translation in Li et al. [24], Bool-slow and Bool-fast correspond to the slow (Sect. 3) and fast (Sect. 4) Boolean translations, and m is the maximum interval length. The vertical dotted lines at 200, 400, and 600 are used to distinguish the different lines for each m (marked with diamond, pentagon, and square) for each of Bool-slow, Bool-fast, and SMT respectively. In (d), Bool-slow and Bool-fast are abbreviated as "slow" and "fast" respectively.

by an increase in m, and the slow translation is affected the most because of its exponential runtime (Lemma 2). At $m = 10^2$ (marked by ◊), the translation times are similar for the three translators.

Figure 1b shows the solving time. Both the Boolean translators show superior performance at all m that we considered. Specifically, at $m = 10^2$ and 10^3, the Boolean translators outperform Li et al.'s [24] SMT translation. Figure 1c shows the total time (adding times from Figs. 1a and 1b) which is mostly dominated by the time in the solving phase for the Bool-fast and the SMT translations, and by the translation time for Bool-slow. From the total time perspective (Fig. 1c), both the Boolean translations outperform the SMT translation at $m = 10^2$ and $m = 10^3$, and the SMT translation seems to perform slightly better at $m = 10^4$. However, this is not the full picture; Fig. 1d shows the number of formulas that

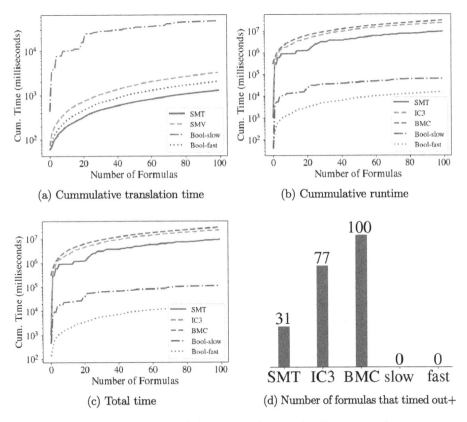

(a) Cummulative translation time

(b) Cummulative runtime

(c) Total time

(d) Number of formulas that timed out+

Fig. 2. Benchmarks of random MaxSAT instances. The cummulative (a) translation, (b) solving, and (c) total (translation + solving) times, and (d) the number of timeouts. SMT denotes the SMT translation in Li et al. [24], and IC3 and BMC correspond to the two SMV approaches in Li et al. Bool-slow and Bool-fast correspond to the slow (Sect. 3) and fast (Sect. 4) Boolean translations. In (d), Bool-slow and Bool-fast are abbreviated as "slow" and "fast" respectively.

timed out (in 5 min) for each m. None of the Boolean translations timed out, whereas in each case several SMT translations timed out. Although we haven't experimented, for $m > 10^4$, we expect a similar trend where Li et al.'s approach has many timeouts, and the boolean translations succeed without timeouts, with an overall better performance of the SMT translation due to a linear encoding time. The timeouts in Li et al.'s approach may be reduced by employing more recent SMT algorithms [2,28].

Figure 2a shows the translation time for the random formulas. Again, Bool-slow takes the longest time, and the SMT translation of Li et al. takes the shortest time. Both Boolean translations perform better than other approaches in the solving phase (Fig. 2b). Figure 2c shows the total time dominated by the solving time in Fig. 2b. Finally, Fig. 2d shows the number of timeouts with each approach. Again, none of the Boolean translations timed out. Notice that the larger number of timeouts indicates that these are harder instances (with a mix of unsatisfiable and satisfiable formulas; see Table 1).

6   Preliminary Results of MLTL MaxSAT

Direct Boolean translations enable using off-the-shelf Boolean MaxSAT solvers to solve the MLTL MaxSAT problem. We summarize the preliminary results of using this approach for MLTL MaxSAT. This problem is very hard (NEXP-Complete), and, to the best of our knowledge, we are the first to present a feasible approach for MLTL MaxSAT. We reconsider the random instances in Sect. 5. Recall that they were made by a conjunction of 16 subformulas, each of length 10. Thus, each instance is a MaxSAT problem with 16 clauses. (For simplicity, we assume that all the clauses have the same weight.) We ran Z3's Boolean MaxSAT solver on all instances to solve for the maximum number of satisfiable clauses. Most random instances in the benchmarks were solvable in time in the order of seconds on our laptop (12th Gen Intel i5-12500H processor), and at most, took 2 min to provide the MaxSAT solution. We then considered tougher formula sets to test the scalability of this approach. We conducted two types of tests; in the first one, we kept the maximum interval length constant and increased the length of each clause ranging from 10 to 50 in steps of 10. We used the same setting as the MLTL-SAT tests in Sect. 5. Tests with clause lengths greater than 20 segment faulted in the MaxSAT phase.

We then considered cases by holding the clause length to 10 and the number of atoms to 5, and tested maximum interval lengths 100, 1000, 10000, and 100000. All tests with $m > 1000$ segment faulted in the solving phase. Table 2 summarizes the successful cases using the Z3 MaxSAT Solver, with a limit of 128 GB memory and a 24-h timeout. There are several directions that could be taken for further investigation of performance. For example, increasing the memory used and using a large instance MaxSAT solver like Volt [26] instead of Z3, will be considered in future work.

Table 2. MLTL MaxSAT on random instances. In all cases, the number of clauses was 16. The fourth column gives the MaxSAT solution, i.e., the number of clauses that are simultaneously satisfiable.

# Atoms	Clause length	Max. interval length	Sol.	Translation (ms)	SAT (ms)
5	10	100	9	370	2148
11	20	100	3	17916	748211
5	10	1000	7	80297	1725711

7   Conclusion and Future Work

MLTL MaxSAT is useful for system design and specification prioritization, and will find great value in engineering aircraft, drones, robots, etc. However, the MLTL MaxSAT is the optimization counterpart of the MLTL-SAT (decision) problem, which is NEXP-Complete, and needs good problem-solving approaches. This work extensively considered an approach that first translates the problem to Boolean logic to leverage off-the-shelf SAT solvers. We developed an efficient parallelizable translation algorithm to Boolean logic, and when complemented with modern MaxSAT solvers, our approach has potential to solve real MLTL MaxSAT instances.

A parallel version of the fast translation can be readily implemented and will be considered in future work. It will also be interesting to incorporate GPU parallelized Boolean pre-processing in the translation phase to simplify (and shorten) the final Boolean expression [30]. Another interesting direction would be to try to reduce the translation time of $\mathcal{O}(|\varphi|^2 m^2)$ to at least linear in the interval length which will certainly improve the overall performance of MLTL MaxSAT. Lastly, we would also consider using MaxSAT solvers better suited for large formulas like Volt [26] to evaluate the scalability of this approach on large interval lengths.

We presented preliminary results for MLTL MaxSAT on random instances. The approach can be readily applied to real instances like the NASA Air Traffic Controller design objectives (real MaxSAT instances) [13,16], but this needs additional work to parse the hard and soft clauses separately to form the partial MLTL MaxSAT problem. These will be considered in future work. Note that the real instances were solvable more easily in the SAT phase compared to the random instances in Sect. 5. Therefore, we expect real MaxSAT instances to be more easily solvable (compared to random instances).

Appendix

A   Proof to Lemma 1

An MLTL formula φ is satisfiable iff the Boolean formula $f(\varphi, 0)$ is satisfiable, i.e., (φ is MLTL-SAT) $\Leftrightarrow$ ($f(\varphi, 0)$ is SAT).

Proof. Let $\mathcal{G} = \{g \mid g : \mathcal{AP}_{Ex} \rightarrow \{\top, \bot\}\}$ denote the set of functions that evaluate the extended atomic propositions to a Boolean value (true/false), and Φ_B be the set of Boolean formulas. Lastly, let $Eval : \Phi_B \times \mathcal{G} \rightarrow \{\bot, \top\}$ take a Boolean formula $\varphi \in \Phi_B$, and a $g \in \mathcal{G}$, and return the evaluation of the Boolean formula, where the atomic propositions are assigned truth values according to g. We prove that

$$(\exists \pi, \ s.t., \ \pi \models \varphi) \ \Leftrightarrow \ (\exists g \in \mathcal{G}, \ s.t., \ Eval(f(\varphi, 0), g) = \top). \tag{8}$$

Forward:

Assume the left side of Eq. (8). For a given trace π, consider a $g \in \mathcal{G}$ defined by:

$$g(p^i) = \begin{cases} \top & \text{if } p \in \pi[i], \\ \bot & \text{otherwise.} \end{cases} \tag{9}$$

We prove that if $(\pi \models \varphi)$ holds, then $Eval(f(\varphi, 0), g) = \top$ by induction on the structure of φ.

Base Case: When $\varphi = p \in \mathcal{AP}$, then if $\pi_i \models p$, then $f(\varphi, i) = f(p, i) = p^i$, and from Eq. (9), $Eval(p^i, g) = \top$.

Now let φ be a formula other than an atomic proposition, and let $(\pi_i \models \varphi_m) \Rightarrow (Eval(f(\varphi_m, i), g) = \top)$ hold for all formulas φ_m at the mth level of the AST of φ. We prove that $(\pi_i \models \varphi_{m-1}) \Rightarrow (Eval(f(\varphi_{m-1}, i), g) = \top)$, that is, whatever $(\pi_i \models \varphi_{m-1})$ evaluates to (i.e., true or false), $(Eval(f(\varphi_{m-1}, i), g) = \top)$ evaluates to the same value, (note that $(Eval(f(\varphi_{m-1}, i), g) = \top)$ is false iff $(Eval(f(\varphi_{m-1}, i), g) = \bot)$ is true).

1. Case when $\varphi_{m-1} = \neg\varphi_m$. From the hypothesis,

$$(\pi_i \models \varphi_m) \Rightarrow (Eval(f(\varphi_m, i), g) = \top),$$
$$\Leftrightarrow (\pi_i \not\models \varphi_m) \Rightarrow (Eval(f(\varphi_m, i), g) = \bot),$$
$$\Leftrightarrow (\pi_i \models \neg\varphi_m) \Rightarrow (Eval(\neg f(\varphi_m, i), g) = \top),$$
$$\Leftrightarrow (\pi_i \models \varphi_{m-1}) \Rightarrow (Eval(f(\neg\varphi_m, i), g) = \top),$$
$$\Leftrightarrow (\pi_i \models \varphi_{m-1}) \Rightarrow (Eval(f(\varphi_{m-1}, i), g) = \top).$$

2. Case when $\varphi_{m-1} = \varphi_m \wedge \varphi'_m$. From the hypothesis, we have for both φ_m and φ'_m,

$$(\pi_i \models \varphi_m) \Rightarrow (Eval(f(\varphi_m, i), g) = \top),$$
$$(\pi_i \models \varphi'_m) \Rightarrow (Eval(f(\varphi'_m, i), g) = \top),$$
$$\Leftrightarrow (\pi_i \models \varphi_m \wedge \varphi'_m) \Rightarrow (Eval(f(\varphi_m \wedge \varphi'_m, i), g) = \top),$$
$$\Leftrightarrow (\pi_i \models \varphi_{m-1}) \Rightarrow (Eval(f(\varphi_{m-1}, i), g) = \top).$$

3. Case when $\varphi_{m-1} = \varphi_m \mathcal{U}_{[lb, ub]} \varphi'_m$. Subcase:

(a) When $ub = 0$, we have that,

$$(\pi_i \models \varphi'_m) \Rightarrow (Eval(\varphi'_m, i), g) = \top),$$
$$\Leftrightarrow (\pi_i \models \varphi_m \mathcal{U}_{[lb,ub]} \varphi'_m) \Rightarrow (Eval(f(\varphi_m \mathcal{U}_{[lb,ub]} \varphi'_m, i), g) = \top),$$
$$\Leftrightarrow (\pi_i \models \varphi_{m-1}) \Rightarrow (Eval(f(\varphi_{m-1}, i), g) = \top).$$

(b) When $lb \geq 0$, for each $k \in [i + lb, i + ub]$, we have from hypothesis that, $(\pi_k \models \varphi_m) \Rightarrow (Eval(f(\varphi_m, k), g) = \top)$. Hence it follows that:

$$\begin{matrix}
(\pi_{i+lb} \models \varphi'_m) \\
\vee((\pi_{i+lb} \models \varphi'_m) \wedge (\pi_{i+lb+1} \models \varphi'_m) \\
\vdots \\
\vee((\pi_{i+ub-1} \models \varphi'_m) \wedge (\pi_{i+ub} \models \varphi'_m)) \\
\cdots))))
\end{matrix}
\Rightarrow
\begin{matrix}
(Eval(f(\varphi'_m, i + lb) \\
\vee(f(\varphi_m, i + lb) \wedge (f(\varphi'_m, i + lb + 1) \\
\vdots \\
\vee(f(\varphi_m, i + ub - 1) \wedge f(\varphi'_m, i + ub)) \\
\cdots)))))), g) = \top)
\end{matrix},$$

$$\Leftrightarrow (\exists j \in [i + lb, i + ub]. (\pi_j \models \varphi'_m \wedge \forall k \in [i + lb, i + ub], k < j, \pi_k \models \varphi_m))$$
$$\Rightarrow (Eval(f(\varphi_m \mathcal{U}_{[0,ub-lb]} \varphi'_m, i + lb), g) = \top),$$
$$\Leftrightarrow (\pi_i \models \varphi_m \mathcal{U}_{[lb,ub]} \varphi'_m) \Rightarrow (Eval(f(\varphi_m \mathcal{U}_{[lb,ub]} \varphi'_m, i), g) = \top),$$
$$\Leftrightarrow (\pi_i \models \varphi_{m-1}) \Rightarrow (Eval(f(\varphi_{m-1}, i), g) = \top).$$

Backward
Given a function g, we can construct a trace π, such that $p \in \pi[i]$ if $g(p^i) = \top$ for all $p \in alp(\varphi)$. The proof is the same as the forward proof with the opposite direction of implication.

Lastly, if a formula φ is MLTL-SAT, then there is a trace such that $\pi \models \varphi$ (by Definition 4), then there is a g such that $Eval(f(\varphi, 0), g) = \top$, and hence $f(\varphi, 0)$ is SAT. Similarly, the converse holds as well.

References

1. Achlioptas, D., Naor, A., Peres, Y.: On the maximum satisfiability of random formulas. J. Assoc. Comput. Mach. **54**(2), 10 (2007). https://doi.org/10.1145/1219092.1219098
2. Arif, M.F., Larraz, D., Echeverria, M., Reynolds, A., Chowdhury, O., Tinelli, C.: SYSLITE: syntax-guided synthesis of PLTL formulas from finite traces. In: 2020 Formal Methods in Computer Aided Design (FMCAD), pp. 93–103 (2020). https://doi.org/10.34727/2020/isbn.978-3-85448-042-6_16
3. Audemard, G., Simon, L.: On the glucose SAT solver. Int. J. Artif. Intell. Tools **27**(01), 1840001 (2018)
4. Aurandt, A., Jones, P., Rozier, K.Y.: Runtime verification triggers real-time, autonomous fault recovery on the CySat-I. In: Proceedings of the 14th NASA Formal Methods Symposium (NFM 2022). Lecture Notes in Computer Science (LNCS), vol. 13260. Springer, Cham (2022). https://doi.org/10.1007/978-3-031-06773-0_45
5. Baier, C., Katoen, J.P.: Principles of Model Checking. MIT press, Cambridge (2008)

6. Barrett, C., Fontaine, P., Tinelli, C.: The Satisfiability Modulo Theories Library (SMT-LIB) (2016). https://www.smt-lib.org/

7. Barrett, C., Stump, A., Tinelli, C., et al.: The SMT-LIB standard: version 2.0. In: Proceedings of the 8th International Workshop on Satisfiability Modulo Theories, Edinburgh, UK, vol. 13, p. 14 (2010)

8. Biere, A., Fazekas, K., Fleury, M., Heisinger, M.: CaDiCaL, kissat, paracooba, plingeling and treengeling entering the SAT competition 2020. In: Balyo, T., Froleyks, N., Heule, M., Iser, M., Järvisalo, M., Suda, M. (eds.) Proceedings of SAT Competition 2020 - Solver and Benchmark Descriptions. Department of Computer Science Report Series B, vol. B-2020-1, pp. 51–53. University of Helsinki (2020)

9. Bjørner, N., Phan, A.-D., Fleckenstein, L.: νZ - an optimizing SMT solver. In: Baier, C., Tinelli, C. (eds.) TACAS 2015. LNCS, vol. 9035, pp. 194–199. Springer, Heidelberg (2015). https://doi.org/10.1007/978-3-662-46681-0_14

10. Cherif, M.S., Habet, D., Terrioux, C.: Proceedings of SAT competition 2021: solver and benchmark descriptions. In: SAT Competition, p. 15 (2021)

11. Coppersmith, D., Gamarnik, D., Hajiaghayi, M., Sorkin, G.B.: Random MAX SAT, random MAX CUT, and their phase transitions. Random Struct. Algor. **24**(4), 502–545 (2004). https://doi.org/10.1002/rsa.20015

12. Cormen, T.H., Leiserson, C.E., Rivest, R.L., Stein, C.: Introduction to Algorithms, 4th edn. MIT press, Cambridge (2022)

13. Dureja, R., Rozier, K.Y.: More scalable LTL model checking via discovering design-space dependencies (D^3). In: Beyer, D., Huisman, M. (eds.) TACAS 2018. LNCS, vol. 10805, pp. 309–327. Springer, Cham (2018). https://doi.org/10.1007/978-3-319-89960-2_17

14. Franceschet, M., Montanari, A., Peron, A., Sciavicco, G.: Definability and decidability of binary predicates for time granularity. J. Appl. Logic **4**(2), 168–191 (2006). https://doi.org/10.1016/j.jal.2005.06.004

15. Froleyks, N., Heule, M., Iser, M., Järvisalo, M., Suda, M.: SAT competition 2020. Artif. Intell. **301**, 103572 (2021)

16. Gario, M., Cimatti, A., Mattarei, C., Tonetta, S., Rozier, K.Y.: Model checking at scale: automated air traffic control design space exploration. In: Chaudhuri, S., Farzan, A. (eds.) CAV 2016. LNCS, vol. 9780, pp. 3–22. Springer, Cham (2016). https://doi.org/10.1007/978-3-319-41540-6_1

17. Geatti, L., Gigante, N., Montanari, A.: A SAT-based encoding of the one-pass and tree-shaped tableau system for LTL. In: Cerrito, S., Popescu, A. (eds.) TABLEAUX 2019. LNCS (LNAI), vol. 11714, pp. 3–20. Springer, Cham (2019). https://doi.org/10.1007/978-3-030-29026-9_1

18. Geist, J., Rozier, K.Y., Schumann, J.: Runtime observer pairs and bayesian network reasoners on-board FPGAs: flight-certifiable system health management for embedded systems. In: Bonakdarpour, B., Smolka, S.A. (eds.) RV 2014. LNCS, vol. 8734, pp. 215–230. Springer, Cham (2014). https://doi.org/10.1007/978-3-319-11164-3_18

19. Grama, A.Y., Gupta, A., Karypis, G., Kumar, V.: Introduction to Parallel Computing Solution Manual. Addison-Wesley Professional, Boston (2003)

20. Hariharan, G., Kempa, B., Wongpiromsarn, T., Jones, P.H., Rozier, K.Y.: MLTL multi-type (MLTLM): a logic for reasoning about signals of different types. In: Proceedings of the 15th International Workshop on Numerical Software Verification (NSV). LNCS, vol. 13466. Springer, Heidelberg (2022). https://doi.org/10.1007/978-3-031-21222-2_11

21. Hertz, B., Luppen, Z., Rozier, K.Y.: Integrating runtime verification into a sounding rocket control system. In: Dutle, A., Moscato, M.M., Titolo, L., Muñoz, C.A., Perez, I. (eds.) NFM 2021. LNCS, vol. 12673, pp. 151–159. Springer, Cham (2021). https://doi.org/10.1007/978-3-030-76384-8_10

22. Kempa, B., Zhang, P., Jones, P.H., Zambreno, J., Rozier, K.Y.: Embedding online runtime verification for fault disambiguation on robonaut2. In: Bertrand, N., Jansen, N. (eds.) FORMATS 2020. LNCS, vol. 12288, pp. 196–214. Springer, Cham (2020). https://doi.org/10.1007/978-3-030-57628-8_12

23. Lago, U.D., Montanari, A., Puppis, G.: On the equivalence of automaton-based representations of time granularities. In: 14th International Symposium on Temporal Representation and Reasoning (TIME 2007), pp. 82–93 (2007). https://doi.org/10.1109/TIME.2007.56

24. Li, J., Vardi, M.Y., Rozier, K.Y.: Satisfiability checking for mission-time LTL. In: Dillig, I., Tasiran, S. (eds.) CAV 2019. LNCS, vol. 11562, pp. 3–22. Springer, Cham (2019). https://doi.org/10.1007/978-3-030-25543-5_1

25. Luppen, Z., Jacks, M., Baughman, N., Hertz, B., Cutler, J., Lee, D.Y., Rozier, K.Y.: Elucidation and analysis of specification patterns in aerospace system telemetry. In: Proceedings of the 14th NASA Formal Methods Symposium (NFM 2022). Lecture Notes in Computer Science (LNCS), vol. 13260. Springer, Cham (2022). https://doi.org/10.1007/978-3-031-06773-0_28

26. Mangal, R., Zhang, X., Nori, A.V., Naik, M.: Volt: a lazy grounding framework for solving very large MaxSAT instances. In: Heule, M., Weaver, S. (eds.) SAT 2015. LNCS, vol. 9340, pp. 299–306. Springer, Cham (2015). https://doi.org/10.1007/978-3-319-24318-4_22

27. Marques-Silva, J., Lynce, I., Malik, S.: Conflict-driven clause learning SAT solvers. In: Handbook of Satisfiability, pp. 133–182. IOS press (2021)

28. Neider, D., Gavran, I.: Learning linear temporal properties. In: 2018 Formal Methods in Computer Aided Design (FMCAD), pp. 1–10 (2018). https://doi.org/10.23919/FMCAD.2018.8603016

29. Okubo, N.: Using R2U2 in JAXA program. Electronic correspondence (November-December 2020), series of emails and zoom call from JAXA to PI with technical questions about embedding R2U2 into an autonomous satellite mission with a provable memory bound of 200 KB (2020)

30. Osama, M., Wijs, A.: GPU acceleration of bounded model checking with ParaFROST. In: Silva, A., Leino, K.R.M. (eds.) CAV 2021. LNCS, vol. 12760, pp. 447–460. Springer, Cham (2021). https://doi.org/10.1007/978-3-030-81688-9_21

31. Reinbacher, T., Rozier, K.Y., Schumann, J.: Temporal-logic based runtime observer pairs for system health management of real-time systems. In: Ábrahám, E., Havelund, K. (eds.) TACAS 2014. LNCS, vol. 8413, pp. 357–372. Springer, Heidelberg (2014). https://doi.org/10.1007/978-3-642-54862-8_24

32. Rozier, K.Y., Schumann, J.: R2U2: tool overview. In: Proceedings of International Workshop on Competitions, Usability, Benchmarks, Evaluation, and Standardisation for Runtime Verification Tools (RV-CUBES), vol. 3, pp. 138–156. Kalpa Publications, Seattle (2017). https://doi.org/10.29007/5pch

33. Schumann, J., Moosbrugger, P., Rozier, K.Y.: Runtime analysis with R2U2: a tool exhibition report. In: Falcone, Y., Sánchez, C. (eds.) RV 2016. LNCS, vol. 10012, pp. 504–509. Springer, Cham (2016). https://doi.org/10.1007/978-3-319-46982-9_35

A Local-Time Semantics for Negotiations

Madhavan Mukund[1,2], Adwitee Roy[1], and B. Srivathsan[1,2(✉)]

[1] Chennai Mathematical Institute, Chennai, India
[2] CNRS IRL, 2000, ReLaX Chennai, India
sri@cmi.ac.in

Abstract. Negotiations, introduced by Esparza et al., are a model for concurrent systems where computations involving a set of agents are described in terms of their interactions. In many situations, it is natural to impose timing constraints between interactions—for instance, to limit the time available to enter the PIN after inserting a card into an ATM. To model this, we introduce a real-time aspect to negotiations. In our model of *local-timed negotiations*, agents have local reference times that evolve independently. Inspired by the model of networks of timed automata, each agent is equipped with a set of local clocks. Similar to timed automata, the outcomes of a negotiation contain guards and resets over the local clocks.

As a new feature, we allow some interactions to force the reference clocks of the participating agents to synchronize. This synchronization constraint allows us to model interesting scenarios. Surprisingly, it also gives unlimited computing power. We show that reachability is undecidable for local-timed negotiations with a mixture of synchronized and unsynchronized interactions. We study restrictions on the use of synchronized interactions that make the problem decidable.

1 Introduction

Computing systems often consist of multiple components that interact with each other to execute a task. For instance, ATMs, online banking platforms, and e-commerce retailers all maintain a coordinated conversation between customers at the front end and data servers at the back end. In many cases, these interactions need to meet timing constraints—for example, a one-time password (OTP) times out if it is not entered within a short window. Hence, when specifying such interactions, it becomes important to accurately describe the interplay between concurrency and timing.

In [9,10], Esparza et al. introduced *negotiations* as a model for describing computations involving a set of agents. Conventional automata-theoretic models focus on states and transitions, and specify how local states of agents determine global behaviours. In negotiations, the basic building blocks are the interactions between the agents. Individual interactions between a set of agents are called *atomic negotiations*. After each atomic negotiation, the participating agents collectively agree on an outcome and move on to participate in other

© The Author(s), under exclusive license to Springer Nature Switzerland AG 2023
L. Petrucci and J. Sproston (Eds.): FORMATS 2023, LNCS 14138, pp. 105–121, 2023.
https://doi.org/10.1007/978-3-031-42626-1_7

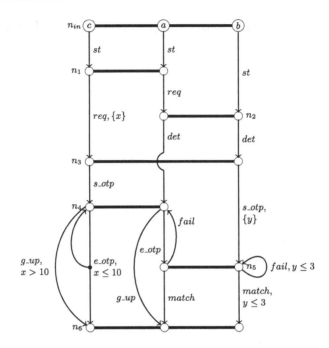

Fig. 1. A local-timed negotiation modeling a transaction between a customer, an ATM and a bank

atomic negotiations. Apart from providing an attractive alternative perspective for modelling concurrent systems, negotiations also admit efficient analysis procedures. For some subclasses, interesting properties can be analyzed in polynomial-time [11,12].

The basic negotiation model does not have any mechanism to incorporate timing constraints between interactions. In [1] a notion of timed negotiations has been proposed, where every outcome is associated with an interval representing the minimum and maximum amount of time required for the interaction to conclude. The work focuses on computing the minimum and maximum execution times for the overall negotiation to complete. This model cannot express constraints on the time between different atomic negotiations. For this, we introduce clocks, as defined in timed automata [3].

A Motivating Example. We use the example in Fig. 1 to introduce our model informally. Consider a time-constrained transaction in an ATM machine (a), where a customer (c) wants to reset her ATM PIN via an OTP received from her bank (b). Here, a, c, and b are the *agents* in the system. Their direct interactions are represented by thick horizontal lines, called nodes. After each interaction, the participating agents decide on an outcome, represented by arrows. Initially, all agents are in the node n_{in} node. They choose the outcome st to start the transaction. Agents a and c go to node n_1 and b goes to n_2. The customer gives her card details and requests for a PIN change in the ATM at node n_1 by choosing the outcome *req*. At n_2, the ATM conveys this request to the bank and sends the details through the outcome *det*. The bank and the customer talk to each other at n_3, and b sends an OTP to the customer through the outcome *s_otp*. At n_4, the customer enters the OTP in the ATM. After entering the OTP, shown by the outcome *e_otp* the customer is ready to engage with the ATM either at n_4 or at n_6, represented by the non-deterministic arc leading to n_4 and n_6. The ATM talks to the bank at n_5 to check the OTP. If it matches, the ATM goes to n_6, otherwise it goes back to n_4.

In this example, we model two time constraints. The bank would like to ensure that at most 3 time units elapse between the sending of the OTP and the final match. This is achieved by resetting a local clock y of the bank and checking that $y \leq 3$ at the outcome *match*. On the other hand, the customer wants at most 10 time units to have elapsed between initiating the request and completing the transaction. This is achieved by resetting a local clock x at the outcome *req* and checking that $x \leq 10$ at the outcome *e_otp*. If more than 10 units elapse, the customer gives up, fires the outcome *g_up*. It is natural to imagine that clocks x and y are local to the customer and to the bank and that they may evolve at different rates. We formalize this behaviour in terms of our local-time semantics. However, as we will see later, in certain interactions, it is useful to force the agents to synchronize their local times. Combining the concurrency present in negotiations with timing constraints and a mechanism to synchronize local times makes the model surprisingly powerful.

Structure of the Paper. We begin by formalizing local-timed negotiations (Sect. 2), with some illustrative examples. We study the reachability problem for this model. We show that when the negotiation has no interactions that synchronize local times, or when all interactions force a synchronization of local times, reachability is PSPACE-complete (Sects. 3 and 4). In the general case when, there is a mix of synchronized and unsynchronized interactions, reachability is undecidable (Sect. 5). Missing proofs can be found in the extended version [19].

Related Work. A local-time semantics was proposed in the context of networks of timed automata in [4]. Recently, the semantics has been applied to the zone-based verification of reachability [13,14] and Büchi reachability properties [16]. Local-time semantics in timed automata has been investigated as a basis for applying partial-order methods. In our current work, we consider local-time semantics as the starting point and make synchronization an option that can be specified explicitly. This allows more independence between the agents and keeps the concurrency between actions of disjoint sets of agents.

Models mixing concurrency and timing have been widely studied: time Petri nets [18], timed-arc Petri nets [15], time-constrained message sequence charts [2] to name a few. Each model offers a different view of the computation. To our knowledge, a notion of a real-time has not yet been considered for negotiations. With similar motivations as local-time semantics, a notion of a partial-order semantics has been studied for networks of timed automata [17] as well as time Petri nets [7,8]. This semantics can be used to compute finite unfoldings which preserve the concurrency and reachability information concisely [5,6].

2   Local-Timed Negotiations

For a finite set S we write $\mathcal{P}(S)$ for the power set containing all subsets of S. Let $\mathbb{R}_{\geq 0}$ denote the set of non-negative reals, and $\mathbb{N}$ the set of natural numbers. For a real number $\alpha \in \mathbb{R}_{\geq 0}$, we write $\lfloor \alpha \rfloor$ for the greatest integer smaller than or equal to α, and $\{\alpha\}$ for the fractional part $\alpha - \lfloor \alpha \rfloor$. A *clock* is a real-valued variable whose values increase along with time and get updated during transitions (exact semantics comes later). Let X be a set of clocks. A *guard* over X is a conjunction of clock constraints of the form $x \bowtie c$ where $x \in X$, $\bowtie \in \{<, \leq, =, >, \geq\}$ and $c \in \mathbb{N}$. We write $\Phi(X)$ for the set of guards over X.

Definition 1 (Local-Timed Negotiations). *Let P be a finite set of agents, Σ a finite set of outcomes and X a finite set of clocks. We assume that X is partitioned as $\{X_p\}_{p \in P}$ with X_p being the* local clocks *for agent p. Further, we associate a special clock t_p to each agent p, called its* reference clock. *This clock is neither used in a guard nor reset. We denote T to be the set $\{t_p \mid p \in P\}$ of reference clocks. A* local-timed negotiation *$\mathcal{N}$ is given by a tuple $(N, dom, \delta, Sync)$ where*

- *N is a finite set of nodes (also called atomic negotiations); there is a special initial node $n_{in} \in N$,*
- *$dom : N \to \mathcal{P}(P)$ maps each node to a non-empty subset of agents; we assume $dom(n_{in}) = P$; for $p \in P$, we let $N_p := \{n \in N \mid p \in dom(n)\}$*
- *$\delta = \{\delta_p\}_{p \in P}$ is a tuple of transition relations, one for each agent, where $\delta_p : N_p \times \Sigma \to \Phi(X) \times \mathcal{P}(N_p) \times \mathcal{P}(X_p)$ maps each node-outcome pair (n, a) to a guard $g \in \Phi(X)$, a set of nodes $M \subseteq N_p$ that p becomes ready to engage in after this outcome, and a set $Y \subseteq X_p$ of clocks that get reset; we will call node-outcome pairs (n, a) as* locations *(as in [12] for untimed negotiations),*
- *$Sync \subseteq N$ is a subset of* synchronizing nodes.

Figure 1 gives an example of a local-timed negotiation over agents $P = \{c, a, b\}$. The set of nodes is given by $N = \{n_{in}, n_1, \ldots, n_6\}$. The domain $dom(n)$ of a node n is represented by the "circles" in each node: for instance, $dom(n_1) = \{c, a\}$ and $dom(n_2) = \{a, b\}$. Agent c has a local clock x, and agent b has a local clock y. As an example of a transition for agent c, we have $\delta_c(n_4, e\_otp) = (x \leq 10, \{n_4, n_6\}, \{\})$. There is a guard $x \leq 10$, the agent is ready to engage in n_4 and n_6 after the outcome, and no clock is reset. In this example, $Sync$ is empty.

Semantics. The semantics of a negotiation is described using *markings* and *valuations*. A marking C is a function assigning each agent p to a subset of N_p. It gives the set of nodes that each agent is ready to engage in. A valuation $v : X \cup T \to \mathbb{R}_{\geq 0}$ maps every clock (including reference clocks) to a non-negative real such that $v(x) \leq v(t_p)$ for all $x \in X_p$, and all agents $p \in P$. The interpretation is that clocks in X_p move at the same pace as t_p, the local reference clock. Since t_p is never reset it gives the local time at agent p. For a constraint $x \bowtie c$ we say $v \models x \bowtie c$ if $v(x) \bowtie c$. We say v satisfies guard $g \in \Phi(X)$, written as $v \models g$, if v satisfies every atomic constraint appearing in g.

A *local-delay* $\Delta \in \mathbb{R}_{\geq 0}^{|P|}$ is a vector of non-negative reals, giving a time elapse for each agent. Each agent can have a different time elapse. Given a valuation v and a local-delay Δ, we write $v + \Delta$ for the valuation obtained as follows: for each agent $p \in P$, we have $(v + \Delta)(y) = v(y) + \Delta(p)$ for every $y \in \{t_p\} \cup X_p$. Notice that all clocks within a process move at the same rate as its reference clock. However, the reference clocks of different agents can move at different speeds. For a set of clocks $Y \subseteq X$, we denote by $v[Y]$ the valuation satisfying $v[Y](y) = 0$ if $y \in Y$ and $v[Y](y) = v(y)$ otherwise.

A configuration is a pair (C, v) consisting of a marking C and a valuation v. The *initial configuration* (C_0, v_0) contains a marking C_0 which maps every agent to n_{in} and valuation v_0 maps all clocks to 0. We write $(C, v) \xrightarrow{\Delta} (C, v + \Delta)$ for the local-delay transition Δ at configuration (C, v). For the negotiation in Fig. 1, an example of a configuration is $(\bar{C}, \bar{v})$ with $\bar{C}(c) = \{n_1\}$, $\bar{C}(a) = \{n_1\}$ and $\bar{C}(b) = \{n_2\}$ and $\bar{v}(t_c) = \bar{v}(x) = 2$, $\bar{v}(t_a) = 1$ and $\bar{v}(t_b) = \bar{v}(y) = 3$. Suppose $\Delta = (c \mapsto 1, a \mapsto 0, b \mapsto 2)$, then $\bar{v} + \Delta$ maps t_c and x to 3, and t_b and y to 5 whereas t_a remains 1.

A location $t = (n, a)$ can be executed at a configuration (C, v) leading to a configuration (C', v'), written as $(C, v) \xrightarrow{t} (C', v')$, provided there is an entry $\delta_p(n, a) = (g_p, M_p, Y_p)$ for all $p \in dom(n)$ such that:

- *current marking enables the negotiation:* $n \in C(p)$ for all $p \in dom(n)$,
- *synchronization condition is met:* if $n \in Sync$, then $v(t_p) = v(t_q)$ for all $p, q \in dom(n)$,
- *guard is satisfied:* $v \models g_p$ for all $p \in dom(n)$,
- *target marking is correct:* $C'(p) = M_p$ for all $p \in dom(n)$, $C'(p) = C(p)$ for $p \notin dom(n)$,
- *resets are performed:* $v'(y) = 0$ for $y \in \bigcup_{p \in dom(n)} Y_p$

For an example, consider Fig. 1 again and a configuration (C^1, v^1) with $C^1 := (\{n_4, n_6\}, \{n_4\}, \{n_6\})$ and $v^1 : \langle t_c = 10, x = 5, t_a = 20, t_b = 5, y = 1 \rangle$. Location (n_4, e_otp) is enabled leading to a configuration (C^2, v^2) where $C^2 := (\{n_4, n_6\}, \{n_6\}, \{n_6\})$ and $v^2 = v^1$, as there are no resets in this location.

We call $(C, v) \xrightarrow{\Delta} (C, v + \Delta) \xrightarrow{t} (C', v')$ a *small step* and write this as $(C, v) \xrightarrow{\Delta, t} (C', v')$ for conciseness. A *run* is a sequence of small steps starting from the initial configuration. We say that a location $t = (n, a)$ is *reachable* (in the negotiation) if there is a run containing a small step that executes t. The *untimed language* of the negotiation $\mathcal{N}$ is the set of all words $w := a_0 a_1 \ldots a_n \in \Sigma^*$ such that there is a run $(C_0, v_0) \xrightarrow{\Delta_0, a_0} (C_1, v_1) \xrightarrow{\Delta_1, a_1} \ldots \xrightarrow{\Delta_n, a_n} (C_{n+1}, v_{n+1})$.

Location-reachability problem. We are interested in the following question: given a local-timed negotiation $\mathcal{N}$ and a location $t = (n, a)$ as inputs, is t reachable in $\mathcal{N}$?

2.1   Some Examples

In the example of Fig. 1, we have seen how local-clocks can be used to constrain interactions. We will now see some examples that show some interesting mechan-

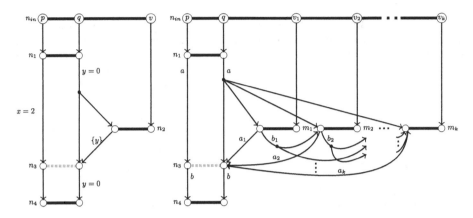

Fig. 2. In the figure on the right, the a transition has guards $x = m$ for p and $y = 0$ for q. Each b_i transition has a guard $y = 1$ and a reset of y to ensure exactly 1 unit of time is spent in the nodes m_i before outcomes b_i. The outcomes a_i have a reset of y. The b transition from n_3 has a guard $y = 0$.

ics of synchronized interactions. The negotiation in the left of Fig. 2 has three agents p, q, v. The outcome at node n_1 results in a non-deterministic choice for agent q: the agent may either decide to talk with p at n_3 or with v at n_2. Suppose at n_3, agent p wants to make sure that q has arrived at n_3 after talking to v. We can imagine that v is a vendor, and p wants to ensure that q has indeed met the vendor between their meetings at n_1 and n_3. To do this, we make use of timing and synchronization constraints as follows.

We first make n_1 and n_3 as synchronization nodes, that is, they are part of $Sync$ for this negotiation. In the picture we represent it as the grey dotted nodes. Suppose x is a clock of agent p and y is a clock of agent q. At n_1, the outcome checks for the guard $x = 2$ and $y = 0$. When this outcome is fired, the local-clock t_p is ahead of t_q by 2 units. Now, we make n_3 a synchronizing node and add a guard $y = 0$ in the outcome of n_3. If q comes to n_3 directly after talking to p at n_1, then we have $t_q = y = 0$, but $t_p = 2$. No time can elapse at q since there is a $y = 0$ guard. But then, the synchronization condition cannot be satisfied. This forces q to meet v at n_2, spend sufficient time (2 units, in this case), reset the clock y and then interact with p at n_3.

This example can be extended to the case where there are multiple vendors $v_1, \ldots v_k$ and p wants q to have met at least m vendors out of them before resynchronizing, as shown in Fig. 2 on the right. We also assume that once q interacts with v_i, she cannot interact with any vendor v_j with $j \leq i$. If each interaction of q with a vendor v_i takes 1 time unit, we can force the clock of p to be at least m at node n_1. Therefore at n_3, the only way for q to ensure synchronization with p, and have $y = 0$ is by finding m other interactions where she can spend time.

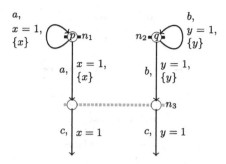

Fig. 3. A local-timed negotiation depicting that the untimed language of the outcome sequences need not be regular. The synchronizing node n_3 forces the number of as and number of bs to be equal.

In Fig. 3 we present an example which has been used in different contexts dealing with a partial-order semantics for timed automata [17] or the local-time semantics for networks of timed automata [14]. Outcomes a and b are local to agents p and q whereas c is the result of a negotiation. We make node n_3 a synchronizing node and ask for the guard $x = 1$ and $y = 1$ at c. If $t_p = n, x = 1$ for agent p, we want $t_q = n, y = 1$ at agent q. This constraint forces the same number of as and bs to have happened locally before p and q interact at n_3. There is no ordering relation between the as and bs, for instance we cannot say that the second a happens after the first b. Therefore the untimed language is simply the language of all words with the same number of as and bs before the c. This shows that the untimed language of the outcome sequences need not even be regular, unlike the case of timed automata.

In an implementation of the model, the synchronization mechanism can be seen as an update of the reference clocks to a larger value determined by the interacting parties.

3   Synchronization-Free Negotiations

Our goal is to study the location reachability problem in local-timed negotiations. Before studying the general case, we look at some restricted versions. The first restriction we look at is a synchronization-free fragment. Fix a negotiation $\mathcal{N} = (N, dom, \delta, Sync)$ for this section.

We say that $\mathcal{N}$ is *synchronization-free* if $Sync = \emptyset$. In such a negotiation, the agents require to elapse sufficient time only to satisfy their local guards (and not to meet any synchronization criteria). For instance, in the example on the left of Fig. 2, if n_3 is not a synchronizing node, then q can come directly to n_3 after node n_1, elapse no time at all, and engage in the only outcome from n_3. In the negotiation of Fig. 3, if the outcome c is not synchronized, the untimed language is the set of wc where $w \in (a + b)^*$ contains at least one a and one b.

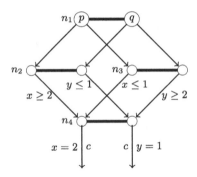

Fig. 4. Example of a synchronization-free local-timed negotiation. If n_3 is fired then the guard $y = 1$ on the transition from n_4 can not be satisfied.

Although the time elapse needed for an agent is to satisfy her own guards, she may need to collaborate with a partner to decide on what amount to elapse. This is because of the combination of guards across the different agents at a location. This is apparent in the negotiation of Fig. 4. For c to be feasible, both the agents have to reach node n_4 via n_2, and not via n_3. Therefore, one can view the time elapse at n_1 as a collective decision between p and q, which impacts their future paths.

The goal of this section is to show that reachability is PSPACE-complete for synchronization-free negotiations. Here is an overview of our proof. Firstly, as there are no synchronization constraints, we observe that the reference clocks are not useful at all in this fragment. We will then quotient the space of valuations by applying the classical region equivalence between clocks of each agent. This generates a finite automaton that accepts all the untimed location sequences that are feasible in the negotiation.

Definition 2 ($\equiv_M^p$ and $\equiv_M$ Equivalences). *Let p be an agent, and let M be the biggest constant appearing in the negotiation. We say $v \equiv_M^p v'$ if for all $x, y \in X_p$:*

- *either $\lfloor v(x) \rfloor = \lfloor v'(x) \rfloor$ or both $\lfloor v(x) \rfloor, \lfloor v'(x) \rfloor > M$,*
- *if $v(x) \leq M$, then $\{v(x)\} = 0$ iff $\{v'(x)\} = 0$*
- *if $v(x) \leq M$ and $v(y) \leq M$, we have $\{v(x)\} \leq \{v(y)\}$ iff $\{v'(x)\} \leq \{v'(y)\}$.*

We define $v \equiv_M v'$ if $v \equiv_M^p v'$ for all agents $p \in P$. We denote by $[v]$ the equivalence class of a valuation v with respect to the $\equiv_M$ equivalence. We will call $\equiv_M$ as the product-region equivalence, and the equivalence classes of $\equiv_M$ as product-regions.

Notice that reference clocks do not appear at all in the above definition. We next state there are finitely many product-regions.

Lemma 3. *The $\equiv_M$ equivalence is of finite index: the number of product-regions is bounded by $\mathcal{O}(|X|! \cdot 2^{|X|} \cdot (2M + 1)^{|X|})$.*

Here are some properties of the product-region equivalence, that follow from the region equivalence.

Lemma 4. *Let v, v' be valuations such that $v \equiv_M v'$. Then, for all local-delays Δ, there exists a local-delay Δ' such that $v + \Delta \equiv_M v' + \Delta'$.*

The next lemma follows by definition.

Lemma 5. *Let v, v' be valuations such that $v \equiv_M v'$. Let g be a guard with constants at most M. Then: (1) $v \models g$ iff $v' \models g$, and (2) for all subsets of local clocks Y, we have $v[Y] \equiv_M v'[Y]$.*

For a valuation v and a product-region r, we write $v \in r$ to mean that r equals $[v]$. We will now build a finite automaton using the product-regions.

Definition 6 (Product-Region Automaton). *States of this NFA are of the form (C, r) where C is a marking and r is a product-region. There is a transition $(C, r) \xrightarrow{(n,a)} (C', r')$ if for some valuation $v \in r$, and for some local-delay Δ, we have $(C, v) \xrightarrow{\Delta,(n,a)} (C', v')$ such that $v' \in r'$. The initial state is the initial marking C_0 and the region r_0 containing the valuation that maps all clocks to 0. We denote the product-region automaton as $\mathsf{ProdRegAut}(\mathcal{N})$.*

Lemma 7. *For every run $(C_0, v_0) \xrightarrow{\Delta_0, \ell_0} (C_1, v_1) \xrightarrow{\Delta_1, \ell_1} \cdots \xrightarrow{\Delta_{m-1}, \ell_{m-1}} (C_m, v_m)$ in the local-timed negotiation $\mathcal{N}$, there is a run $(C_0, [v_0]) \xrightarrow{\ell_0} (C_1, [v_1]) \xrightarrow{\ell_1} \cdots \xrightarrow{\ell_{m-1}} (C_m, [v_m])$ in $\mathsf{ProdRegAut}(\mathcal{N})$.*

Conversely, for every run $(C_0, r_0) \xrightarrow{\ell_0} (C_1, r_1) \xrightarrow{\ell_1} \cdots \xrightarrow{\ell_{m-1}} (C_m, r_m)$ in the product-region automaton $\mathsf{ProdRegAut}(\mathcal{N})$, there is a run $(C_0, v_0) \xrightarrow{\Delta_0, \ell_0} (C_1, v_1) \xrightarrow{\Delta_1, \ell_1} \cdots \xrightarrow{\Delta_{m-1}, \ell_{m-1}} (C_m, v_m)$ in $\mathcal{N}$ such that $v_i \in r_i$ for each $0 \leq i \leq m$.

Theorem 8. *Location reachability is PSPACE-complete for synchronization-free local-timed negotiations.*

Proof. A location $\ell = (n, a)$ is reachable in $\mathcal{N}$ iff it is reachable in $\mathsf{ProdRegAut}(\mathcal{N})$, thanks to Lemma 7. Let K be the size of the negotiation counted as the sum of the number of nodes, outcomes, clocks and the sum of the binary encoding of each constant appearing in the guards. Both the number of markings and the number of product-regions is $2^{\mathcal{O}(K)}$ (Lemma 3). Hence the size of the product-region graph is $2^{\mathcal{O}(K)}$. From the fact that st-connectivity is in LOGSPACE [20], we get the PSPACE upper bound for our problem.

PSPACE-hardness follows from the hardness of timed automata reachability [3]. Each timed automaton can be seen as a negotiation involving a single agent (with a single agent, both notions of local-time and global-time coincide). □

4   Always-Synchronizing Negotiations

We will now look at the fragment where every interaction forces a synchronization. We say that a local-timed negotiation is *always-synchronizing* if every node is a synchronization node, that is $Sync = N$. The negotiation in Fig. 3 can be seen as an always-synchronizing negotiation (in nodes that are local to one agent, the synchronization condition is vacuously true). We first remark that a region based argument is not immediate in this fragment. In order to satisfy the synchronization constraint, we check conditions of the form $t_p = t_q$. Therefore, we cannot decouple the time elapse of p and q completely, as in the previous section. Instead, we need to keep track of the difference $t_p - t_q$ in the equivalence. But then, there is no bound M' that allows us to club together all valuations with $t_p - t_q > M'$. This is because, t_q can perform local delays to catch up with p, and in particular, from $t_p - t_q > M'$ we may get to a situation where $t_p - t_q \leq M'$. This kind of a mechanics does not happen in classical timed automata, where once a clock is beyond M it always stays beyond M until the next reset. In the previous section, we avoided this problem since we did not need to keep track of the reference clocks.

We will make use of a different argument altogether, which is used in the proof of equivalence between the local-time and global-time semantics for networks of timed automata [4,13]. In always-synchronizing negotiations, every location (n, a) is executed at a unique timestamp given by the reference clock value of the participating processes. For example, the sequence $aabbc$ in the negotiation of Fig. 3 can be associated with the timestamp 12123: the first a occurs at $t_p = 1$, the second a at $t_p = 2$, the first b at $t_q = 1$ and the c occurs when both $t_p = t_q = 3$. The main observation is that whenever there is a $t_i t_{i+1}$ in this sequence with $t_{i+1} < t_i$, we can reorder the actions corresponding to them, and still get a valid run. For example, the run $(a, 1)(a, 2)(b, 1)(b, 2)(c, 3)$ described above can be reordered as $(a, 1)(b, 1)(a, 2)(b, 2)(c, 3)$ which is still a feasible run of the negotiation.

We will first show that every run of an always-synchronizing sequence can be reordered to a "monotonic" run. Next, we describe a timed automaton that accepts all monotonic runs of the negotiation. This gives a procedure for reachability, as reachability in the negotiation reduces to checking whether there is a run of a timed automaton that fires an edge.

Definition 9. *Let $\mathcal{N}$ be an always-synchronizing negotiation. Consider a run*
$$\rho := (C_0, v_0) \xrightarrow{\Delta_0, \ell_0} (C_1, v_1) \xrightarrow{\Delta_1, \ell_1} \cdots \xrightarrow{\Delta_{m-1}, \ell_{m-1}} (C_m, v_m), \text{ where } \ell_i = (n_i, a_i)$$
for every i.

We associate timestamps $\theta_i^\rho := v_i(t_p) + \Delta_i(p)$ where p is some agent participating in the negotiation n_i. The run ρ is monotonic if $\theta_i^\rho \leq \theta_j^\rho$ for every $i \leq j$.

Fix an always-synchronizing negotiation $\mathcal{N}$ for the rest of this section.

Lemma 10. *For every location (n, a) that is reachable, there is a monotonic run containing a small step that executes (n, a).*

Definition 11. *For an always-synchronizing negotiation $\mathcal{N}$ we define a timed automaton $\mathsf{TA}(\mathcal{N})$ as follows. States are the set of all markings possible in $\mathcal{N}$. There is a transition $C \xrightarrow{g,(n,a),Y} C'$ on guard g, action (n,a) and reset Y if (1) n is enabled in C, (2) there are transitions $\delta_p(n,a) = (g_p, M_p, Y_p)$ for all $p \in dom(n)$, and g is the conjunction of all g_p, and Y is the union of all Y_p, (3) $C'(p) = M_p$ for $p \in dom(n)$ and $C'(p) = C(p)$ otherwise.*

Lemma 12. *Let $\mathcal{N}$ be an always-synchronizing negotiation. A location (n,a) is reachable in $\mathcal{N}$ iff there is a run in the timed automaton $\mathsf{TA}(\mathcal{N})$ that executes an edge labeled with (n,a).*

Theorem 13. *Location-reachability is PSACE-complete for always-synchronizing negotiations.*

Proof. From Lemma 12, it is enough to check reachability of a certain edge in $\mathsf{TA}(\mathcal{N})$. We cannot directly use the fact that reachability in a timed automaton is in PSPACE, since the size of $\mathsf{TA}(\mathcal{N})$ is exponential in the size of $\mathcal{N}$. However, we next show that the size of the region automaton of $\mathsf{TA}(\mathcal{N})$ is $2^{\mathcal{O}(K)}$. Once again, using st-connectivity is in LOGSPACE gives the PSPACE upper bound. Let K be the size of the negotiation $\mathcal{N}$ which includes the number of nodes, outcomes, clocks and the sum of the binary encodings of the constants present. The number of states of $\mathsf{TA}(\mathcal{N})$ is $2^{\mathcal{O}(K)}$. The set of clocks is the same as that of $\mathcal{N}$. Therefore, the number of regions for $\mathsf{TA}(\mathcal{N})$ is still $2^{\mathcal{O}(K)}$. The product of states and regions remains to be $2^{\mathcal{O}(K)}$. Lower bound follows once again from the hardness of timed automata, which is simply a negotiation with a single agent. Synchronization is vacuously true at every node. □

5   Reachability Is Undecidable for Local-Timed Negotiations

When we allow both synchronized and unsynchronized nodes, we are unable to use either of the techniques of the previous two sections. In fact, reachability turns out to be undecidable. Since local-times are independent of each other, it is possible to have an unbounded drift between the reference clocks of two agents. This helps store counter values as differences between the local times. The main challenge is the check for zero. This is where we require a combination of synchronized and unsynchronized interactions. We will now show how to simulate a counter machine using a local-timed negotiation.

Theorem 14. *Location-reachability is undecidable for local-timed negotiations.*

The rest of the section is devoted to proving Theorem 14. We will encode the halting problem of a 2-counter machine as the reachability problem for a local-timed negotiation.

Counter Machines. A 2-counter machine M is a program that manipulates two counters, C_1 and C_2, each of which can hold a non-negative number. The machine is given as a sequence of labelled instructions $\ell : I$, where I is one of the following for some $i \in \{1, 2\}$:

increment $C_i + +$, which increments the value of the counter C_i and goes to the next instruction $\ell + 1$.

decrement if $C_i > 0$ then $C_i - -$, which decrements C_i and continues with the next instruction $\ell + 1$. If the value of C_i is 0, then the program is blocked.

jump-on-zero if $C_i == 0$ goto ℓ', which transfers control to the instruction labelled ℓ' if counter C_i is 0 for $i \in \{1, 2\}$. If $C_i > 0$, it continues to the instruction $\ell + 1$.

The counter machine is said to halt if it reaches the final instruction. A configuration of M is a triple (ℓ, c_1, c_2) representing the current instruction ℓ that needs to be executed and the current values $c_1, c_2 \geq 0$ of the counters C_1, C_2 respectively. The transitions $(\ell, c_1, c_2) \rightarrow (\ell', c_1', c_2')$ follow naturally from the description above.

Overview of the Reduction. The negotiation $\mathcal{N}_M$ that we construct will have 6 agents $p_1, q_1, r_1, p_2, q_2, r_2$. Agents p_1, q_1, r_1 simulate counter C_1, and the rest simulate C_2. Let $i \in \{1, 2\}$. The local clocks of p_i, q_i, r_i are respectively $\{x_{p_i}\}$, $\{x_{q_i}, x_{q_i}'\}$ and $\{x_{r_i}\}$. Additionally, we have the reference clocks t_α for each agent α. For every instruction ℓ, we will have a node n_ℓ in which all the six agents participate. A configuration (C, v) of $\mathcal{N}_M$ is said to encode configuration (ℓ, c_1, c_2) of M if:

- $C(\alpha) = \{n_\ell\}$ for every agent α,
- $v(x) = 0$ for all local clocks (and reference clocks can take any value),
- $v(t_{r_1}) \leq v(t_{q_1}) \leq v(t_{p_1})$ and $v(t_{r_2}) \leq v(t_{q_2}) \leq v(t_{p_2})$, and
- $v(t_{p_1} - t_{q_1}) = c_1$ and $v(t_{p_2} - t_{q_2}) = c_2$,

The initial configuration of $\mathcal{N}_M$ has every agent in n_{ℓ_0}, where ℓ_0 is the first instruction in M and every clock (including reference clocks) to be 0.

We will have a gadget in $\mathcal{N}_M$ corresponding to each instruction in the counter machine. Let $(C, v), (C', v')$ be configurations that encode (ℓ, c_1, c_2) and (ℓ', c_1', c_2') respectively. A run $(C, v) \rightarrow \cdots \rightarrow (C', v')$ such that none of the intermediate configurations encodes any counter machine configuration will be called a *big step*. We denote a big step as $(C, v) \Rightarrow (C', v')$. Our gadgets will ensure the following two properties.

- Let $(\ell, c_1, c_2) \rightarrow (\ell', c_1', c_2')$ in M. Then from every configuration (C, v) that encodes (ℓ, c_1, c_2), there is a big step $(C, v) \Rightarrow (C', v')$ to some configuration (C', v') that encodes (ℓ', c_1', c_2').
- Let $(C, v), (C', v')$ be arbitrary configurations of $\mathcal{N}_M$ that encode (ℓ, c_1, c_2) and (ℓ', c_1', c_2') respectively. If $(C, v) \Rightarrow (C', v')$ is a big step, then $(\ell, c_1, c_2) \rightarrow (\ell', c_1', c_2')$ in M.

The first property ensures that for every path $(\ell^0, c_1^0, c_2^0) \rightarrow (\ell^1, c_1^1, c_2^1) \rightarrow \cdots$, there is a sequence of big steps $(C_0, v_0) \Rightarrow (C_1, v_1) \Rightarrow \cdots$ such that (C_i, v_i) encodes (ℓ^i, c_1^i, c_2^i). The second property ensures the reverse: from a sequence of big steps, we get a corresponding run in counter machine. We will now describe each gadget and show that the two properties are satisfied.

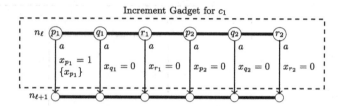

Fig. 5. Gadget for implementing increment instruction on c_1

Increment. Assume an instruction $\ell : C_1 + +$ with ℓ not being the final instruction. The case with $C_2 + +$ is symmetric. Every configuration (ℓ, c_1, c_2) on executing this instruction goes to $(\ell + 1, c_1 + 1, c_2)$. Figure 5 shows the gadget for the increment instruction. All agents other than p_1 cannot elapse time due to the guard checking local clocks to 0. Agent p_1 elapses exactly one time unit, after which clock x_{p_1} is reset. It is easy to see that the configuration (C', v') that results from (C, v) encodes $(\ell', c_1 + 1, c_2)$. The big step $(C, v) \Rightarrow (C', v')$ is in fact a single transition. Both the properties are easily seen to be satisfied.

Decrement. Consider a decrement instruction: if $C_1 > 0$ then $C_1 - -$. We have $(\ell, c_1, c_2) \to (\ell + 1, c_1 - 1, c_2)$ if $c_1 > 0$. The first task is to check if $c_1 > 0$. Recall that in the negotiation the difference $t_{p_1} - t_{q_1}$ gives the value of c_1. Our idea is to let q_1 elapse time to synchronize with p_1 and check if this time elapse needed for synchronization is strictly above 0 or not. However, in this process, we lose the actual value of the counter. In order to maintain the same difference between t_{p_1} and t_{q_1}, we make use of the auxiliary process r_1.

Consider a configuration (C, v) that encodes (ℓ, c_1, c_2). By our definition, $v(t_{r_1}) \le v(t_{p_1})$ and $v(t_{p_1} - t_{q_1}) = c_1$.

- We first let r_1 synchronize with p_1, while p_1 elapses no time.
- Next, we keep moving both p_1 and q_1 by 1 unit each until q_1 synchronizes with r_1. In this entire process r_1 is not allowed to elapse time.

By the end of this, we will get a valuation v' with the same difference $v'(t_{p_1} - t_{q_1}) = c_1$ since both the agents were moved by the same amount. Moreover, we can use an additional clock to check whether in the process of q_1 synchronizing with r_1, a non-zero time had elapsed in q_1.

The gadget is depicted in Fig. 6. For simplicity, we do not index the intermediate nodes n_1, n_2, n_3, n_4 by ℓ. The computation proceeds in three phases. Below, we show the run of $\mathcal{N}_M$ along this gadget, restricted to the agents p_1, q_1, r_1. The other three agents simply move to the next possible instruction (this is not shown in the figure for simplicity).

Phase 1. Synchronize r_1 with p_1 maintaining no time elapse in p_1 as follows: $((n_\ell, n_\ell, n_\ell), v) \to ((n_1, n_2, n_1), v_1) \to ((n_2, n_2, n_3), v_3)$. After the last action, agents p_1 and r_1 are synchronized, that is, $v_3(t_{p_1}) = v_3(t_{r_1})$. This is due to the node n_1 being a synchronization node. Moreover, $v_3(t_{p_1}) = v(t_{p_1})$, due to the guard $x_{p_1} = 0$. Similarly, $v_3(t_{q_1}) = v(t_{q_1})$ due to $x_{q_1} = 0$.

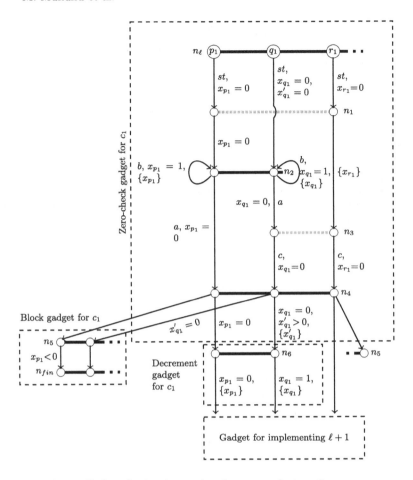

Fig. 6. Gadget for implementing decrement instruction on c_1

Phase 2. Move p_1 and q_1 repeatedly by one unit each: $((n_2, n_2, n_3), v_3) \xrightarrow{b}$ $((n_2, n_2, n_3), v_3^1) \xrightarrow{b} \cdots \xrightarrow{b} ((n_2, n_2, n_3), v_3^k)$. By the end of k iterations of b, we have $v_3^k(t_{p_1}) = v(t_{p_1}) + k$ and $v_3^k(t_{q_1}) = v(t_{q_1}) + k$.

Phase 3. Check if the reference clocks of q_1 and r_1 are equal: $((n_2, n_2, n_3), v_3^k)$ $\xrightarrow{a} ((n_4, n_3, n_3), v_4) \xrightarrow{c} ((n_4, n_4, n_4), v_5)$. The outcome c at n_4 can be fired only if the reference clocks of q_1 and r_1 are equal: that is, $v_4(t_{q_1}) = v_4(t_{r_1})$. Due to the guard checking for 0 at a and c, we have $v_5(t_{q_1}) = v_4(t_{q_1}) = v_3^k(t_{q_1})$. From Phase 2, this value equals $v(t_{q_1}) + k$. Secondly, notice that $v_4(t_{r_1}) = v_3(t_{r_1})$, which from Phase 1 equals $v(t_{p_1})$. From the equality $v_4(t_{q_1}) = v_4(t_{r_1})$, we get $v(t_{q_1}) + k = v(t_{p_1})$. This shows that $k = v(t_{p_1}) - v(t_{q_1})$. The number of times the loop b is done equals the difference between t_{p_1} and t_{q_1} at the start of this gadget. If the number of b iterations is more than this value or less than this value, location (n_3, c) cannot be executed and the negotiation cannot proceed further.

When action c is done, the clock x'_{q_1} holds the time between st and c for agent q_1, and this is exactly k. If $k > 0$ the value of t_{q_1} is increased by 1, resulting in the counter value getting decremented and the agents move to the next instruction (shown as the decrement gadget in the figure). Otherwise, the agents are sent to a gadget from which there is no run (shown as the block gadget in the figure). Notice the interplay between synchronized and unsynchronized nodes in this gadget. It is crucial that n_2 is unsynchronized, whereas nodes n_1, n_3 need to be. *Jump-on-Zero.* This gadget is similar to the decrement gadget, where the first part was to check if C_1 is 0 or not. When $C_1 == 0$, the gadget jumps to the relevant instruction, otherwise it moves to the next instruction in sequence. The gadget is shown in [19].

6   Conclusion

We have presented a model of local-timed negotiations. This is motivated by the need for expressing timing constraints between interactions in a negotiation. We have chosen a local-time model and incorporated a synchronization constraint as part of the model. We have shown that reachability is decidable when there is no mix of synchronized and unsynchronized interactions. This mix creates situations where one agent needs to fire a number of outcomes before synchronizing with a second agent, and in this process forces a third agent to elapse time. We have used this in the gadget explained for the decrement instruction. As future work, we would like to study non-trivial restrictions which contain a mix of synchronized and unsynchronized interactions and are yet decidable.

We would like to remark that such a synchronization constraint can be added in the local-time semantics for networks of timed automata. Currently, the local-time semantics forces every shared action to be synchronized. The main reason is that the definition gives equivalence with the global-time semantics for reachability and Büchi reachability. For networks of timed automata, global-time semantics is considered the gold standard. The local-time semantics is studied as a heuristic to solve reachability and Büchi reachability, since this has better independence properties and is therefore amenable to partial-order methods. In our case with negotiations, we consider local-time as the original semantics and make synchronization as an option to be specified in the model. This allows more independence between the agents and makes it more attractive for partial-order methods. Having a decidable fragment with controlled use of synchronization would be interesting in this regard.

References

1. Akshay, S., Genest, B., Hélouët, L., Mital, S.: Timed negotiations. In: Proceedings of the 23rd International Conference on Foundations of Software Science and Computation Structures, FOSSACS 2020, Dublin, 25–30 April 2020, pp. 37–56 (2020)

2. Akshay, S., Mukund, M., Narayan Kumar, K.: Checking coverage for infinite collections of timed scenarios. In: Proceedings of the 18th International Conference on Concurrency Theory, CONCUR 2007, Lisbon, 3–8 September 2007, pp. 181–196 (2007)

3. Alur, R., Dill, D.L.: A theory of timed automata. Theor. Comput. Sci. **126**(2), 183–235 (1994)

4. Bengtsson, J., Jonsson, B., Lilius, J., Yi, W.: Partial order reductions for timed systems. In: Proceedings of the 9th International Conference on Concurrency Theory, CONCUR 1998, Nice, 8–11 September 1998, pp. 485–500 (1998)

5. Bouyer, P., Haddad, S., Reynier, P.-A.: Timed unfoldings for networks of timed automata. In: Graf, S., Zhang, W. (eds.) ATVA 2006. LNCS, vol. 4218, pp. 292–306. Springer, Heidelberg (2006). https://doi.org/10.1007/11901914_23

6. Cassez, F., Chatain, T., Jard, C.: Symbolic unfoldings for networks of timed automata. In: Graf, S., Zhang, W. (eds.) ATVA 2006. LNCS, vol. 4218, pp. 307–321. Springer, Heidelberg (2006). https://doi.org/10.1007/11901914_24

7. Chatain, T., Jard, C.: Time supervision of concurrent systems using symbolic unfoldings of time petri nets. In: Pettersson, P., Yi, W. (eds.) FORMATS 2005. LNCS, vol. 3829, pp. 196–210. Springer, Heidelberg (2005). https://doi.org/10.1007/11603009_16

8. Chatain, T., Jard, C.: Complete finite prefixes of symbolic unfoldings of safe time petri nets. In: Donatelli, S., Thiagarajan, P.S. (eds.) ICATPN 2006. LNCS, vol. 4024, pp. 125–145. Springer, Heidelberg (2006). https://doi.org/10.1007/11767589_8 125–145. Springer, 2006

9. Desel, J., Esparza, J., Hoffmann, P.: Negotiation as concurrency primitive. Acta Informatica **56**(2), 93–159 (2019)

10. Esparza, J., Desel, J.: On negotiation as concurrency primitive. In: Proceedings of the 24th International Conference on Concurrency Theory, CONCUR 2013, Buenos Aires, Argentina, 27–30 August 2013, pp. 440–454 (2013)

11. Esparza, J., Kuperberg, D., Muscholl, A., Walukiewicz, I.: Soundness in negotiations. Log. Methods Comput. Sci. **14**(1) (2018)

12. Esparza, J., Muscholl, A., Walukiewicz, I.: Static analysis of deterministic negotiations. In: Proceedings of the 32nd Annual ACM/IEEE Symposium on Logic in Computer Science, LICS 2017, Reykjavik, 20–23 June 2017, pp. 1–12 (2017)

13. Govind, R., Herbreteau, F., Srivathsan, B., Walukiewicz, I.: Revisiting local time semantics for networks of timed automata. In: Proceedings of the 30th International Conference on Concurrency Theory, CONCUR 2019, Amsterdam, 27–30 August 2019, pp. 16:1–16:15 (2019)

14. Govind, R., Herbreteau, F., Srivathsan, B., Walukiewicz, I.: Abstractions for the local-time semantics of timed automata: a foundation for partial-order methods. In: Proceedings of the 37th Annual ACM/IEEE Symposium on Logic in Computer Science, LICS 2022, Haifa, 2–5 August 2022, pp. 24:1–24:14 (2022)

15. Hanisch, H.-M.: Analysis of place/transition nets with timed arcs and its application to batch process control. In: Proceedings of the 14th International Conference on Application and Theory of Petri Nets 1993, Chicago, 21–25 June 1993, pp. 282–299 (1993)

16. Herbreteau, F., Srivathsan, B., Walukiewicz, I.: Checking timed büchi automata emptiness using the local-time semantics. In: Proceedings of the 33rd International Conference on Concurrency Theory, CONCUR 2022, Warsaw, 12–16 September 2022, pp. 12:1–12:24 (2022)

17. Lugiez, D., Niebert, P., Zennou, S.: A partial order semantics approach to the clock explosion problem of timed automata. Theor. Comput. Sci. **345**(1), 27–59 (2005)

18. Merlin, P.M.: A Study of the Recoverability of Computing Systems. Ph.D. thesis, University of California, Irvine (1974). AAI7511026
19. Mukund, M., Roy, A., Srivathsan, B.: A local-time semantics for negotiations. arXiv preprint arXiv:2307.06691 (2023)
20. Savitch, W.J.: Relationships between nondeterministic and deterministic tape complexities. J. Comput. Syst. Sci. **4**(2), 177–192 (1970)

Timed Non-interference Under Partial Observability and Bounded Memory

Anthony Spriet[✉], Didier Lime, and Olivier H. Roux

Nantes Université, École Centrale Nantes, CNRS,
LS2N, UMR 6004, 44000 Nantes, France
Anthony.Spriet@ec-nantes.fr

Abstract. We investigate a timed non-interference property for security systems modeled as timed automata, in which a low-security level user should not be able to deduce the occurrence of some high-security level actions. We assume an attack model in which the malicious (low-level) user has the ability to partially observe and memorize the set of runs of the timed automaton modeling the system.

We first formalize a non-interference property that ensures the system security under such an attack model and we then prove the undecidability of that property when the attacker can have an arbitrarily big memory, i.e., when they are able to memorize sequences of previous observations, with time-stamps, of any length. We next assume bounded memory for the attacker and show that the property can then be decided in PSPACE for a subclass of timed automata ensuring finite duration between distinct observations.

Keywords: Non-interference · Timed Automata · Partial observability

1 Introduction

Information leakage is a type of software vulnerability in which information is unintentionally accessible to unauthorized party, potentially aiding malicious attackers or leading to malfunction of systems. Various information flow properties have been defined in the literature such as anonymity, non-interference, secrecy, privacy, opacity, non-deducibility. These properties intersect with each other and formal comparisons have been made as in [BKMR08] between opacity, anonymity, (trace-based) non-interference and non-deducibility. We focus here on non-interference properties that could thus be written as opacity.

A system is said to be non-interferent [GM84] if the information available on the interface of the system is not sufficient to infer some classified internal information. That is to say, the information available in the low-level channel (not classified, observable by most users) does not contain any clues about the information only available on the high-level channel (classified information, only

---

This work has been partially funded by ANR project ProMiS ANR-19-CE25-0015.

L. Petrucci and J. Sproston (Eds.): FORMATS 2023, LNCS 14138, pp. 122–137, 2023.
https://doi.org/10.1007/978-3-031-42626-1_8

accessible to some or no users). Another way to put it is that a sequence of low-level inputs will always produce the same low-level outputs, regardless of what happens on high-level inputs. It has been shown that additional information that is not directly provided by the system can be used to make inferences on what happens on the high-level channel. In particular, a system may be non-interferent when considering sequences of low-level inputs and outputs but interferent when the dates of each observation of the different inputs and outputs are measured and memorized by a malicious observer [Koc96, FS00, BB07, KPJJ13].

In [BT03], Barbuti *et al* proposed two notions of timed non-interference in systems modeled by timed automata. One is a trace-based notion in which the attacker can observe the consecutive actions performed by the system and tries to guess if a hidden action has occurred. The trace-based approach has since been refined by taking simulation properties into account or by providing control synthesis algorithms [GMR07, BCLR15, GSB18]. The other approach is state-based: the attacker can observe the state of the system directly but does not see any action. If the observed state is not reachable using only low-level actions, the attacker is able to infer the use of a high-level action. The state-based approach has also been refined since by being extended to parametric timed automata [AK20]. Other notions of non-interference have also been proposed, a common framework involves ensuring that no information is leaked through the execution time of a timed automaton with final locations [ALMS22, WZ18, AETYM21].

Contributions We introduce a new state-based non interference property (POS-NNI) and discuss its relevance when it comes to modeling realistic attackers. We prove that the POS-NNI verification problem is undecidable when the attacker memory is infinite. We provide a subclass of timed automata for which this property is decidable for attackers with finite memory of any length and we prove that its verification is PSPACE-complete.

In Sect. 2, we recall definitions used to formalize the timed non-interference property and present some basic constructions over timed automata used to model the systems and the information flow. In Sect. 3, we introduce the POS-NNI property and we prove its undecidability when the attacker memory is infinite. Lastly, in Sect. 4, we provide a subclass of timed automata for attackers with finite memory of any length for which the POS-NNI verification problem is PSPACE-complete.

2   Definitions

2.1   Timed Automata

Timed automata [AD94] are one of the many formalism to model real-time systems, they consist in adding real-valued clocks to finite automata in order to capture timed behaviors accurately. We consider here *security automata*, in which the set of actions is partitioned into two subsets, modeling two users with different access privileges to information or commands.

Definition 1 (Clocks and Valuations). *A clocks is a real-valued variable that evolves at rate 1 w.r.t. time. We define a set $\mathbb{X} = \{x_1, x_2, ..., x_H\}$ of clocks.*

A clock valuation is a function $\nu : \mathbb{X} \to \mathbb{R}_{\geq 0}$. We denote by $\mathbb{R}_{\geq 0}^{\mathbb{X}}$ the set of valuations.

Given $d \in \mathbb{R}_{\geq 0}, \nu + d$ denotes the valuation s. t. $(\nu + d)(x) = \nu(x) + d$. Given $R \subseteq \mathbb{X}$, we define the reset of a valuation ν, denoted by $[\nu]_R$ s. t. $[\nu]_R(x) = 0$ if $x \in R$, and $[\nu]_R(x) = \nu(x)$ otherwise.

Definition 2 (Clock Constraint). *A clock constraint g is a constraint over $\mathbb{X}$ defined by a conjunction of inequalities of the form $x \bowtie d$ with $d \in \mathbb{N}$ and $\bowtie \in \{\leq, <, >, \geq\}$.*

Given g, we write $\nu \models g$ iff each inequality in g evaluates to true when each clock x is replaced with its value $\nu(x)$.

Definition 3 (ϵ-Timed Automatons (ϵ-TA) *An ϵ-TA $\mathcal{A}$ is a tuple $\mathcal{A} = (\Sigma \cup \{\epsilon\}, L, l_0, \mathbb{X}, I, E)$ where: Σ is a finite set of actions, ϵ is the unique "silent action", L is a finite set of locations, l_0 is the initial location, $\mathbb{X}$ is a finite set of clocks, I assigns to every $l \in L$ a clock constraint $I(l)$ called* invariant, *E is a finite set of edges $e = (l, g, a, R, l')$ where $l, l' \in L$ are respectively the source and target locations, $a \in \Sigma \cup \{\epsilon\}, R \subseteq \mathbb{X}$ is a set of clocks to be reset, and g is a clock constraint.*

Definition 4 (Semantics of Timed Automata). *Given an ϵ-TA $\mathcal{A} = (\Sigma \cup \{\epsilon\}, L, l_0, \mathbb{X}, I, E)$, the semantics of $\mathcal{A}$ is given by the timed transition system $(S, s_0, \to)$, with:*

- *$S = \{(l, \nu) \in L \times \mathbb{R}_{\geq 0}^{\mathbb{X}} \mid \nu \models I(l)\}$*
- *$s_0 = (l_0, \mathbf{0})$ with $\mathbf{0}$ the valuation of clocks with all clocks equal to 0.*
- *$\to$ consists of the discrete and continuous delay transitions:*
  - *discrete transitions: $(l, \nu) \xrightarrow{a} (l', \nu')$ with $(l, \nu), (l', \nu') \in S$ and there exists $e = (l, g, a, R, l') \in E$ such that $\nu' = [\nu]_R$ and $\nu \models g$*
  - *delay transitions: $(l, \nu) \xrightarrow{d} (l, \nu + d)$ with $d \in \mathbb{R}_{\geq 0}$ if $\forall d' \in [0, d], (l, \nu + d') \in S$*

Definition 5 (Run). *Let $\mathcal{A} = (\Sigma \cup \{\epsilon\}, L, l_0, \mathbb{X}, I, E)$ be a ϵ-TA and $(S, s_0, \to)$ its semantics. A (finite) run ρ of $\mathcal{A}$ is a finite sequence $\rho = s_0 e_0 s_1 e_1 \cdots s_n$ with $\forall i, s_i \in S$ and $(s_i, e_i, s_{i+1}) \in \to$, which we will also write $\rho = s_0 \xrightarrow{e_0} s_1 \xrightarrow{e_1} \cdots \xrightarrow{e_{n-1}} s_n$.*

A run ρ can always be put in the form:$\rho = s_0 \xrightarrow{d_1} s_1 \xrightarrow{a_2 \ d_2} s_2 \xrightarrow{a_2} ... s_{n-1} \xrightarrow{a_n \ d_n} s_n$ where delays and actions strictly alternate. we have omitted some state names for brevity.

We write $\Psi(\mathcal{A})$ the set of all runs of $\mathcal{A}$. We say that a state s is reachable in $\mathcal{A}$ if there exists a run $\rho \in \Psi(\mathcal{A})$ s.t. $s \in \rho$. We write $Q^{\mathcal{A}}$ set of all the reachable states in $\mathcal{A}$

2.2   Timed Language

Sequences of actions generated by a TA, together with their dates, describe the behavior of the automaton.

Definition 6 (Timed Word and Trace). *A timed word over the alphabet Σ is a finite sequence $w = (a_0, t_0)(a_1, t_1)...(a_n, t_n)$ so that $\forall i \geq 0, a_i \in \Sigma, t_i \in \mathbb{R}_{\geq 0}$.*

Given a run $\rho = s_0 \xrightarrow{d_1} s_1 \xrightarrow{a_2, d_2} s_2 \xrightarrow{a_2} ...s_{n-1} \xrightarrow{a_n, d_n} s_n$, its trace is the timed word $(a_1, d_1)(a_2, d_1 + d_2) \cdots (a_n, \sum_{i=1}^{n-1} d_i)$

We denote $\mathcal{U}(\Sigma)$ the set of all timed words over the alphabet Σ

Definition 7 (Timed Language). *For a given ϵ-TA $\mathcal{A}$, its timed language $\mathcal{L}(\mathcal{A})$ is the set of the traces of all its runs.*

2.3   Security Timed Automata

Definition 8 (Security Timed Automaton). *A Security Timed Automaton $\mathcal{A} = (\Sigma \cup \{\epsilon\}, L, l_0, \mathbb{X}, I, E)$ is an ϵ-TA whose set of (visible) actions Σ is partitioned in two subsets Σ_{low} and Σ_{high} such that $\Sigma_{\text{low}} \cap \Sigma_{\text{high}} = \emptyset$ and $\Sigma_{\text{low}} \cup \Sigma_{\text{high}} = \Sigma$.*

In order to compare high-level behaviors and low-level behaviors by removing all the high-level information we define restricted timed automata as follows. Figure 1 shows a security TA $\mathcal{A}$ and its restriction $\mathcal{A}_{\backslash \Sigma_{\text{high}}}$.

Definition 9 (Restricted Timed Automata). *Let $\mathcal{A} = (\Sigma, L, l_0, \mathbb{X}, I, E)$ be a TA and $\Gamma \subseteq \Sigma$. We define the Γ-restriction TA $\mathcal{A}_{\backslash \Gamma} = (\Sigma \backslash \Gamma, L, l_0, \mathbb{X}, I, E_{\backslash \Gamma})$ where $(l, g, a, R, l') \in E_{\backslash \Gamma}$ iff $a \in (\Sigma \backslash \Gamma)$ and $(l, g, a, R, l') \in E$.*

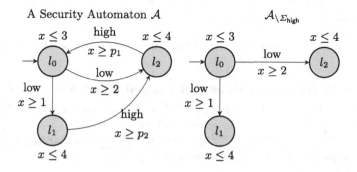

Fig. 1. A security TA $\mathcal{A}$ and $\mathcal{A}_{\backslash \Sigma_{\text{high}}}$

3   State-Based Non-interference Properties

3.1   Already Existing State-Based Non-interference Properties

To our knowledge, the first proposal of a state-based non-interference property for timed automata comes from Barbuti and Tesei, [BT03] and has later been refined by Gardey *et al* [GMR07]. To define a state-based property of non-interference we can picture a memoryless attacker who is able to fully observe the system states (both location and clocks valuation) and tries to guess if a high-level action has occurred. Because they are memoryless, they have to make their guess based on a single observation of the system, which intuitively corresponds to the property called *St-NNI* (State non-interference) by Gardey *et al* [GMR07]: a security automaton $\mathcal{A}$ satisfies St-NNI iff $Q^{\mathcal{A}} = Q^{\mathcal{A} \backslash \Sigma_{\text{high}}}$

3.2   A More Realistic Property

As we described St-NNI can be seen as a model for a really powerful attacker, in the sense that they can fully observe the system states, but with the minimal deductive abilities due to their memorylessness. If we were to give memory to the attacker, in the sense that the attacker would have access to all their previous observations, while keeping their ability to observe the state directly: we would end up with an unrealistically high standard for security. We therefore propose an attacker that has memory and is able to continuously observe the system but is only able to observe part of the information, in the sense that they cannot observe systems clocks and that some locations are indistinguishable to them. Formally, we do so by attributing a value to each location, the attacker being able to observe this value and associate it with a time-stamp.

Definition 10 (Observation Functions). *Let Ω be a finite set with $|\Omega| \leq |L|$. We call the elements of Ω observations. An observation function is a function $\mathcal{O} : L \rightarrow \Omega$. If $\mathcal{O}(l) = \mathcal{O}(l')$ (resp: $\mathcal{O}(l) \neq \mathcal{O}(l')$) we say that l and l' are indistinguishable (resp: distinguishable).*

We now use the observation to define the runs from the attacker point of view.

Definition 11 (Observed Runs and Events). *Given a run $\rho = (l_0, 0) \xrightarrow{d_1} (l_1, \nu_1) \xrightarrow{a_2, d_2} (l_2, \nu_2) \dots (l_{n-1}, \nu_{n-1}) \xrightarrow{a_n, d_n} (l_n, \nu_n)$ and an observation function $\mathcal{O}$. We define the projecting operator $\mathcal{O}$ as:*
$$\mathcal{O}(\rho) = (\mathcal{O}(l_{i_0}), 0)(\mathcal{O}(l_{i_1}), \sum_{k=1}^{i_1 - 1} d_k) \dots (\mathcal{O}(l_{i_{m-1}}), \sum_{k=1}^{i_m - 1} d_k)(\mathcal{O}(l_{i_m}), \sum_{k=1}^{i_m} d_k),$$
where the sequence $(i_0, i_1, ..., i_m)$ is defined as follows:

- *$i_0 = 0$*
- *for $1 \leq k < m$, i_k is the smallest index $j > i_{k-1}$ such that $\mathcal{O}(l_{i_{k-1}}) \neq \mathcal{O}(l_j)$*
- *$i_m = n$*

We call $\mathcal{O}(\rho)$ an observed run of $\mathcal{A}$ (with respect to $\mathcal{O}$). We note $\mathcal{O}(\mathcal{A})$ the set of observed runs of $\mathcal{A}$.

*When the observed run $\mathcal{O}(\rho)$ of a run ρ contains an element (a, t) we say that an **observed event** occured at time t in the run.*

To put it simply, because attackers are able to continuously observe the system, they are therefore able to memorize the absolute date of the events (when a discrete transition between distinguishable locations occurs). The last element of the observed run is there to model the time elapsed since the last event, by construction $\mathcal{O}(l_{i_m}) = \mathcal{O}(l_{i_{m-1}})$. If an observed run is possible both with and without high-level actions, an attacker cannot deduce anything from this observed run. Therefore, ensuring that no observed run is possible only for high-level users guarantees security.

Example 1 (A run and its associated observed run). Given a run $\rho = (l_0, \mathbf{0}) \xrightarrow{d_1, a_1} (l_1, \nu_1) \xrightarrow{d_2, a_2} (l_2, \nu_2) \xrightarrow{d_3, a_3} (l_3, \nu_3) \xrightarrow{d_4, a_4} (l_4, \nu_4) \xrightarrow{d_5, a_5} (l_5, \nu_5) \xrightarrow{d_6}$
(l_5, ν_6) with $\mathcal{O}(l_0) = \mathcal{O}(l_1) = \mathcal{O}(l_3) = \mathcal{O}(l_4) = o_1, \mathcal{O}(l_2) = o_2$ and $\mathcal{O}(l_5) = o_3$.
We have $\mathcal{O}(\rho) = (o_1, 0)(o_2, d_1 + d_2)(o_1, d_1 + d_2 + d_3)(o_3, \sum_{k=1}^{5} d_k)(o_3, \sum_{k=1}^{6} d_k)$

We say that observed events occurred at time $0, d_1, \sum_{k=1}^{2} d_k, \sum_{k=1}^{4} d_k$ and $\sum_{k=1}^{5} d_k$. No event occurred at $\sum_{k=1}^{6} d_k$, the last term is to account for the time elapsed since the last event.

Definition 12 (Partial Observability State-Based Non-interference (POS-NNI)). *A security automaton $\mathcal{A}$ satisfies POS-NNI with respect to the observation function $\mathcal{O}$ if and only if $\mathcal{O}(\mathcal{A}) = \mathcal{O}(\mathcal{A}_{\backslash \Sigma_{\text{high}}})$*

We now show that verifying POS-NNI is undecidable by reducing to it the problem of timed language universality, which is known to be undecidable [AD94]. We do so in the following way: we first define a transformation $\mathcal{T}$ on TAs that allows us to define an observation function so that there is a one to one correspondence between the observed run set of $\mathcal{T}(\mathcal{A})$ and the timed language of $\mathcal{A}$. Then for any TA $\mathcal{A}$, we define an augmented security automaton that is equal to $\mathcal{T}(\mathcal{A})$ when restricted to low-level actions (therefore having the same language) but has the universal language when not restricted. The augmented automaton therefore satisfies POS-NNI with respect to our observation function if and only if the timed language of $\mathcal{A}$ is the universal language.

Definition 13 (Transformation $\mathcal{T}$). *Given a TA $\mathcal{A} = (\Sigma, L, l_0, \mathbb{X}, I, E)$, we define $\mathcal{T}(\mathcal{A}) = (\Sigma, L_{\mathcal{T}(\mathcal{A})}, l_{0_{\mathcal{T}(\mathcal{A})}}, \mathbb{X}, I_{\mathcal{T}(\mathcal{A})}, E_{\mathcal{T}(\mathcal{A})})$ with:*

- $l_{0_{\mathcal{T}}} = (l_0, \epsilon, 0)$
- $L_{\mathcal{T}} = \{L\} \times \{\Sigma \cup \{\epsilon\}\} \times \{0; 1\}$
- $\forall l \in L, \forall a \in \Sigma, \forall i \in \{0, 1\}, (l, a, i) \in L_{\mathcal{T}(\mathcal{A})} \land I_{\mathcal{T}(\mathcal{A})}((l, a, i)) = I(l)$
- $E_{\mathcal{T}(\mathcal{A})}$ *is the smallest set such that* $\forall e = (l, g, a, R, l') \in E$:
  - $\forall b \in (\Sigma \cup \{\epsilon\}), ((l, b, 0), g, a, R, (l', a, 1)) \in E_{\mathcal{T}(\mathcal{A})}$
  - $\forall b \in (\Sigma \cup \{\epsilon\}), ((l, b, 1), g, a, R, (l', a, 0)) \in E_{\mathcal{T}(\mathcal{A})}$

The idea of transformation T is to preserve the language while augmenting the set of locations by splitting it into triplets (l, σ, b). When using a discrete transition labeled σ, the automaton $T(\mathcal{A})$ necessarily reaches a location labeled σ as well. The parameter b is a boolean value ensuring the absence of self-loop transitions in $T(\mathcal{A})$, any discrete transition available from a locality marked with 0 would reach a locality marked with 1 and vice-versa. This way, we are able to define an observation function on $T(\mathcal{A})$ so that every transition of a run is associated with an observed event and every observation is associated with a unique transition label.

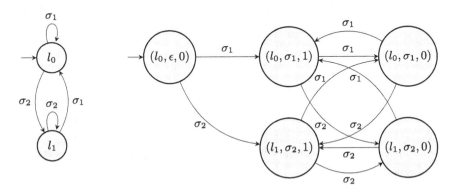

Fig. 2. A timed automaton and its transformation with T (clock constraints are omitted)

Proposition 1. *Given a TA $\mathcal{A}$ defined over the alphabet Σ and its transformation $T(\mathcal{A})$, the following properties holds:*

i) $\mathcal{L}(\mathcal{A}) = \mathcal{L}(T(\mathcal{A}))$
ii) $\forall((l_s, \sigma_s, j_s), g, a, R, (l_t, \sigma_t, j_t)) \in E_{T(\mathcal{A})}, a = \sigma_t$
iii) $\forall((l_s, \sigma_s, j_s), g, a, R, (l_t, \sigma_t, j_t)), \in E_{T(\mathcal{A})}, j_s \neq j_t$
iv) *There is no self-loop edge in $E_{T(\mathcal{A})}$*

Proof. i) First we recall that by definition of T, $\forall l' = (l, a, i) \in L_{T(\mathcal{A})}, I_{T(\mathcal{A})}(l') = I(l)$. Then we notice that $\forall e = (l_s, g, a, R, l_t) \in E, \exists e' = ((l_s, \sigma_s, j_s), g, a, R, (l_t, a, j_t)) \in E_{T(\mathcal{A})}$ for any pair (σ_s, j_s) and for some j_t, which implies $\mathcal{L}(\mathcal{A}) \subseteq \mathcal{L}(T(\mathcal{A}))$. Conversely, $\forall e = ((l_s, \sigma_s, j_s), g, a, R, (l_t, a, j_t)) \in E_{T(\mathcal{A})}, \exists e' = (l_s, g, a, R, l_t) \in E$ which implies $\mathcal{L}(T(\mathcal{A})) \subseteq \mathcal{L}(\mathcal{A})$.

ii) By definition of T, there is no edge of the form $((l_s, \sigma_s, j_s), g, a, R, (l_t, \sigma_t, j_t))$ with $a \neq \sigma_t$ in the set $E_{T(\mathcal{A})}$. In other words, each location of $T(\mathcal{A})$ is associated with a unique letter of Σ and can only be reached using an edge labeled with this letter.

iii) By definition of $E_{T(\mathcal{A})}$, there is no edge of the form $((l_s, \sigma_s, 0), g, \sigma_t, R, (l_t, \sigma_t, 0))$ or $((l_s, \sigma_s, 1), g, \sigma_t, R, (l_t, \sigma_t, 1))$.

iv) Is a direct consequence of (iii).   □

Theorem 1. *The verification problem associated with POS-NNI is undecidable.*

Proof (sketch). Given a TA $\mathcal{A}$ defined over the alphabet Σ, we define a trivially universal automaton $\mathcal{U} = (\Sigma, l_u, l_u, \emptyset, I(l_u) = true, (l_u, \emptyset, \Sigma, \emptyset, l_u))$. We then define a security TA $\mathcal{A}^*$ that is the union of $\mathcal{T}(\mathcal{A})$ and $\mathcal{T}(\mathcal{U})$ with only one high-level edge going from the initial location of $\mathcal{T}(\mathcal{A})$ to the initial location of $\mathcal{T}(\mathcal{U})$. To this TA we associate an observation function so that all locations are distinguishable from every other except the two initial locations of $\mathcal{T}(\mathcal{A})$ and $\mathcal{T}(\mathcal{U})$. This way, the high-level location does not appear in the set of observed runs (no event occurs when using it). By choosing the initial location of $\mathcal{T}(\mathcal{A})$ to be the initial location of $\mathcal{A}^*$ we show that $\mathcal{A}^*$ has the language of $\mathcal{U}$ when not restricted but the language of $\mathcal{A}$ when restricted to low-level actions. Using the absence of self-loops in $\mathcal{T}(\mathcal{A})$ and $\mathcal{T}(\mathcal{U})$ (Proposition 1), we show that any low-level action (actions of Σ) corresponds to an observed event, it allows us to provide a bijection between the set of projected runs and the language, showing the reduction of POS-NNI to language universality. □

4   A Decidable Sub-problem

We now consider that the attacker has a bounded memory, which seems not unreasonable.

Such an attacker could choose between various policies to store and discard information. As a first approach we choose to model an attacker who uses a first-in/first-out policy, only keeping the most recent information and discarding the oldest one each time new information is available to them. This can be modeled by taking the suffixes of observed runs (and relabeling with new time-stamps).

Definition 14 (Observed Runs with Memory k).

Given an observation function $\mathcal{O}$, a run ρ and its observed run of $\mathcal{O}(\rho) = (o_1, t_1 = 0)(o_2, t_2) \ldots (o_n, t_n)(o_n, t_{n+1})$, the observed run of memory size k associated with ρ, noted $\mathcal{O}_k(\rho)$, is the sequence defined by:

if $n \leq k$: $\mathcal{O}_k(\rho) = \mathcal{O}(\rho)$
if $n > k$: $\mathcal{O}_k(\rho) = (o_{n-k}, 0)(o_{n-k+1}, t_{n-k+1} - t_{n-k}) \ldots (o_n, t_n - t_{n-k})(o_n, t_{n+1} - t_{n-k})$

We note $\mathcal{O}_k(\mathcal{A})$ the set of observed runs with memory k for every run of $\mathcal{A}$

Similar to observed runs (with infinite memory), observed runs with memory k contain $k + 1$ elements as one is added to keep track of the time elapsed since the last event.

Example 2 (An observed run and its associated observed run with memory 3).
Let us go back to example 1, given a run ρ and its associated projected run:
$\mathcal{O}(\rho) = (o_1, 0)(o_2, d_1 + d_2)(o_1, d_1 + d_2 + d_3)(o_3, \sum_{k=1}^{5} d_k)(o_3, \sum_{k=1}^{6} d_k)$ We have
$\mathcal{O}_3(\rho) = (o_2, 0)(o_1, d_3)(o_3, \sum_{k=3}^{5} d_k)(o_3, \sum_{k=3}^{6} d_k)$.

This gives rise to an updated version of the non-interference property adapted to attackers with finite memory.

Definition 15 (Partial Observability State-Based Non-interference with Finite Memory of Size k (k-POS-NNI)). *A security automaton $\mathcal{A}$ satisfies k-POS-NNI with respect to the observation $\mathcal{O}$ if and only if $\mathcal{O}_k(\mathcal{A}) = \mathcal{O}_k(\mathcal{A}_{\setminus \Sigma_{high}})$*

Remark 1. If $k = 0$, any run ρ ending in a location l would have the same observed run with memory 0: $\mathcal{O}_0(\rho) = (\mathcal{O}(l), 0)$. It is therefore clear that 0-POS-NNI is equivalent to the reachability of locations, which is decidable [AD94].

If $k = 1$, observed runs of memory k are reduced to a measurement of the time elapsed since the last observed event of the run. It follows that 1-POS-NNI is decidable as well, since the (possibly infinite) maximal time that can be elapsed in a set of indistinguishable locations is computable (see, e. g., Sect. 4.2).

4.1   First Approach to 2-POS-NNI

One intuitive way to solve 2-POS-NNI is to add two attacker clocks x_{old} and x_{new} to the system to model the time elapsed since the last two observed events and to synchronize on transitions associated with observable events the security automaton with another automaton modeling the last sequence of observations of the attacker. As the last two events occur, the attacker clocks are successively reset to zero.

An automaton with two observations A and B, and a single clock x (left) and its associated attacker automaton with 2 clocks x_{old} and x_{new} (right) are given in Fig. 3. Location l_A and $l_{A'}$ are observed as A and location l_B is observed as B.

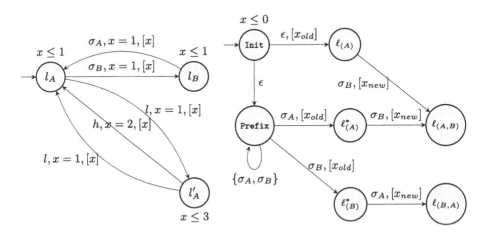

Fig. 3. A TA and a TA modeling the attacker memory ([] denote clock resets)

The automata shown in Fig. 3 illustrate how 2-POS-NNI can be reduced to a state reachability problem. For instance, having $(\ell_{(A,B)}; x_{old} = 2.5, x_{new} = 0.5)$ reachable on the attacker automaton is equivalent to the existence of a run so that at some point 2 time units elapse in l_A and l'_A, followed by 0.5 time unit elapsed in l_B. Conversely, for any run with n observed events ($n > 2$) there exists one run of the attacker automaton that loops $n - 2$ times on location before reaching $\ell^*_{(A)}$ followed by $\ell_{(A,B)}$ (or $\ell^*_{(B)}$ followed by $\ell_{(B,A)}$), resetting the attacker clocks along the way. Location $\ell_{(A)}$ is meant to account for runs with two or less events by "skipping" the cycle. However, in a run with $n \geq 2$ events, the corresponding run on the attacker automaton could cycle n times or $n - 1$ times on location so that it ends in location , $\ell^*_{(A)}$ or $\ell^*_{(B)}$ instead of $\ell_{(A,B)}$ or $\ell_{(B,A)}$. Therefore, clock valuations on these locations do not correspond to any observed runs.

This method can be generalized to any observation function: when one of the last two observable events occurs, we add the new observation to the sequence memorized by the attacker. Previous events are accounted for by cycling on location .

However, the region graph (or zone-based graphs) does not faithfully represent all reachable states of a given automaton because it relies for finiteness on the use of some maximal constant above which the property that if some valuation in a region is reachable, then all valuations in the region are, does not hold. And it may well be that interfering states have some clock values above the maximal constant found in clock constraints of the automaton.

For instance, for the automaton introduced in Fig. 3, we get the possible clock valuations associated with the location $\ell_{(A,B)}$ (clock x is omitted) depicted in Fig. 4[1] [2].

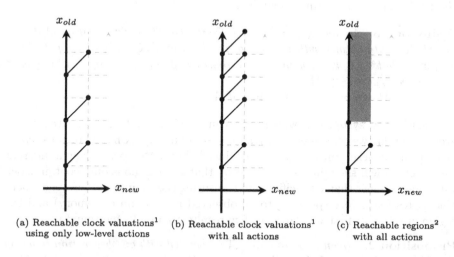

(a) Reachable clock valuations[1]   (b) Reachable clock valuations[1]   (c) Reachable regions[2]
    using only low-level actions   with all actions   with all actions

Fig. 4. Reachable states and Reachable regions location $\ell_{(A,B)}$ of Fig. 3

---

[1] Regions without c-approximation, i.e. each point represent a reachable state of location $\ell_{(A,B)}$ associated with given values of x_{new} and x_{old}

[2] On this figure, regions are represented according to the original definition proposed by Alur & Dill ([AD94]), that is with c-approximation, c being the largest synthaxic value used to define the automaton)

We see that the interfering behaviors occur at the earliest when $x_{old} = 4$, after the maximal constant, which is 3. Here this could therefore be solved by taking 4 instead of 3 as the constant for the definition of regions. However we can define automata with more complex behaviors. For instance, changing the 2 with a 3 and every 1s by 2s in the automaton of Fig. 3 would change the required maximal constant of regions to 6 instead of 4. By adding more locations to the automata the maximal constant can be pushed even further from the largest constant of the syntax. We found no trivial relation between the size of the automaton and the necessary constant to ensure the validity of this approach.

Remark 2. Note that this example also shows that the claims of [BT03, GMR07] that n-state-non-interference and St-NNI are decidable in the general case by computing the set of reachable states of the considered automata do not hold, unless the clocks are bounded.

This issue only gets worse when we extend this method to any memory size or when the security automaton uses more clocks. This kind of example highlights the need for automata with bounded time between events (i.e. bounded attacker clocks) to decide k-POS-NNI.

4.2   Finite Duration Observation Automata (FDO Automata)

In this part, we provide a class of automata for which k-POS-NNI is decidable. It consists of automata for which the time elapsed between two consecutive observed events of any run is bounded.

Definition 16. *An automaton $\mathcal{A}$ is a Finite Duration Observation Automaton (FDO Automaton) with respect to an observation $\mathcal{O}$[3] if and only if $\exists M \in \mathbb{R}_{\geq 0}$ such that $\forall \rho \in \Psi(\mathcal{A})$ with $\mathcal{O}(\rho) = (o_0, t_0 = 0)(o_1, t_1) \cdots (o_n, t_n)$, $\forall 0 \leq k < n$, we have $t_{k+1} - t_k \leq M$.*
We call M the observation bound *of $\mathcal{A}$.*

By focusing on systems in which time cannot elapse indefinitely without any event occurring we get systems with a finite set of unapproximated regions reachable on the attacker automaton as introduced above. Moreover, using a different construct we will show in the next section that these regions only contain clock valuations smaller than a specific bound, ensuring the equivalence between reachable states (each corresponding to an observed runs of finite memory) and the region graph. But first we provide a few results about FDO automata.

Proposition 2. *Given an automaton $\mathcal{A}$ associated with an observation function $\mathcal{O}$. The membership of $\mathcal{A}$ in the set of FDO automata with respect to $\mathcal{O}$ is decidable.*

Proof (sketch). Given a TA $\mathcal{A}$ with a set of clocks $\mathbb{X}$ and an observation function $\mathcal{O}$, we define the TA $\mathcal{A}_{\mathcal{O}}$ as $\mathcal{A}$ but with an extra clock y and a self-loop edge on

---

[3] We also say the automaton is FDO w.r.t. $\mathcal{O}$.

every location to reset this clock. We then compute the region graph $\mathcal{RG}$ of $\mathcal{A_O}$ using standard techniques. We define $\mathcal{RG}^-$ by removing every discrete transition between two distinguishable locations from $\mathcal{RG}$. Let R be a region of $\mathcal{RG}^-$ in which $y = 0$. We call *unit cycle* a path in $\mathcal{RG}^-$ starting in R and ending in a region R' with $y \geq 1$ and all other clocks satisfying the same constraints as in R. Given any observation bound M, if there is a *unit cycle* in the region graph there is a run executing the *unit cycle* at least $M + 1$ time, showing that the maximal elapsed time between events is not bounded by M, hence $\mathcal{A}$ is not FDO w.r.t. $\mathcal{O}$. We now suppose that $\mathcal{A}$ does not contain any *unit cycle* yet is not FDO w.r.t $\mathcal{O}$. Because $\mathcal{A}$ is not FDO, for any $M \in \mathbb{R}_{\geq 0}$ there exists $\rho \in \Psi(\mathcal{A})$ s.t. $\mathcal{O}_1(\rho) = (o, 0)(o, t > M)$. Let us call s the state reached when the event leading to observation o occurs. Because of the absence of *unit cycles*, neither s nor any state contained in the same region as s is ever reached in ρ after one time unit has elapsed unless an observed event occurred. Because we can take $M > 1$, it follows that at least one state s' contained in a different region than s has to be reached at some point in ρ after s'. Because the same argument applies to s' by taking $M > 2$. Inductively, it follows that after $M + 1$ time unit elapsed, at least M regions of the state-space are not reachable unless a event occurred. Because the amount of regions (defined with c-approx) is finite, it follows that $\mathcal{A}$ is FDO w.r.t. $\mathcal{O}$ with an observation bound less than the number of regions, which is a contradiction. This proves that $\mathcal{A}$ is FDO w.r.t. $\mathcal{O}$ if and only if it has no *unit cycle* in its region graph, which is decidable. □

Corollary 1. *Given an observation $\mathcal{O}$ associated to the automaton $\mathcal{A}$ with x clocks, c the largest integer used in clock constraints and L the size of the set of locations. If $\mathcal{A}$ is FDO w.r.t. $\mathcal{O}$, then its observation bound M verifies the relation:*

$$M \leq x!(2c + 2)^x L$$

Proof. As previously demonstrated, $\mathcal{A}$ is FDO w.r.t. $\mathcal{O}$ iff it has no *unit cycle*. Furthermore, we showed that the observation bound of an FDO automaton is bounded by its number of region. Using the bound on the number of regions given in [AD94], the relation follows. □

Corollary 2. *Given an observation $\mathcal{O}$ associated to the automaton $\mathcal{A}$. If $\mathcal{A}$ is FDO w.r.t. $\mathcal{O}$, then its observation bound M can be computed.*

Proof. By adding a clock y to $\mathcal{A}$ (with x clocks, L locations and c its largest constant used in clock constraints) and replacing any transition of the form (l, g, a, R, l') with $\mathcal{O}(l) \neq \mathcal{O}(l')$ by $(l, g, a, R \cup \{y\}, l')$, the cumulated time elapsed in a run since the last observed event always corresponds to the value of y. Thanks to the previous corollary we know that defining regions using constant $(x!(2c + 2)^x L + 1)$ instead of c will provide a region-graph of $\mathcal{A}$ that does not approximate the value of y. The maximal value of y can therefore be computed by taking the smallest value M so that no region in the latter region graph contains valuations of y greater than M. □

4.3   Deciding K-POS-NNI for FDO Automata

In this section we generalize and formalize the construction proposed in Sect. 4.1.

Given a sequence u, we note $u(i)$ the i-th element of u, $u[a, b]$ the subset of u ranging from index a to index b, both $u(a)$ and $u(b)$ being included.

Given a security automaton $\mathcal{A} = (\Sigma_{\mathsf{low}} \cup \Sigma_{\mathsf{high}}, L, l_0, \mathbb{X}, I, E)$ associated with observation $\mathcal{O} : L \mapsto \Omega$ and an attacker memory k. We define Ω^j the set of sequences of observations from Ω of length j.

We define the attacker automaton $\mathcal{B}_k = (\{\epsilon\} \cup \Sigma_\Omega, L_{\mathcal{B}_k}, \mathtt{Init}, Y, I_{\mathcal{B}_k}, E_{\mathcal{B}_k})$:

- $\Sigma_\Omega = \{\sigma_o \mid o \in \Omega\}$
- $L_{\mathcal{B}_k} = \{\mathtt{Init}\} \cup \{\} \cup \{\ell_\omega^* \mid \omega \in \Omega^j, j \in [\![1, k-1]\!]\} \cup \{\ell_\omega \mid \omega \in \Omega^j, j \in [\![1, k]\!]\}$
- $I_{\mathcal{B}_k}(\mathtt{Init}) = (Y = 0), I_{\mathcal{B}_k}(l \neq \mathtt{Init}) = \mathtt{true}$
- $Y = (y_i)_{i \in [\![1,k]\!]}$, where the y_i are some new clocks;
- $E_{\mathcal{B}_k}$ is defined as follows:
  (a) **initialization** $(\mathtt{Init}, \emptyset, \epsilon, [y_1], \ell_{\mathcal{O}(l_0)})$
  (a) **event** $\forall j \in [\![2, k]\!], \forall \omega \in \Omega^j, (\ell_{\omega[1, j-1]}, \emptyset, \sigma_{\omega[j]}, y_j, \ell_\omega) \in E_{\mathcal{B}_k}$
  (b) **initialization** $(\mathtt{Init}, \emptyset, \epsilon, \emptyset,)$
  (b) **prefix event** $(, \emptyset, \Sigma_\Omega, \emptyset,)$
  (b) **first event** $\forall o \in \Omega, (, \emptyset, \sigma_o, [y_1], \ell_o^*) \in E_{\mathcal{B}_k}$
  (b) **intermediary event** $\forall j \in [\![2, k-1]\!], \forall \omega \in \Omega^j, (\ell_{\omega[1, j-1]}^*, \emptyset, \sigma_{\omega[j]}, y_j, \ell_\omega^*) \in E_{\mathcal{B}_k}$
  (b) **last event** $\forall \omega \in \Omega^k, (\ell_{\omega[1, k-1]}^*, \emptyset, \sigma_{\omega[k]}, [y_k], \ell_\omega) \in E_{\mathcal{B}_k}$

$\mathcal{B}_k$ is simply the generalization of the attacker automaton proposed in Example 3. In the example, the **(a) initialization** transition is the one going from location $\mathtt{Init}$ to location $\ell_{(A)}$, it is used for runs with k events or less (again, counting the initialization of the observed system as an event); the **(b) initialization** transition is the one going from $\mathtt{Init}$ to location , it is used for runs with more than k events; the transitions going from to $\ell_{(A)}^*$ or $\ell_{(B)}^*$ are **(b) first event** transitions; the transitions going from $\ell_{(A)}^*$ (resp. $\ell_{(B)}^*$) to $\ell_{(A,B)}$ (resp. $\ell_{(B,A)}$) are **(b) last event** transitions; the **(b) intermediary event** type is absent in the example as it only appears when $k \geq 3$ where intermediary locations would be necessary between $\ell_{(A)}^*$ (resp. $\ell_{(B)}^*$) and $\ell_{(A,B)}$ (resp. $\ell_{(B,A)}$) to account for more time-stamps memorized. Lastly, the **(a) event** transitions correspond to the transition between $\ell_{(A)}$ and $\ell_{(A,B)}$. Overall, the **(a)**-transitions serve the purpose of memorizing time-stamps in short runs whereas the **(b)**-transitions serve the same purpose for longer runs by allowing the attacker to ignore information about the part of the run they would discard anyway (by cycling on the location) so that only the last k events are associated with clocks $(y_i)_{i \in [\![1,k]\!]}$.

Because $\mathcal{A}$ and $\mathcal{B}_k$ do not use the same alphabet, we define the ϵ-automaton $\mathcal{A}^{\mathcal{O}} = (\{\epsilon\} \cup \Sigma_\Omega, L, l_0, \mathbb{X}, E^{\mathcal{O}})$ so that $\mathcal{O}_k(\mathcal{A}) = \mathcal{O}_k(\mathcal{A}^{\mathcal{O}})$ as follows:

$$\forall e = (l, g, a, R, l') \in E :$$
$$\mathcal{O}(l) = \mathcal{O}(l') \implies (l, g, \epsilon, R, l') \in E^{\mathcal{O}}$$
$$\mathcal{O}(l) \neq \mathcal{O}(l') \implies (l, g, \sigma_{\mathcal{O}(l')}, R, l') \in E^{\mathcal{O}}$$

We note $\mathcal{A}||_\Sigma \mathcal{B}$ the synchronized product à la Arnold Nivat ([Arn94]) of $\mathcal{A}$ with $\mathcal{B}$ on the set of action Σ.

Lemma 1. $(o_1, t_1 = 0)(o_2, t_2)\ldots(o_j, t_j)(o_j, t_{j+1}) \in \mathcal{O}_k(\mathcal{A})$ *iff* $\exists l \in L$, *and a valuation* ν *on* $Y \cup X$ *such that* $\forall i \in [\![1, j]\!], \nu(y_i) = t_{j+1} - t_i$ *and* $((l, \ell_{(o_1,\ldots,o_j)}), \nu) \in Q^{\mathcal{A}^{\mathcal{O}}||_{\Sigma_\Omega} \mathcal{B}_k}$.

Proof (sketch). We first notice that $\mathcal{B}_k$ is universal on alphabet Σ_Ω. This is sufficient to show that any reachable state of $\mathcal{A}^{\mathcal{O}}$ is also a reachable state of $\mathcal{A}^{\mathcal{O}}||_{\Sigma_\Omega} \mathcal{B}_k$. We use this to associate to any run ρ of $\mathcal{A}$ a run ρ' of $\mathcal{A}^{\mathcal{O}}||_{\Sigma_\Omega} \mathcal{B}_k$ ending in a location of the form $(l \in L, \ell_{(o_1,\ldots,o_n)})$ for some $n \leq k$. We ensure that such a run exists by splitting cases based on the number of events of ρ. If ρ contains $j \leq k$ events we simply consider the a run ρ' starting with the **(a) initialization** transition. If ρ contains $j > k$ events we consider a run ρ' starting with the **(b) initialization** transition and cycling on $k - j$ times. By the definition of $E^{\mathcal{O}}$ and $E_{\mathcal{B}_k}$, a new location of the form ℓ_ω or ℓ_ω^* can only be reached when an observed event would occur in the run of $\mathcal{A}$ that $\mathcal{A}^{\mathcal{O}}||_{\Sigma_\Omega} \mathcal{B}_k$ is reproducing. It follows that the values of clocks y_i are such that the difference between consecutive clocks are equal to the time elapsed between observable events of the run. The relation between time-stamps of the observed run with memory k of $\mathcal{A}$ and the clock valuations follows.

The other direction of the equivalence boils down to the same idea. To each state of $\mathcal{A}^{\mathcal{O}}||_{\Sigma_\Omega} \mathcal{B}_k$ can be associated plenty of runs of $\mathcal{A}$, possibly mapping to multiple observed runs, but to only a single observed run with memory k. □

Theorem 2. $\forall k \in \mathbb{N}$, k-*POS-NNI associated with an observation* $\mathcal{O}$ *is decidable for FDO automata w.r.t.* $\mathcal{O}$.

Proof (sketch). Given an FDO security automata $\mathcal{A}$ and its observation bound M, we can show that for any state $((l, \ell_\omega), \nu)$ reachable in $\mathcal{A}^{\mathcal{O}}||_{\Sigma_\Omega} \mathcal{B}_k$, $\forall i < |\omega|, \nu(y_i) < kM$. Therefore, the clocks y_i that are relevant to Lemma 1 do not suffer from the kind of "loss of information" caused by the region abstraction described on Fig. 4 if the constant used to define regions is greater than kM.

For any $\omega \in \Omega^j$ for some $j < k$, we can compute a set Γ_ω of pairs (ω, ν) for every ν that is the projection on clocks $\{y_i, \ldots, y_{|\omega|}\}$ of a valuation contained in any region R such that a vertex $((l, \ell_\omega), R)$ is reachable in the region graph of $\mathcal{A}^{\mathcal{O}}||_{\Sigma_\Omega} \mathcal{B}_k$. by Lemma 1, Γ_ω is in bijection with the set of observed runs with memory k of the form $(\omega[1], 0) \ldots (\omega[|\omega|], t_{|\omega|})(\omega[|\omega|], t_{|\omega|+1})$. Because there is a finite amount of possible ω, the set $\Gamma = \bigcup_\omega \Gamma_\omega$ is in bijection with $\mathcal{O}_k(\mathcal{A})$

Repeating this process for $\mathcal{A}_{\backslash \Sigma_{\text{high}}}$ provides a set $\Gamma^{\backslash \Sigma_{\text{high}}}$ in bijection with $\mathcal{O}_k(\mathcal{A}_{\backslash \Sigma_{\text{high}}})$. Therefore, $\mathcal{A}$ verifies k-POS-NNI if and only if $\Gamma^{\backslash \Sigma_{\text{high}}} = \Gamma$, which can be computed using standard techniques on polyhedra, because those infinite sets can be represented by finite unions of regions. □

Although the method given above would not be efficient if implemented as it is, a PSPACE algorithm can be found.

Theorem 3. *With k represented in unary, k-POS-NNI for FDO automata is PSPACE-complete.*

Proof (sketch). To prove PSPACE-membership we use the PSPACE-membership of region reachability in a region-graph. Because $\mathcal{B}_k$ is only defined with respect to $\mathcal{O}$ and k it is not necessary to compute it explicitly, instead the transition function of the Turing machine can account for the sequence of observations as $\mathcal{O}$ is given in the input. Because the sequence of observation has to be memorized, an overhead of size linear with k is induced, hence the necessity for k to be represented in unary to preserve PSPACE complexity.

To prove PSPACE-hardness we reduce from location reachability in TAs. Given a TA with a given target location, we create an augmented TA with an extra location associated with a unique observation. We ensure this additional location is reachable either by using a high-level action or be using a low-level action from the target location so that this unique observation appears in the set of observed runs restricted to low level actions if and only if the target location is reachable. Some other details are added to ensure the augmented automaton is FDO and to ensure the strict equality between observed runs.

5   Discussion and Future Work

We have introduced a new property of state-based non-interference. We believe that this property is more realistic than previously studied state-based approach to non-interference as it models a smarter attacker with a more reasonable observation power. We have shown that this property is not decidable in the general case. However, we have provided a decidable class of automata for which the property is decidable given a finite memory of any length. We can also decide membership in that class.

For future work consists first in investigating other policies for observation replacement in the memory of the attacker. We also want to find more efficient, e.g. DBM-based, algorithms to decide k-POS-NNI for FDO automata.

Lastly, we want to settle the general case of k-POS-NNI decidability for non-FDO automata, and of the related problem of the decidability of St-NNI when clocks are not bounded which, as we have shown, is actually still open.

References

AD94.   Alur, R., Dill, D.L.: A theory of timed automata. Theor. Comput. Sci. **126**(2), 183–235 (1994)

AETYM21.   Ammar, I., El Touati, Y., Yeddes, M., Mullins, J.: Bounded opacity for timed systems. J. Inf. Secur. Appl. **61**, 102926 (2021)

AK20.   André, É., Kryukov, A.: Parametric non-interference in timed automata. In: Proceedings of the 2020 25th International Conference on Engineering of Complex Computer Systems (ICECCS), pp. 37–42. IEEE (2020)

ALMS22. André, É., Lime, D., Marinho, D., Sun, J.: Guaranteeing timed opacity using parametric timed model checking. ACM Trans. Softw. Eng. Methodol. **31**(4), 1–36 (2022)

Arn94. Arnold, A.: Finite Transition Systems. Prentice Hall (1994)

BB07. Bortz, A., Boneh, D.: Exposing private information by timing web applications. In: Proceedings of the 16th International Conference on World Wide Web, pp. 621–628 (2007)

BCLR15. Benattar, G., Cassez, F., Lime, D., Roux, O.H.: Control and synthesis of non-interferent timed systems. Int. J. Control **88**(2), 217–236 (2015)

BKMR08. Bryans, J., Koutny, M., Mazare, L., Ryan, Peter, Y.A.: Opacity generalised to transition systems. Int. J. Inf. Secur. **7**(6), 421–435 (2008)

BT03. Barbuti, R., Tesei, L.: A decidable notion of timed non-interference. Fundam. Inform. **54**(2–3), 137–150 (2003)

FS00. Felten, E.W., Schneider, M.A.: Timing attacks on web privacy. In: Proceedings of the 7th ACM Conference on Computer and Communications Security, CCS 2000, pp. 25–32. Association for Computing Machinery, New York (2000)

GM84. Goguen, J.A., Meseguer, J.: Unwinding and inference control. In: Proceedings of the 1984 IEEE Symposium on Security and Privacy, pp. 75–75. IEEE (1984)

GMR07. Gardey, G., Mullins, J., Roux, O.H.: Non-interference control synthesis for security timed automata. Electron. Notes Theor. Comput. Sci. **180**(1), 35–53 (2007)

GSB18. Gerking, C., Schubert, D., Bodden, E.: Model checking the information flow security of real-time systems. In: Payer, M., Rashid, A., Such, J.M. (eds.) ESSoS 2018. LNCS, vol. 10953, pp. 27–43. Springer, Cham (2018). https://doi.org/10.1007/978-3-319-94496-8_3

Koc96. Kocher, PC.: Timing attacks on implementations of Diffie-Hellman, RSA, DSS, and other systems. In: Koblitz, N. (ed.) CRYPTO 1996. LNCS, vol. 1109, pp. 104–113. Springer, Heidelberg (1996). https://doi.org/10.1007/3-540-68697-5_9

KPJJ13. Kotcher, R., Pei, Y., Jumde, P., Jackson, C.: Cross-origin pixel stealing: timing attacks using CSS filters. In: Proceedings of the 2013 ACM SIGSAC conference on Computer & Communications Security, pp. 1055–1062 (2013)

WZ18. Wang, L., Zhan, N.: Decidability of the initial-state opacity of real-time automata. In: Jones, C., Wang, J., Zhan, N. (eds.) Symposium on Real-Time and Hybrid Systems. LNCS, vol. 11180, pp. 44–60. Springer, Cham (2018). https://doi.org/10.1007/978-3-030-01461-2_3

Special Track on Monitoring
of Cyber-Physical Systems

Usage-and Risk-Aware Falsification Testing for Cyber-Physical Systems

Andrej Kiviriga[1], Kim Guldstrand Larsen[1], Dejan Nickovic[2(✉)],
and Ulrik Nyman[1]

[1] Aalborg University, Aalborg, Denmark
{kiviriga,kgl,ulrik}@cs.aau.dk
[2] AIT Austrian Institute of Technology, Vienna, Austria
Dejan.Nickovic@ait.ac.at

Abstract. Falsification testing is a popular method for efficiently identifying inputs that witness the violation of cyber-physical system (CPS) specifications. The generated counterexamples are used to locate and explain faults and debug the system. However, CPS rarely operate in unconstrained environments and not all counterexamples have the same value. On one hand, faults resulting from common system usage are more likely to happen in practice than faults triggered by esoteric inputs. On the other hand, some faults can have more severe consequences than others. Together, the probability and the severity of a fault determine its *risk*, an important aspect that is neglected by the existing falsification testing techniques. We propose a new falsification testing methodology that is aware of the system's expected usage and the severity associated to different faulty behaviors. Given a user profile in the form of a stochastic hybrid automaton, an associated severity degree measure, an executable black-box implementation of the CPS and its formalized requirements, we provide a test generation method that (1) uses efficient randomized methods to generate multiple violating traces, and (2) estimates the probability and the expected severity, and hence the expected risk of each counterexample, thus providing their ranking to the engineer.

Keywords: Cyber-physical systems · counterexample · black-box testing · randomized testing · falsification-based testing

1 Introduction

Falsification testing (FT) [17] is a popular simulation-based method for systematically identifying requirement violations in cyber-physical systems (CPS). FT uses quantitative monitoring of formal specifications to guide the system-under-

This research received funding from the Villum Investigator Grant S4OS of Professor Kim G. Larsen.

L. Petrucci and J. Sproston (Eds.): FORMATS 2023, LNCS 14138, pp. 141–157, 2023.
https://doi.org/10.1007/978-3-031-42626-1_9

test (SUT) to the violation of its requirements, whenever possible. The resulting witness of the requirement falsification is used to locate and explain the fault and hence to facilitate the system debugging task.

FT typically finds one counterexample among possibly many of them. However, CPS often operate in constrained environments with assumptions on their usage in which not all counterexamples have the same value. On one hand, a fault triggered by a common usage of the system has a higher *probability* to happen than another fault resulting from some esoteric input sequence. On the other hand, a rare fault can have more *severe* consequences. The probability and the severeness define together the *expected risk* of a counterexample, an important aspect for prioritizing debugging tasks under time and budget constraints. The impact of counterexamples in the form of their expected risk has been nevertheless largely neglected by the existing FT techniques.

We introduce a new methodology for *usage-* and *risk-aware* FT to remedy the above situation. The inputs to our approach are: (1) a user profile model that describes the system's intended usage in the form of a stochastic hybrid automaton, (2) a severity degree specification, (3) an SUT provided in the form of an executable black-box implementation, and (4) requirements formalized using temporal logic. We first use a randomized accelerator procedure to generate test inputs from the user profile model. We then feed the input vector to the SUT and execute it. We use the temporal logic monitor to detect potential violation of requirements. Whenever we find a counterexample, we use statistical model checking (SMC) [7,20,23], and more specifically importance splitting (IS) [11], to estimate the likelihood of the counterexample. We combine the estimated probability of every counterexample with its severity, to estimate the overall risk of the faulty behavior. We finally rank faulty behaviors according to their expected risk, thus facilitating prioritization of the debugging tasks.

We instantiated and implemented our usage- and risk- aware FT methodology (Sect. 2) with concrete methods and tools. We adopted UPPAAL SMC [5] to model stochastic hybrid automata (Sect. 3), MATLAB Simulink [6] to implement the SUTs, signal temporal logic (STL) [16] to formalize CPS requirements (Sect. 3) and a severity degree measure where the earlier a violation of the CPS requirement occurs, the more severe it is. We developed a modified variant of the randomized reachability analysis (RRA) [12] to efficiently find counterexamples (Sect. 4) and adapted a version of the IS algorithm to estimate counterexample probabilities and severity (Sect. 5), integrating both methods to the UPPAAL SMC engine. We used MATLAB Simulink's to simulate generated input sequences and the RTAMT [18] runtime verification library to monitor the resulting simulation traces against STL requirements. We used a thermal model of a house as our case study (Sect. 6) to evaluate our approach (Sect. 7).

Related Work

Falsification Testing. (FT) [17] is a test generation method that uses formal specifications with quantitative semantics to guide the search for behaviors that violate the formalized requirements. In that work, the authors propose to use deterministic assumptions for restricting the test search space. The test search space can be additionally restricted using symbolic reachability methods [4]. The classical FT approaches also stop the generation of tests after finding the first violation of a requirement. The adaptive FT method [3] remedies this situation by introducing the notion of specification coverage and providing means to generate multiple qualitatively different counterexamples. None of these works allow one to compare violation witnesses according to their likelihood to happen. To contrast, we introduce probabilistic user profile models of the SUT and a severity specifications to estimate the risk of counterexamples and enable their ranking.

Counterexamples in Probabilistic Model Checking. have received considerable attention in the last two decades, see [1] for a survey on methods for generating probabilistic counterexamples. We mention the early work from Han and Katoen [10], who propose a method for finding the strongest evidence, i.e. the most likely counterexample violating an until-specification as a hop-constrained shortest path problem. The tool DiPro [2] allows generating probabilistic counterexamples discrete time Markov chains, continuous time Markov chains and Markov decision processes. In the work on probabilistic model checking, the model of the SUT is available as a white-box, which allows precise computation of counterexample probabilities but limits the scalability of the approach to the systems of small size and complexity. In our approach, we consider SUTs as black-box without a-priori assumptions on their size and complexity, and use simulation-based methods to detect counterexamples and estimate their probabilities.

Statistical and Randomized Testing: Statistical model checking (SMC) is a Monte Carlo method used to estimate the probability of violating formal requirements. Reliable estimation of rare events remains difficult and is typically addressed by the *importance splitting* (IS) [13,19]. IS divides the goal with small probability into a sequence of intermediate goals that are easier to reach. An alternative way to address the problem of rare-event simulation is to use *randomized reachability analysis* (RRA) [12]. RRA discards the stochastic semantics of the model to increase the chance of exercising a rare event. While RRA can efficiently find a counterexample, it cannot be used alone to estimate its probability. On the other hand, SMC and IS can reason about the probability that a given SUT violates a property, but are less appropriate to estimate the probability of a single counterexample. In addition, none of these methods takes notions of risk into account. In our work, we combine SMC, IS and RRA to achieve efficient falsification while enabling the risk estimation of counterexamples. STL robustness risk approximation [14,15], i.e. the risk of lacking robustness against failure, is a method for estimating upper bounds of risk in stochastic systems. In contrast to this work, our approach focuses on efficient generation and ranking of counterexamples according to our risk estimate that incorporates both the likelihood of a behavior and its impact.

2 Methodology

In this section, we describe our user- and risk-aware falsification testing methodology. The input to our approach are: a *user profile* model, a black-box implementation of the *system-under-test (SUT)*, a *formalized requirement* and a *severity specification*. The output is a set of test cases that lead to the falsification of the requirement ranked according to their estimated risk.

The user profile is a stochastic hybrid automaton that models the expected use of the SUT. It allows for rich dynamics and stochastic behavior. Straightforward simulations of the user profile can be performed to generate inputs for the SUT. Generated simulations follow the underlying stochastic semantics of the model, which allows them to mimic the behavior of the real user and supports reasoning about the probability of generating a particular input sequence.

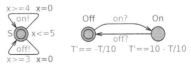

$$\varphi = \Box_{[0,20]}(T < 75)$$
$$SD = (D - \min_{t \in [0,D]} T(t) \geq 75)/D$$

Fig. 1. Example: user profile model (top left), heater controller (top right), formal requirement φ and severity degree SD (bottom).

The SUT is a dynamic system, which consumes an input sequence to generate another sequence of observable outputs. We assume an executable black-box implementation of the SUT, whose behavior can be only observed at its input/output interface. The formalized requirement is given in the form of a temporal logic specification. It defines the expected system behavior and is used as an oracle to discriminate behaviors that satisfy the requirement from those that violate it. The severity specification maps a behavior that violates the formalized requirement to the interval $[0,1]$, indicating its degree of severity.

We illustrate our methodology with a simplified heat controller example, depicted in Fig. 1. The simplified heat controller follows a deterministic implementation (Fig. 1 top right) has a single continuous state variable, the temperature T and consists of two discrete modes, Off and On. In the Off mode, the temperature decreases according to the differential equation $T' = -\frac{T}{10}$. Conversely, the temperature increases in the On mode according to the differential equation $T' = 10 - \frac{T}{10}$. The temperature range is limited to the interval between 0 and 100 degrees (not shown in the figure). The change between the two heater's modes is triggered by actions on and off provided by an external environment. We note that while the implementation is given in the form of a hybrid automaton for illustration purposes, we assume that it is seen as a black box to the tester, i.e. the tester can only provide the actions off and on and observe the temperature T. The stochastic user profile (Fig. 1 top left) models the expected generation of the off and on actions. The clock x measures the time between two consecutive actions. After an action happens, x is reset to 0 and a time delay between 0 and 5 is sampled according to the uniform distribution. If the time delay is in the interval $[0,3)$ no action is enabled and an additional time

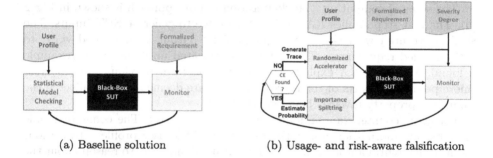

(a) Baseline solution   (b) Usage- and risk-aware falsification

Fig. 2. Methodology workflow for falsification of black-box CPS.

delay must be taken. If it is in the interval $[3, 4)$, the action off is taken with probability 1. If the time delay is in the interval $[4, 5)$, the actions off and on are triggered, each with probability 0.5. It follows that the action off is likely to happen three times more often then the action on. The formalized requirement φ (Fig. 1 bottom) states that within 20 time units, the temperature T must continuously remain within 75 degrees. Finally, the severity degree SD (Fig. 1 bottom) is defined as the ratio between the earliest violation time of φ and the total duration D of the behavior.

Baseline Solution: We first propose a simple baseline solution to estimate the risk of an error in the system with SMC [21,22]. The core idea of SMC is to generate simulations of a stochastic model and then statistically analyze them to estimate the probability that the system violates requirements with some degree of confidence. Figure 2 (a) shows the workflow using SMC in our setting – the input sequences are generated by the user profile and the outputs from SUT are analyzed by SMC to conclude on probability estimate of an error.

This simple approach has two disadvantages. First, SMC requires many simulations to discover *rare* events. Second, SMC allows to estimate the overall probability of a bug, but cannot reason about probabilities nor estimate the risk of individual faulty behaviors.

Proposed Solution: We now present a procedure that (1) allows efficient identification of a faulty behavior, and (2) an estimate of its probability, severity and hence its risk. It utilizes the Randomized Accelerator (RA) which is a modified version of the randomized reachability analysis algorithm, initially proposed in [12] as an efficient error detection method for timed and stopwatch automata models. Among the modifications, we extend the algorithm to support the rich dynamics of hybrid automaton models to allow simulation of the user profile. In contrast to SMC, RA discards the underlying stochastic semantics to favor exploration of otherwise unlikely to reach parts of the model. As a consequence, RA cannot reason about the probability of its generated simulations, but excels at finding "exotic" traces fast. In their study, [12] have shown their randomized reachability analysis to be up to three orders of magnitude faster than SMC at discovering bugs.

The steps of computing a single iteration in our approach is shown in Fig. 2 (b). The first step applies RA on the user profile to generate SUT inputs. The SUT is executed with the given input and its output is monitored w.r.t. to its formalized requirement. These steps are repeated until the counterexample is found. Moreover, RA exploits the information from previous runs to favor "more promising" parts of the user profile that are deemed to have affected the monitored property towards being violated.

For every counterexample found, we estimate its risk. The counterexample contains the information about the execution of the user profile – transitions taken in the hybrid automaton and the resulting dynamics. To reason about the probability of counterexamples we use the Importance Splitting (IS) from [13]. IS allows efficient probability estimation of rare. We use IS to estimate the probability of following the qualitative trace from the user profile, i.e. focusing on executing transitions of the user profile model in the sequence commanded by the trace. Additionally, a run of IS generates multiple traces with different timing behaviors w.r.t to the stochastic semantics. Since the timing behavior might have a crucial impact on the property satisfaction, we check all the traces generated by IS against SUT to estimate the ratio of traces violating the property. For each trace that violates the property, we compute its severity degree according to the specification. We combine the computed probability and severity of the counterexample to estimate its risk. The result of our approach is a list of counterexamples ranked according to their estimated risk.

3 Stochastic Hybrid Systems and Formal Specifications

In this section, we recall the definition of hybrid automata with stochastic semantics [8] that we use to model the user profiles. We also define formal requirements in the form of Signal Temporal Logic (STL) [16] formulas and introduce the notion of severity specifications. Let X be a finite set of continuous variables. A variable valuation over X is a mapping $v : X \to \mathbb{R}$. We write $\mathbb{R}^X$ for the set of valuations over X. Valuations over X evolve over time according to a delay function $F : \mathbb{R}_{\geq 0} \times \mathbb{R}^X \to \mathbb{R}^X$, where for a delay d and valuation v, $F(d, v)$ provides the new valuation after a delay of d. As is the case for delays in timed automata, delay functions are assumed to be time additive in the sense that $F(d_1, F(d_2, v)) = F(d_1 + d_2, v)$. To allow for communication between different hybrid automata we assume a set of actions Σ, which is partitioned into disjoint sets of input and output actions, i.e. $\Sigma = \Sigma_i \uplus \Sigma_o$.

Definition 1.
A Hybrid Automaton (HA) $\mathcal{H}$ is a tuple $\mathcal{H} = (L, l_0, X, \Sigma, E, F, I)$, where (1) L is a finite set of locations, (2) l_0 is an initial location s.t. $l_0 \in L$, (3) X is a finite set of continuous variables, (4) Σ is a finite set of actions partitioned into inputs (Σ_i) and outputs (Σ_o) s.t. $\Sigma = \Sigma_i \uplus \Sigma_o$, (5) E is a finite set of edges of the form (l, g, σ, r, l') where $l, l' \in L$, g is a predicate on $\mathbb{R}^X$ which acts as a guard that must be satisfied, $a \in \Sigma$ is an action label and u is a binary relation

on $\mathbb{R}^X$ which acts as an update, (6) $F(l)$ is a delay function for each location $l \in L$, and (7) I assigns invariant predicates $I(l)$ to any location $l \in L$.

The semantics of a HA $\mathcal{H}$ is a timed labeled transition system, whose states are pairs $(l, v) \in L \times \mathbb{R}^X$ with $v \models I(l)$, and whose transitions are either delay transitions $(l, v) \xrightarrow{d} (l, v')$ with $d \in \mathbb{R}_{\geq 0}$ and $v' = F(d, v)$, or discrete transitions $(l, v) \xrightarrow{a} (l', v')$ if there is an edge (l, g, a, u, l') such that $v \models g$ and $u(v, v')$. The effect of the delay function F may be specified by a set of ODEs that govern the evolution of the continuous variables in time.

We denote by $\omega = s_0 d_1 a_1 s_1 d_2 a_2 \ldots$ a *timed word* where for all $i, s_i \in S$, $a_i \in \Sigma$, $s_i \xrightarrow{d_{i+1}} \xrightarrow{a_{i+1}} s_{i+1}$ and $d_i \in \mathbb{R}_{\geq 0}$. If ω is a finite timed word, we write $|\omega| = n$ to denote the length. We write $\omega[i]$ to denote a prefix run of ω up to i such that $\omega[i] = s d_1 a_1 s_1 \ldots d_i a_i s_i$. Last, we denote by $\Omega(\mathcal{H})$ the entire set of timed words over $\mathcal{H}$.

Figure 3 (a) shows the resulting evolution of the continuous temperature variable from the SUT from Fig. 1 induced by the example input sequence (timed word) $3.7 \cdot \mathsf{off} \cdot 4.1 \cdot \mathsf{on} \cdot 3.1 \cdot \mathsf{off} \cdot 4.5 \cdot \mathsf{off} \cdot 4 \cdot \mathsf{off}$. The property φ holds as the temperature stays under 75 degrees throughout the simulation.

Hybrid Automata may be given a stochastic semantics by refining the non-deterministic choices of transitions and delays by probabilistic and stochastic distributions. For each state $s = (l, v)$ of HA $\mathcal{H}$ there exists:

- the *delay density function* μ_s gives a probability distribution over delays in $\mathbb{R}_{\geq 0}$ that can be taken by a component, such that $\int \mu_s(t) dt = 1$,
- the *output probability function* γ_s gives a probability of taking an output $o \in \Sigma_o^j$ such that $\sum_o \gamma_s(o) = 1$, and
- the *next-state density function* η_s^a gives a probability distribution on the next state $s' = (l', v') \in \mathbb{R}^X$ given an action a such that $\int_{s'} \eta_s^a(s') = 1$.

Consider $\mathcal{H}$ to be a stochastic HA. For $s \in S$ and $a_1 a_2 \ldots a_k \in \Sigma^*$ we denote a *timed cylinder* $\pi(s, a_1 a_2 \ldots a_k)$ to be the set of all timed words from s with a prefix $t_1 a_1 t_2 a_2 \ldots t_k a_k$ for some $t_1, \ldots, t_n \in \mathbb{R}_{\geq 0}$. An infinite timed word $\omega = s_0 d_1 a_1^\omega s_1 d_2 a_2^\omega \ldots d_k a_k^\omega s_k \ldots$ belongs to the timed cylinder, written as $\omega \in \pi(s, a_1, a_2, \ldots, a_k)$, if $a_i^\omega = a_i$ for all i up to k and $s_0 = s$. Figure 3 (b) shows two timed words belonging to the same timed cylinder $\pi(s, \mathsf{off}, \mathsf{off}, \mathsf{on}, \mathsf{off}, \mathsf{off})$, where $s = (\mathsf{S}, \mathsf{x=0})$ is the initial state.

Providing the basic elements of a Sigma-algebra we now recall from [8] the inductively defined measure for such timed cylinders:

$$\mathbb{P}_{\mathcal{H}}(\pi(s, a_1 a_2 \ldots a_k)) = \int_{t \geq 0} \mu_s(t) \cdot \gamma_{st}(a_1) \cdot \int_{s'} \left(\eta_{st}^{a_1}(s') \cdot \mathbb{P}_{\mathcal{H}}(\pi(s', a_2 \ldots a_k)) ds' \right) dt \qquad (1)$$

The probability of following a timed cylinder π is computed by integrating over the initial delays t in the outermost level. Next, we take the probability of outputting a_i. The last part integrates over all successors s' and takes a product of probabilities for stochastic state changed after taking the delay t and output a_1, and the probability of following the remainder of the timed cylinder.

A general system can be represented as a network of HA. Under the assumption of input-enabledness, an arbitrary number of HA can be composed into a network where the individual components communicate with each other and all together act as a single system. A race-based stochastic semantics determines which of the components in the network gets to perform an output such that the winning component is the one with the smallest chosen delay. Here we skip the definition of networks of HA and their stochastic semantics, and refer the interested reader to [8] for in-depth details. We now proceed with formalized requirements for HA.

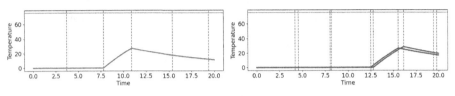

(a) Timed word example   (b) Two timed words in the same cylinder

Fig. 3. A timed word with on and off actions represented by green and red vertical dashes lines, respectively. The temperature dynamics of SUT (blue line(s)) and φ threshold of 75 degrees (red line) is shown.

Let $\mathcal{F}(\omega_\downarrow) = y$ be a function representing a black-box nonlinear hybrid system that gives a real-valued output y on the given projection of a timed word $\omega \in \Omega(\mathcal{H})$ of a stochastic HA $\mathcal{H}$, denoted as $\omega_\downarrow$ which represents a simulation output of the model $\mathcal{H}$ w.r.t. to the stochastic semantics.

Our formal property φ is expressed in a Signal Temporal Logic (STL) language [16]. STL supports quantitative semantics [9] with the help of function $\rho(\varphi, y, t)$ which gives *robustness*, i.e. degree of satisfaction of the formula φ for the input y at time t. The formula is satisfied if the robustness is positive and vice versa. Given a *robustness* function ρ, when $\rho(\varphi, y)$ is positive it indicates that y satisfies φ, written as $y \models \varphi$.

Let **Error** $\in S$ be a set of error states of HA $\mathcal{H}$. An infinite timed run $\omega = s_0 \xrightarrow{d_1\ a_1} s_1 \xrightarrow{d_2\ a_2} \ldots$ is an *error run* if $\exists i. \exists \tau \le d_i. s_{i-1}^\tau \in$ **Error**, where $\tau \in \mathbb{R}_{\ge 0}$ and s_{i-1}^τ is the state such that $s_{i-1} \xrightarrow{\tau} s_{i-1}^\tau$. We say that ω has an error at i'th transition and show it as $\mathcal{F}(\omega[i]_\downarrow) \not\models \varphi$. In this case, clearly any ω' such that $\omega' = \omega[i]\omega_n$ is also an error run.

We now define formally the *severity degree* that an input timed word ω induces w.r.t. the specification φ as the function $\mathrm{SD}(\omega, \varphi)$ that maps ω and φ to a real value in the interval $[0, 1]$, such that $\mathrm{SD}(\omega, \varphi) = 0$ if $y \models \varphi$ for $y = \mathcal{F}(\omega_\downarrow)$, and $\mathrm{SD}(\omega, \varphi) > 0$ otherwise. Intuitively, the higher the value is, the more severe the violation of φ induced by ω and witnessed by y is. We can extend the notion of severity degree $\mathrm{SD}(\omega, \varphi)$ to the *expected risk* $\mathbb{ER}(\pi(\omega), \varphi)$ that the timed cylinder $\pi(\omega)$ induces on the specification φ as shown in Eq. 2.

$$\mathbb{E}(\mathrm{R}(\pi(\omega), \varphi)) = \int_{\omega' \in \pi(\omega)} \mathrm{SD}(\omega', \varphi) d\omega'. \tag{2}$$

4 Falsification Testing with Randomized Accelerator

In this section, we describe our FBT approach for discovery of traces that violate requirements. In order to efficiently find counterexamples, we use the modified version of the randomized reachability analysis (RRA) initially proposed by [12] as a lightweight, quick and efficient error detection technique for timed systems. The core idea of RRA is to discard the underlying stochastic semantics of the model in an attempt to exercise an "exotic" behavior faster than with UPPAAL SMC. The method is based on exploring the model by means of repeated *random walks* that operate on concrete states and delays, and avoid expensive computations of symbolic, zone-based abstractions.

RRA simulation produces a timed word $w \in \Sigma$ of HA $\mathcal{H}$ where the last state satisfies some simulation termination condition (e.g. time bound). For our running example, Fig. 4 shows a RRA generated timed word that violates the requirement φ. In this study we use RRA as our RA (randomized accelerator from Sect. 2) as a

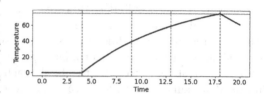

Fig. 4. A timed word witnessing violation.

mean of accelerating discovery of rare events in the user profile model. In the remainder of this section, we discuss improvements over the vanilla version of the RRA algorithm.

The RA from our methodology is applied for a number of iterations until a violating trace (counterexample) ω is discovered, i.e. until the robustness of the formula becomes negative $\rho(\varphi, \omega_\downarrow) < 0$. Clearly, in practice not all of the RA generated traces will violate the property, but some of them are likely to be close. Since evaluation of the generated input against SUT is expensive, we are interested in minimizing the number of RA iterations. Thus, we guide our RA towards the areas of the state space of HA which are deemed to be "promising" according to the previous runs. More specifically, for non-violating runs we analyze the robustness of the output and search for robustness that lays outside its standard deviation and towards a violation. The corresponding actions of HA are then identified and prioritized over other actions in the following RA iteration. To avoid actions that lead to robustness local minima, the "promising" actions are used only for a single iteration of our methodology and are discarded if the property is not violated. Afterwards, an unguided run of RA is carried out and new promising transitions are recorded for the next RA iteration in the similar fashion. Hence, only every even non-violating run of RA is guided.

Short counterexamples are not only more probable to occur in practice but also easier to debug. For those reasons, we employ an adaptive simulation duration (ASD) that may change with each discovered counterexample. First, a user profile is simulated for an initial duration. When a counterexample is found, we detect the time of first violation. In the next iteration the simulation duration is limited to that time. Intuitively, this is similar to the search for the shortest trace. However, at some point we may end up reducing the simulation time to a point where no counterexamples exist. Hence, we increase the current simulation time by 10% after a certain number of iterations is spent without finding a violation. We define that number of iterations to be the average number of iterations among so far discovered counterexamples plus a constant to ensure "enough" effort is spent before increasing the simulation duration.

5   Estimating Expected Severity

The probability of a timed cylinder is given by Eq. 1. Unfortunately, it is a theoretical construct that we cannot compute efficiently in practice. Alternatively, we can use simulation-based methods, such as SMC, to estimate the probability of following a timed cylinder. However, for rare events, SMC cannot estimate such probability reliably as simply too many simulations would be required to achieve a reasonable confidence. As a solution to this problem we use a rare event simulating technique known as *importance splitting* (IS).

The idea of IS is to split the final reachability goal δ_f into a number of intermediate sub-goals $\delta_1, \delta_2, \ldots, \delta_n$ that eventually lead to the main goal, i.e. $\delta_n = \delta_f$. The sub-goals are called *levels* that each get closer to the goal which naturally can be ensured by a *score function*. The score of each subsequent goal is required to be larger than that of a previous one. In our case a score function is a binary function that helps to ensure that the timed cylinder is followed, i.e. the action transitions are taken strictly in a sequence defined by π.

The probability estimate of reaching the level i from level $i-1$ is then $\frac{\mathsf{Successors}_i}{m}$, where $\mathsf{Successors}_i$ are successors of level i obtained from level $i-1$ by following action a_i from the timed cylinder, and m is a fixed number of simulations performed at each level. Repeating this process for all levels n allows to estimate a probability of a timed cylinder of a HA $\mathcal{H}$ as follows:

$$\mathbb{P}_{\mathcal{H}}(\pi(s, a_1 a_2 \ldots a_n)) \simeq \prod_{i=1}^{n} \frac{|\mathsf{Successors}_i|}{m} \tag{3}$$

With the help of IS, we can now estimate the probability of the timed cylinder $\mathbb{P}(\pi(s, a_1, a_2, \ldots, a_n))$ which was generated by our RA. To ease the notation we sometimes write (π_n) instead of $\pi(s, a_1, a_2, \ldots, a_n)$. A run of IS also produces a number of concrete simulations that all follow the timed cylinder and are generated according to the stochastic semantics of the underlying HA. During a run of IS, each successor has its predecessor recorded together with the delay and broadcast action that lead to that successor. The concrete simulations are obtained by back-tracing from the successors that made it to the very last level and back to the starting state. We define a finite set of timed words (traces) w generated by IS from a timed cylinder π_n as $\Gamma_{\pi_n} \subseteq \pi_n$ such that $|\Gamma_{\pi_n}| \leq m$, where m is the effort allocated per level of IS fixed effort scheme.

Even though all traces in Γ_{π_n} follow the same timed cylinder, the differences in the timing behavior (chosen delays) may influence the dynamics of the user profile to a large degree. Violation (or satisfaction) of the property monitored for SUT - as well as the level at which a violation appear - is therefore not guaranteed to be identical for all traces Γ_{π_n} reported by IS.

We first estimate the probability of violating the STL property with a timed cylinder π_n, i.e. $\mathbb{P}(\omega \in \pi_n \wedge \mathcal{F}(\omega_\downarrow) \not\models \varphi)$. In the following let m be a number of IS simulation per level and let $\texttt{Successors}_i$ be the successors of each level i in IS. Considering the IS sampled traces Γ_{π_n} and their (varying) violation of the monitored property, we may estimate this probability as follows:

$$\mathbb{P}(\omega \in \pi_n \wedge \mathcal{F}(\omega_\downarrow) \not\models \varphi) = \mathbb{P}(\pi_n) \cdot \mathbb{P}(\omega \in \pi_n \wedge \mathcal{F}(\omega_\downarrow) \not\models \varphi \mid \pi_n) \simeq$$

$$\prod_{i=1}^{n} \left(\frac{|\texttt{Successors}_i|}{m} \right) \cdot \left(\sum_{\omega \in \Gamma_{\pi_n}} \mathcal{F}(\omega_\downarrow) \not\models \varphi \right) \cdot \frac{1}{|\Gamma_{\pi_n}|} \tag{4}$$

Also we estimate the *expected* risk as follows:

$$\mathbb{E}(\mathrm{R}(\pi(\omega), \varphi)) \simeq \prod_{i=1}^{n} \left(\frac{|\texttt{Successors}_i|}{m} \right) \cdot \left(\sum_{\omega \in \Gamma_{\pi_n}} \mathrm{SD}(\omega, \varphi) \right) \cdot \frac{1}{|\Gamma_{\pi_n}|} \tag{5}$$

where the last two factors of the equation are the *expected* severity (of the cylinder π) according to the severity measure SD.

For our running example, we consider 100 traces generated by IS (Fig. 5) for a timed cylinder with on, on, on, off, on action sequence. Violation of 75 degrees threshold is observed in 9 (out of 100). The probability estimate of Eq. 4 is then $\left(\frac{23}{100} \cdot \frac{27}{100} \cdot \frac{25}{100} \cdot \frac{77}{100} \right) \cdot \frac{9}{100} \approx 0.001$, where the parenthesis give IS probability estimate of the cylinder with 4 steps. The estimated expected risk evaluates

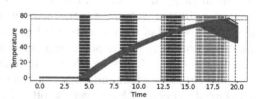

Fig. 5. One hundred traces generated by IS. Blue line traces satisfy the property and purple line ones violate.

to $\left(\frac{23}{100} \cdot \frac{27}{100} \cdot \frac{25}{100} \cdot \frac{77}{100} \right) \cdot (0.07 + 0.09 + 0.10 + 0.08 + 0.06 + 0.07 + 0.10 + 0.09 + 0.10)/100 \approx 8.7 \cdot 10^{-5}$.

6   Case Study

We use a Thermal Model of a House[1], shown in Fig. 6, as our black-box SUT $\mathcal{F}$. The model accounts for the heating system, thermal dynamics of the house, the outdoor environment and additional properties such as house geometry and heater flow rate. The heating of the house is controlled by the thermostat that turns on/off the heater once the temperature is below/above specified thresholds. The inside temperature is calculated by considering the heat flow from the heater and the heat losses to the environment through the insulation of the house.

[1] https://se.mathworks.com/help/simulink/slref/thermal-model-of-a-house.html.

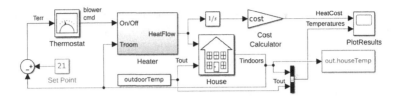

Fig. 6. Simulink Thermal Model of a House.

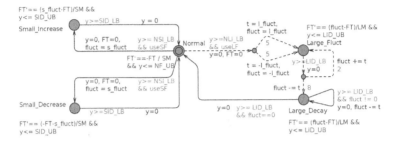

Fig. 7. Weather profile hybrid automaton model.

To simulate the outdoor environment for the thermal house system, we use the HA weather model shown in Fig. 7. The daily and yearly temperature fluctuations are modelled by sinusoidal waves with varying phase, amplitude and biases. In our experiments we simulate the weather model for a period of 1 year while the starting period of the simulation being January 1st; therefore, the waves are adjusted accordingly and depend on an elapsing, observing clock x that we use to model the time in hours. In addition to daily and yearly temperature changes the model supports small and large "anomalous" temperature fluctuations that are enforced to occur at least every so often by `guards` and `invariants` on edges and locations, respectively. Each fluctuation results in a temperature change of the magnitude and dynamics governed by ODEs. A number of large fluctuations can happen sequentially, representing e.g. a heat wave or a sudden temperature drop. The type of a fluctuation, as well as its duration, which largely affects the dynamics, is decided during the simulation and in accordance with the stochastic semantics described in Sect. 3. The likelihood of an additional large fluctuation taking place right after a previous one is defined by discrete probabilities 8 and 2 on the outgoing transition from the **Large_Fluct** location. Even though no restrictions are made on the maximal number of large fluctuations happening sequentially, the probability of additional n sequential large fluctuations (after the initial one) is $(\frac{2}{8+2})^n = 0.2^n$.

We use RTAMT [18] as our STL monitoring library. The inside temperature of the house is monitored in an offline setting to measure the property robustness. We monitor the property $\varphi = \Box(T \leq 16 \rightarrow \Diamond_{[0,24]}(T \geq 18))$, i.e. it is required that the temperature, if it drops below 16 degrees, always recovers to at least 18 degrees within 24 h. We finally instantiate the severity degree measurement with $SD(\omega, \varphi) = (D - \inf_{t \in [0,D]}(y \not\models \varphi))/D$, where D is the duration of the timed word ω and $y = \mathcal{F}(\omega_\downarrow)$.

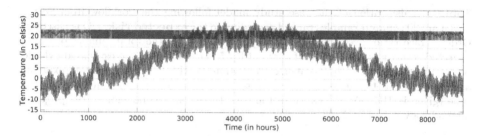

Fig. 8. Simulink Thermal House indoor (red) and outdoor (blue) temperatures simulated for 1 year (Color figure online) (8736 h hours).

7 Experiments

We use SMC as a baseline and compare it to the performance of our falsification methodology. The two approaches are rather different as SMC cannot reason about probability of each individual violating trace. Rather, SMC estimates an overall property violation probability which lays within some approximation interval $p \pm \epsilon$ with a confidence $1 - \alpha$. The amount of simulations N required to produce an approximation interval given ϵ and α can be computed using Chernoff-Hoeffding inequality with $N \geq \frac{\log(2/\alpha)}{2\epsilon^2}$. To accurately estimate a very improbable error in the system, the probability uncertainty ϵ must be sufficiently small. As can be seen in Table 2, the growth of the required simulations is logarithmic and exponential in relation to α and ϵ, respectively. However, in practice this approach is too conservative. As an alternative, UPPAAL SMC uses a sequential approach of Clopper-Pearson that computes the approximation interval with each iteration (for given α) and until the target ϵ is reached. Moreover, the further away a true probability is from $\frac{1}{2}$, the fewer simulations are needed. Empirical evidence[2] suggests that a true probability in range $[0, 10^{-5}]$ in practice requires roughly around 10% simulations (depending on α) of what Chernoff-Hoeffding inequality suggests. Nonetheless, for $\alpha = 0.01$ and $\epsilon = 5 \times 10^{-4}$ around as many as 10^6 simulations would be required.

In our experiments we only give an estimate of the time required by SMC to derive approximation intervals for a sufficiently small ϵ and α as each simulation is costly due to the execution of the Simulink model. To estimate the time of one iteration of the workflow from Fig. 2a we ran 20,000 SMC simulations with 220 of them violating the

Table 2. Number of simulations required for an approximation interval $[p - \epsilon, p + \epsilon]$ with confidence $1 - \alpha$ using Chernoff-Hoeffding inequality.

Confidence α	Probability uncertainty ϵ			
	0.05	5×10^{-3}	5×10^{-4}	5×10^{-5}
0.1	600	59,915	5,991,465	599,146,455
0.05	738	73,778	7,377,759	737,775,891
0.01	1,060	105,967	10,596,635	1,059,663,474

---

[2] https://docs.uppaal.org/language-reference/requirements-specification/ci_estimation/.

Table 1. Falsification of the case study model following the workflow from Sect. 2. Given are 20 counterexamples ranked according to the **expected risk**. DO is Discovery Order, Trace ratio gives the ratio between violating and the total number of traces, expected severity is the last two factors of Eq. 5 (i.e. excluding the estimated cylinder probability), #Tran. is the number of transitions in HA for a given counterexample, and #RA Iter. is the number of RA iterations to find the counterexample. Execution time (given in HH:MM:SS) captures the time to run all components of the proposed methodology from Fig. 2 (b).

DO	Exact cylinder pr.	Estimated cylinder pr. (Equation 3)	Trace ratio	Estimated violation pr. (Equation 4)	Expected severity	Estimated exp. risk (Equation 5)	#Tran. in HA	#RA Iter.	Execution time
16	7.9012e-04	6.1200e-04	44/80	3.3660e-04	0.530	**3.2409e-04**	6	46	00:01:41
4	3.5556e-04	3.0121e-04	73/73	3.0121e-04	0.973	**2.9311e-04**	5	39	00:01:08
10	3.5117e-04	5.2745e-04	46/81	2.9954e-04	0.538	**2.8400e-04**	8	35	00:01:30
20	3.5117e-04	2.4857e-04	50/79	1.5732e-04	0.601	**1.4941e-04**	8	70	00:01:59
6	4.4444e-04	2.0995e-04	9/13	1.4535e-04	0.676	**1.4189e-04**	4	2	00:00:12
7	1.7778e-03	2.4472e-04	39/76	1.2558e-04	0.499	**1.2212e-04**	4	95	00:02:05
5	8.8889e-05	8.6184e-05	16/16	8.6184e-05	0.975	**8.4000e-05**	5	37	00:00:35
18	8.7791e-05	1.2667e-04	15/25	7.5999e-05	0.569	**7.2102e-05**	8	20	00:00:36
17	1.5802e-05	6.5331e-05	82/82	6.5331e-05	0.953	**6.2273e-05**	8	107	00:02:14
13	1.5803e-04	6.3690e-05	79/79	6.3690e-05	0.960	**6.1112e-05**	7	87	00:01:47
19	8.7791e-05	1.1980e-04	11/23	5.7297e-05	0.455	**5.4494e-05**	8	22	00:00:35
12	3.9506e-05	4.7904e-05	18/18	4.7904e-05	0.960	**4.5973e-05**	7	27	00:00:34
14	8.7791e-05	4.3612e-05	8/17	2.0523e-05	0.447	**1.9474e-05**	8	57	00:00:58
9	1.9753e-05	2.4394e-05	18/22	1.9958e-05	0.781	**1.9046e-05**	7	36	00:00:42
8	1.9753e-04	2.7846e-05	8/13	1.7136e-05	0.594	**1.6542e-05**	6	6	00:00:16
11	3.1605e-05	8.2675e-06	100/100	8.2675e-06	0.963	**7.9637e-06**	9	5	00:00:17
15	8.7791e-05	2.2050e-05	2/10	4.4100e-06	0.191	**4.2162e-06**	8	16	00:00:18
3	1.0114e-09	2.8638e-10	100/100	2.8638e-10	0.975	**2.7934e-10**	24	5	00:00:12
2	3.1179e-17	6.3463e-18	9/9	6.3463e-18	0.859	**5.4489e-18**	46	2	00:00:10
1	4.1829e-49	1.5479e-48	100/100	1.5479e-48	0.695	**1.0762e-48**	141	3	00:00:26
Total:	4.9725e-03	2.7796e-03	-	1.8323e-03	-	**1.7618e-03**	-	717	00:18:24

Time estimate of 10^4 SMC iterations ($\alpha = 0.01$, $\epsilon = 5 \times 10^{-3}$) based on Table 2.   **08:48:00**

property. With the total time of 17 h 36 m 20 s, a single iteration in average takes 3.169 s. Figure 8 gives black-box SUT dynamics of one such iteration that includes outdoor ambient temperature (input) and a resulting indoor temperature (output). As UPPAAL SMC primarily exercises common behavior of the weather profile, we observe no requirement violation in the output from SUT.

In addition to IS that is used to estimate the probability to follow a timed cylinder, we implement an exact method for probability computation. This method supports only a subset of HA models where all clocks are reset in every transition (this is the case for our weather profile). It enables us to compare how far the estimated probability is away from the true one.

We perform an experiment to determine to which degree the variance in the probability estimates produced by IS is affected by the number of simulations m performed per level by IS. The results do not show any clear pattern indicating the amount of IS simulations per level to significantly affect the variance of the probability estimates. Since the execution time taken is roughly proportional to

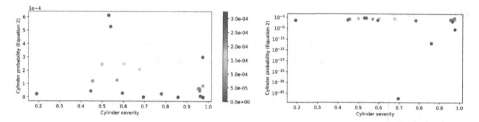

Fig. 9. Expected risk of counteraxamples from Table 1 (color of points in the heatmap) as a relation between cylinder probability and expected severity. Linear (left) and logarithmic scale (right) views.

the number of IS simulations, in further experiments we fix the number of IS simulations per level to 100.

Finally, we evaluate our FBT methodology on the proposed case study and report the results in Table 1. Due to ASD, the quality of discovered errors tends to increase over time as the length (# transitions) of counterexamples decreases. The ratio between violating and total traces (TR) confirms that the timing behavior within the timed cylinder may influence the violation of the monitored property to a large degree. We estimate the time needed for SMC to find violation with the probability uncertainty of 10^{-3} which is in the same order of magnitude as the sum of estimated expected risks of all the 20 counterexamples (1.46×10^{-3}). The discovery, evaluation and ranking of 20 bugs with our approach is an order of magnitude faster than with SMC – a technique often used for falsification in cases where alternative methods for analysis of HA are infeasible. However, SMC is only able to estimate the overall probability of violation and cannot rank individual counterexamples unlike our falsification framework.

Figure 9 shows the relation between the probability of a cylinder and its severity. Multiplication of the two measures gives us expected risk (Eq. 5), which we depict in Fig. 9 using a heatmap. We observe that the counterexample(s) with the highest (cylinder) probability are in fact similar in "value" to the counterexample with the lower (cylinder) probability but higher severity. This indicates that both measures have high importance in ranking counterexamples.

8 Conclusion and Future Work

We introduced a new approach for usage-aware FT of CPS. It combines stochastic HA modeling, randomized reachability analysis, SMC, importance splitting and runtime verification to efficiently generate tests that lead to the violation of the requirements, while estimating their risk in the real usage of the system. We believe that the proposed methodology can significantly help the debugging effort by enabling to prioritize bugs with higher impact.

As future work, we plan to 1) develop more sophisticated guiding for our randomized accelerator, 2) introduce a state coverage metric, and 3) explore symbolic reachability techniques for HA.

References

1. Ábrahám, E., Becker, B., Dehnert, C., Jansen, N., Katoen, J., Wimmer, R.: Counterexample generation for discrete-time markov models: An introductory survey. In: Formal Methods for Executable Software Models - 14th International School on Formal Methods for the Design of Computer, Communication, and Software Systems, SFM 2014, Bertinoro, Italy, June 16–20, 2014, Advanced Lectures, pp. 65–121 (2014)
2. Aljazzar, H., Leitner-Fischer, F., Leue, S., Simeonov, D.: Dipro - A tool for probabilistic counterexample generation. In: Model Checking Software - 18th International SPIN Workshop, Snowbird, UT, USA, July 14–15, 2011. Proceedings, pp. 183–187 (2011)
3. Bartocci, E., Bloem, R., Maderbacher, B., Manjunath, N., Nickovic, D.: Adaptive testing for specification coverage in CPS models. In: 7th IFAC Conference on Analysis and Design of Hybrid Systems, ADHS 2021, Brussels, Belgium, July 7–9, 2021, pp. 229–234 (2021)
4. Bogomolov, S., Frehse, G., Gurung, A., Li, D., Martius, G., Ray, R.: Falsification of hybrid systems using symbolic reachability and trajectory splicing. In: Proceedings of the 22nd ACM International Conference on Hybrid Systems: Computation and Control, HSCC 2019, Montreal, QC, Canada, April 16–18, 2019, pp. 1–10 (2019)
5. Bulychev, P.E., et al.: UPPAAL-SMC: statistical model checking for priced timed automata. In: Proceedings 10th Workshop on Quantitative Aspects of Programming Languages and Systems, QAPL 2012, Tallinn, Estonia, 31 March and 1 April 2012, pp. 1–16 (2012)
6. Chaturvedi, D.K.: Modeling and simulation of systems using MATLAB® and Simulink®. CRC Press (2017)
7. Clarke, E.M., Zuliani, P.: Statistical model checking for cyber-physical systems. In: Automated Technology for Verification and Analysis, 9th International Symposium, ATVA 2011, Taipei, Taiwan, October 11–14, 2011. Proceedings, pp. 1–12 (2011)
8. David, A., et al.: Statistical model checking for stochastic hybrid systems. Electron. Proc. Theor. Comput. Sci. **92**, 122–136 (2012). https://doi.org/10.4204/eptcs.92.9
9. Donzé, A., Maler, O.: Robust satisfaction of temporal logic over real-valued signals. In: Chatterjee, K., Henzinger, T.A. (eds.) Formal Modeling and Analysis of Timed Systems, pp. 92–106. Springer, Berlin Heidelberg, Berlin, Heidelberg (2010)
10. Han, T., Katoen, J.: Counterexamples in probabilistic model checking. In: Tools and Algorithms for the Construction and Analysis of Systems, 13th International Conference, TACAS 2007, Held as Part of the Joint European Conferences on Theory and Practice of Software, ETAPS 2007 Braga, Portugal, March 24 - April 1, 2007, Proceedings, pp. 72–86 (2007)
11. Jégourel, C., Legay, A., Sedwards, S.: Importance splitting for statistical model checking rare properties. In: Computer Aided Verification - 25th International Conference, CAV 2013, Saint Petersburg, Russia, July 13–19, 2013. Proceedings, pp. 576–591 (2013)
12. Kiviriga, A., Larsen, K.G., Nyman, U.: Randomized reachability analysis in uppaal: Fast error detection in timed systems. In: Lluch Lafuente, A., Mavridou, A. (eds.) Formal Methods for Industrial Critical Systems, pp. 149–166. Springer International Publishing, Cham (2021)

13. Larsen, K.G., Legay, A., Mikucionis, M., Poulsen, D.B.: Importance splitting in uppaal. In: Margaria, T., Steffen, B. (eds.) Leveraging Applications of Formal Methods, Verification and Validation. Adaptation and Learning - 11th International Symposium, ISoLA 2022, Rhodes, Greece, October 22–30, 2022, Proceedings, Part III. Lecture Notes in Computer Science, vol. 13703, pp. 433–447. Springer (2022). https://doi.org/10.1007/978-3-031-19759-8_26
14. Lindemann, L., Jiang, L., Matni, N., Pappas, G.J.: Risk of stochastic systems for temporal logic specifications. ACM Trans. Embed. Comput. Syst. **22**(3), 54:1–54:31 (2023). https://doi.org/10.1145/3580490
15. Lindemann, L., Matni, N., Pappas, G.J.: STL robustness risk over discrete-time stochastic processes. In: 2021 60th IEEE Conference on Decision and Control (CDC), Austin, TX, USA, December 14–17, 2021, pp. 1329–1335 (2021)
16. Maler, O., Nickovic, D.: Monitoring temporal properties of continuous signals. In: Lakhnech, Y., Yovine, S. (eds.) Formal Techniques, Modelling and Analysis of Timed and Fault-Tolerant Systems, pp. 152–166. Springer, Berlin Heidelberg, Berlin, Heidelberg (2004)
17. Nghiem, T., Sankaranarayanan, S., Fainekos, G., Ivancic, F., Gupta, A., Pappas, G.J.: Monte-carlo techniques for falsification of temporal properties of non-linear hybrid systems. In: Proceedings of the 13th ACM International Conference on Hybrid Systems: Computation and Control, HSCC 2010, Stockholm, Sweden, April 12–15, 2010, pp. 211–220 (2010)
18. Ničković, D., Yamaguchi, T.: Rtamt: online robustness monitors from STL. In: Hung, D.V., Sokolsky, O. (eds.) Automated Technology for Verification and Analysis, pp. 564–571. Springer International Publishing, Cham (2020)
19. Rubino, G., Tuffin, B.: Rare event simulation using Monte Carlo methods. John Wiley & Sons (2009)
20. Sen, K., Viswanathan, M., Agha, G.: Statistical model checking of black-box probabilistic systems. In: Computer Aided Verification, 16th International Conference, CAV 2004, Boston, MA, USA, July 13–17, 2004, Proceedings, pp. 202–215 (2004)
21. Sen, K., Viswanathan, M., Agha, G.: Statistical model checking of black-box probabilistic systems. In: Alur, R., Peled, D.A. (eds.) Computer Aided Verification, pp. 202–215. Springer, Berlin Heidelberg, Berlin, Heidelberg (2004)
22. Younes, H.L.S.: Verification and Planning for Stochastic Processes with Asynchronous Events. Ph.D. thesis (2004)
23. Younes, H.L.S., Simmons, R.G.: Probabilistic verification of discrete event systems using acceptance sampling. In: Computer Aided Verification, 14th International Conference, CAV 2002, Copenhagen, Denmark, July 27–31, 2002, Proceedings, pp. 223–235 (2002)

Model Predictive Runtime Verification for Cyber-Physical Systems with Real-Time Deadlines

Pei Zhang[1]([✉])[ID], Alexis Aurandt[1][ID], Rohit Dureja[2][ID], Phillip H. Jones[1][ID], and Kristin Yvonne Rozier[1][ID]

[1] Iowa State University, Ames, USA
{peizhang,aurandt,phjones,kyrozier}@iastate.edu
[2] IBM Corporation, Armonk, USA

Abstract. Cyber-physical systems often require fault detection of future events in order to mitigate the fault before failure occurs. Effective on-board runtime verification (RV) will need to not only determine the system's current state but also predict future faults by predetermined mitigation trigger deadlines. For example, if it takes three seconds to deploy the parachute of an Unmanned Aerial System (UAS), the deployment of the parachute must be triggered three seconds before it is needed to mitigate the impending crash. To allow for the detection of future faults by deadlines, we design a real-time Model Predictive Runtime Verification (MPRV) algorithm that uniquely uses current data traces whenever possible, predicting only the minimum horizon needed to make an on-deadline evaluation. Although MPRV is extensible to other RV engines, we deploy the algorithm on the R2U2 RV engine due to R2U2's resource-aware architecture, real-time guarantees, and deployment history. We demonstrate the utility of the MPRV algorithm through a quadcopter case study and evaluate the effectiveness of our implementation by conducting memory usage and runtime performance analysis in a resource-constrained FPGA environment.

1 Introduction

Modern cyber-physical systems such as Unmanned Aerial Systems (UAS), autonomous driving systems, and human-interactive robots require runtime verification (RV) to ensure that they uphold design requirements and react to unanticipated events during deployment [11]. On-board RV can detect violations of system requirements and trigger appropriate mitigation actions. For RV to be effective, some element of prediction is often required; waiting until sensor data confirms a fault occurred can limit mitigation options.

Predictive RV was first introduced in [36,63], but these works focus only on the prediction of *untimed* properties. In [47], the idea of synthesizing online monitors to predict

Supported by NSF:CPS Award 2038903. Artifacts at https://zenodo.org/record/8076503.

R. Dureja—Work performed as a graduate student at Iowa State University.

L. Petrucci and J. Sproston (Eds.): FORMATS 2023, LNCS 14138, pp. 158–180, 2023.
https://doi.org/10.1007/978-3-031-42626-1_10

timed properties is introduced. However, the system model must be known and represented as a deterministic timed automaton, which is not compositional, resource-aware, or executable in real-time or in hardware. As a result, this approach is not scalable or applicable to many system models or applications. We introduce Model Predictive Runtime Verification (MPRV), which monitors *timed* properties but allows for integration with *any* user-defined model predictor.

In more recent work, several apply knowledge of the system to produce a model predictor [19, 23, 60, 61], while others address generating a model predictor when a model is not known a priori (i.e., black-box systems) or when a system is subject to perturbations [6–8, 24]. Others also take into consideration the uncertainty of the model predictor when considering the supervisory controller's actions [38, 57, 60]. To the best of our knowledge, these tools are all restricted to software implementations and have not been deployed on resource-constrained, real-time systems. We prove resource and time constraints for the MPRV algorithm that demonstrate its adaptability to RV in resource-constrained environments with real-time requirements.

Cyber-physical systems often deploy with a small, finite set of possible mitigation actions should a fault occur, and each action typically has a known deployment time. For example, a UAS may have a parachute that takes three seconds to unfurl, but the parachute must be fully unfurled within two seconds after motor failure to be effective. If the parachute does not unfurl in time, an unsafe crash will occur. We can define a mitigation trigger deadline d as the deadline by which a mitigation decision needs to be determined. In this case, d is one second before motor failure occurs (i.e., $d = -1$). Note that d can change with the property being monitored or during the mission. With our example, the same mission property may require evaluation with an earlier d when the UAS is flying at low altitudes, but then with no d at all when the UAS is flying so low to the ground that a parachute would not be useful. We may monitor with a later d when the UAS is flying at a high altitude; in this case, there may even be time to rigorously confirm the motor failure without any predicted data.

MPRV answers the following question: *by a given mitigation trigger deadline d, what is the two-valued verdict (*true *or* false*) of a given timed property φ based on maximum real data?* **No other tool or algorithm answers this question** in an implementation independent, real-time, online setting, much less in a resource-aware, on-board embeddable fashion, such as on an FPGA. Additionally, the deadline d may vary across different properties or in one property across different operational modes (e.g., UAS flying at low altitudes versus high altitudes); therefore, a modular, generalizable algorithm is required. Effective mitigation triggering depends upon making the most accurate decision by the deadline d. In most cases, real data is more accurate than predicted data (assuming the RV engine is also monitoring for sensor malfunctions); therefore, MPRV uniquely uses real data up to time d with the minimal necessary predicted data to make a decision by d.

As the NASA Lunar Gateway team's 2021 survey confirms [20], only two RV engines run in real-time on embedded platforms, R2U2 [48, 50] and LOLA [3, 21], but neither of them provides prediction. Many RV designers have recognized the need for hardware implementations suitable for real-time embedded systems [30, 32, 34, 39, 43, 46, 55, 56, 58]; however, R2U2 is the only one that has a currently-maintained implementation, evaluates both true and false verdicts (versus only property failure) over a future-time logic without evaluation delay, and monitors formulas (versus analysis requiring software instrumentation). R2U2 also has a history of being deployed on several mission-critical, resource-constrained, flight-certified systems [5,17,31,34]. We exemplify the R2U2 extension and leave the LOLA extension to future work. We choose Mission-time Linear Temporal Logic (MLTL) for property specification as it intuitively captures our quadcopter case study's requirements, is a timed logic, and R2U2 encodes it natively. We also introduce a new MLTL semantics that incorporates deadlines to accurately represent our MPRV specifications. However, MPRV is *extensible* to other logics and RV engines.

Our contributions include (**1**) MLTL semantics with deadline (Definition 10), (**2**) a formal definition of MPRV (Definition 13), (**3**) a generic algorithm for MPRV and proof of its correctness (Algorithm 1 and Theorem 1), (**4**) a specialized algorithm for implementing MPRV utilizing the R2U2 framework (Algorithm 2) and analysis of its worst-case execution time and memory usage (Sect. 3.3), (**5**) application in a quadcopter case study (Sect. 4), and (**6**) memory usage and runtime performance analysis of MPRV in a resource-constrained FPGA environment (Sect. 5).

2   Preliminaries

2.1   Mission-Time Linear Temporal Logic (MLTL) [37,48]

Definition 1 *(MLTL Syntax). The syntax of an MLTL formula φ over a set of atomic propositions $\mathcal{AP}$ is recursively defined as:*

$$\varphi ::= \text{true} \mid \text{false} \mid p \mid \neg\varphi \mid \varphi_1 \wedge \varphi_2 \mid \varphi_1 \vee \varphi_2 \mid \Box_I \varphi \mid \Diamond_I \varphi \mid \varphi_1 \, \mathcal{U}_I \, \varphi_2 \mid \varphi_1 \, \mathcal{R}_I \, \varphi_2$$

where $p \in \mathcal{AP}$ is an atom and φ_1, φ_2 are MLTL formulas. I is a closed interval $[lb, ub]$ where $lb \leq ub$ and $lb, ub \in \mathbb{N}_0$, or simply $[ub]$ if $lb = 0$.

Definition 2 *(MLTL Semantics). The semantics of an MLTL formula over atomic propositions $\mathcal{AP}$ is interpreted over a bounded finite trace π. Every position $\pi(i)$ (where $i \geq 0$) is an assignment over $\in 2^{\mathcal{AP}}$. $|\pi|$ denotes the length of π (where $|\pi| < \infty$), and $\pi[m, n]$ denotes the trace segment $\pi(m), \pi(m+1), ..., \pi(n)$. Given two MLTL formulas φ_1 and φ_2, $\varphi_1 \equiv \varphi_2$ denotes that they are semantically equivalent. MLTL keeps the standard operator equivalences from LTL, including $\text{false} \equiv \neg\text{true}$, $\varphi_1 \vee \varphi_2 \equiv \neg(\neg\varphi_1 \wedge \neg\varphi_2)$, $\neg(\varphi_1 \mathcal{U}_I \varphi_2) \equiv (\neg\varphi_1 \mathcal{R}_I \neg\varphi_2)$, $\neg\Diamond_I \varphi \equiv \Box_I \neg\varphi$, $\Diamond_I \varphi \equiv (\text{true} \, \mathcal{U}_I \varphi)$, and $(\Box_I \varphi) \equiv (\text{false} \, \mathcal{R}_I \varphi)$. (Notably, MLTL discards the next ($\mathcal{X}$) operator, which is essential in LTL, since $\mathcal{X}\varphi$ is semantically equivalent to $\Box_{[1,1]}\varphi$ [37]). We recursively define $\pi, i \models \varphi$ (trace π starting from time index $i \geq 0$ satisfies, or "models" MLTL formula φ) as*

- $\pi, i \models \text{true}$,
- $\pi, i \models p$ *for* $p \in \mathcal{AP}$ *iff* $p \in \pi(i)$,
- $\pi, i \models \neg\varphi$ *iff* $\pi, i \not\models \varphi$,
- $\pi, i \models \varphi_1 \wedge \varphi_2$ *iff* $\pi, i \models \varphi_1$ *and* $\pi, i \models \varphi_2$,

- $\pi, i \models \varphi_1 \, \mathcal{U}_{[lb,ub]} \, \varphi_2$ *iff* $|\pi| \geq i + lb$ *and* $\exists j \in [i + lb, i + ub]$ *such that* $\pi, j \models \varphi_2$ *and for every* $k < j$ *and* $k \in [i + lb, i + ub]$ *we have* $\pi, k \models \varphi_1$

Definition 3 *(MLTL Satisfiability [37]). Given an MLTL formula* φ*, the satisfiability problem asks whether there exists a finite trace* π *starting at time index* i*, such that* $\pi, i \models \varphi$*.*

Propagation Delay. To evaluate the satisfiability of a future-time MLTL formula φ at time index i in a trace π, the RV engine may need to know the evaluation of atomic propositions at future time stamps, e.g., if $a \in \mathcal{AP}$ is false at time 0 in π, then we can evaluate that $\pi, 0 \not\models \Box_{[0,5]} a$ at time 0. However, if a is always true in π, we cannot make the assertion that $\pi, 0 \models \Box_{[0,5]} a$ until time 5. In this example, the best-case propagation delay of φ is 0, and the worst-case propagation delay is 5.

Definition 4 *(Propagation Delay). Given an MLTL formula* φ *and trace* π *starting from time index* $i \geq 0$*, let* k *be the time stamp when the satisfiability of* $\pi, i \models \varphi$ *is determinable. The propagation delay of formula* φ*, denoted* $\varphi.pd$ *is the number of time stamps between* i *and* k*, i.e.,* $\varphi.pd = k - i$*.*

Definition 5 *(Best-case Propagation Delay). The best-case propagation delay of an MLTL formula* φ*, denoted* $\varphi.bpd$*, is the minimum propagation delay required to determine the satisfiability of* $\pi, i \models \varphi$*, i.e.,* $\varphi.bpd = min(\varphi.pd)$*.*

Definition 6 *(Worst-case Propagation Delay). The worst-case propagation delay of an MLTL formula* φ*, denoted* $\varphi.wpd$*, is the maximum propagation delay required to determine the satisfiability of* $\pi, i \models \varphi$*, i.e.,* $\varphi.wpd = max(\varphi.pd)$*.*

Definition 7 *(Propagation Delay Semantics). The best- and worst-case propagation delay for an MLTL formula* φ *is structurally defined as follows:*

- $\varphi \in \mathcal{AP}$: $\begin{cases} \varphi.wpd = 0 \\ \varphi.bpd = 0 \end{cases}$
  $\qquad$ $\varphi = \neg\psi$: $\begin{cases} \varphi.wpd = \psi.wpd \\ \varphi.bpd = \psi.bpd \end{cases}$

- $\varphi = \Box_{[lb,ub]}\psi \, or \, \varphi = \Diamond_{[lb,ub]}\psi$: $\begin{cases} \varphi.wpd = \psi.wpd + ub \\ \varphi.bpd = \psi.bpd + lb \end{cases}$

- $\varphi = \varphi_1 \vee \varphi_2 \, or \, \varphi = \varphi_1 \wedge \varphi_2$: $\begin{cases} \varphi.wpd = max(\varphi_1.wpd, \varphi_2.wpd) \\ \varphi.bpd = min(\varphi_1.bpd, \varphi_2.bpd) \end{cases}$

- $\varphi = \varphi_1 \mathcal{U}_{[lb,ub]}\varphi_2 \, or \, \varphi = \varphi_1 \mathcal{R}_{[lb,ub]}\varphi_2$: $\begin{cases} \varphi.wpd = max(\varphi_1.wpd, \varphi_2.wpd) + ub \\ \varphi.bpd = min(\varphi_1.bpd, \varphi_2.bpd) + lb \end{cases}$

where $\mathcal{AP}$ *is the set of atomic propositions and* lb *and* ub *stand for the lower and upper bounds of an interval, respectively.*

2.2 Abstract Syntax Tree

R2U2 [34,48,50,51] decomposes the formula φ into subformulas using a parse tree. It computes the satisfaction of every subformula from the bottom up and propagates the verification results to the root-level formula φ. R2U2 uses optimized automatic code generation to synthesize asynchronous (event-triggered) observers that output *execution sequences* over finite time stamps.

Definition 8 (*Execution Sequence for Asynchronous Observers* [48]). *An execution sequence for an MLTL formula* φ, *denoted* $\langle T_\varphi \rangle$, *over trace* π *is a sequence of tuples* $T_\varphi = (v, \tau)$, *where* $\tau \in \mathbb{N}_0$ *is a time index and* $v \in \{\text{true}, \text{false}\}$ *is a verdict.*

We use an integer superscript to access a particular tuple in $\langle T_\varphi \rangle$, e.g., T_φ^0 is the first tuple in $\langle T_\varphi \rangle$. Elements in T_φ are referenced as $T_\varphi.\tau$ and $T_\varphi.v$. We say T_φ holds if $T_\varphi.v$ is true, and T_φ does not hold if $T_\varphi.v$ is false. For a given execution sequence $\langle T_\varphi \rangle = T_\varphi^0, T_\varphi^1, T_\varphi^2, T_\varphi^3, \ldots$, the tuple accessed by T_φ^n corresponds to a section of satisfaction of φ such that $T_\varphi^n.v$ is true if and only if $\forall i \in [T_\varphi^{n-1}.\tau + 1, T_\varphi^n.\tau]$, we have $\pi, i \models \varphi$. Similarly, $T_\varphi^n.v$ is false if there $\exists i \in [T_\varphi^{n-1}.\tau + 1, T_\varphi^n.\tau]$ such that $\pi, i \not\models \varphi$. We say an execution sequence tuple T_φ is *produced* by the observer for φ when $T_\varphi.\tau \geq i$ and $T_\varphi.v \in \{\text{true}, \text{false}\}$ according to $\pi, i \models \varphi$.

Abstract Syntax Tree Construction. A compiler parses the user-specified MLTL formula into an Abstract Syntax Tree (AST) of subformulas, where each node in the AST handles one MLTL operator. Every node explicitly exposes the logical connection between the subformulas. R2U2 automatically synthesizes a runtime observer for every non-leaf node in the tree (i.e., for every MLTL operator) that takes an input execution sequence from child nodes and produces an output execution sequence for the parent node. R2U2 determines the satisfaction of the MLTL formula on an input trace by evaluating the output of the observers from the leaf nodes to the root of the tree. Figure 1 shows the AST for MLTL formula $\varphi = (\square_{[0,2]} a0) \wedge a1$, and Fig. 2 shows the corresponding compiled instructions. The leaf nodes are atomic proposition load operators

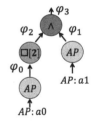

Fig. 1.   AST   for $\varphi = (\square_{[0,2]} a0) \wedge a1$

that output an execution sequence that combines the values of the atomic propositions in the trace π with time index τ. The output sequence of the root node corresponds to the verification result of the MLTL specification φ at every time stamp.

Abstract Syntax Tree Evaluation. Let t_R be the current time stamp during runtime. Note that $t_R = 0$ indicates the start of execution. Table 1 shows the execution sequences generated by the observers when evaluating the MLTL formula $\varphi = (\square_{[0,2]} a0) \wedge a1$ over the assignments shown in Fig. 3. The atomic proposition load operators capture hardware signals at the beginning of each

Line0: $\varphi_0 \leftarrow load(a0)$
Line1: $\varphi_1 \leftarrow load(a1)$
Line2: $\varphi_2 \leftarrow \square[0,2](\varphi_0)$
Line3: $\varphi_3 \leftarrow \wedge(\varphi_1, \varphi_2)$

Fig. 2. Instructions compiled from AST

time stamp (shown as event edges in Fig. 3) and output the corresponding execution sequence tuple. For example, at time stamp $t_R = 3$, $a1 = $ false and $T_{\varphi_1} = $ (false, 3). The verdicts in an execution sequence provide an evaluation of a future-time MLTL formula for every time stamp, sometimes by aggregating multiple consecutive verdicts from an input execution sequence. For example, at time stamp $t_R = 2$, $\langle T_{\varphi_0} \rangle = \langle$ (true, 0), (true, 1), (true, 2)$\rangle$ and $\langle T_{\varphi_2} \rangle = \langle$ (true, 0)$\rangle$; in other words, whether φ_2 holds at time index $\tau = 0$ cannot be known until $t_R = 2$. In this example, the trace π does not always satisfy φ; note that the tuple (false, 3) in T_φ (indicating that φ is false from time 2 to time 3) is produced at time stamp $t_R = 3$.

Table 1. Output of observers as an execution sequence ($\top \equiv$ true and $\bot \equiv$ false) at time stamps t_R.

MLTL	t_R				
	0	1	2	3	4
$T_{\varphi_0} (\varphi_0 = load(a0))$	$(\top, 0)$	$(\top, 1)$	$(\top, 2)$	$(\top, 3)$	$(\top, 4)$
$T_{\varphi_1} (\varphi_1 = load(a1))$	$(\top, 0)$	$(\top, 1)$	$(\bot, 2)$	$(\bot, 3)$	$(\top, 4)$
$T_{\varphi_2} (\varphi_2 = \Box_{[0,2]} \varphi_0)$	-	-	$(\top, 0)$	$(\top, 1)$	$(\top, 2)$
$T_\varphi (\varphi = \varphi_1 \wedge \varphi_2)$	-	-	$(\top, 0)$	$(\top, 1)(\bot, 3)$	-

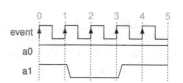

Fig. 3. Assignment to propositions $a0$ and $a1$ at event edges.

3 Model Predictive Runtime Verification (MPRV)

Overview. A high-level overview of MRPV is shown in Fig. 4. The future-time monitor utilizes current sensor data and model predictions to evaluate the satisfiability of formula φ by deadline d. The prediction's accuracy depends on the type of predictor and its modeling inaccuracies. We design MPRV generically; the user may choose *any* model predictor, weighing the trade-offs between accuracy and timing for the system-under-verification. The goal of MPRV is to make a decision on $\pi, i \models \varphi$ such that

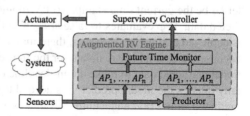

Fig. 4. High-level overview of MPRV. The blue and yellow arrows represent real and predicted data values, respectively. (Color figure online)

the supervisory controller can take the appropriate mitigation action by deadline d.

Definition 9 *(Deadline). Given an MLTL formula φ and trace π starting from time index $i \geq 0$, the deadline $d \in \mathbb{Z}$ is the number of time steps measured relative to i by which the satisfiability result of $\pi, i \models \varphi$ must be evaluated such that $0 \leq i + d \leq M$, where M denotes the end of the mission (i.e., $\pi, i \models \varphi$ cannot be evaluated before the mission begins or after the mission ends).*

Definition 10 *(MLTL Semantics with Deadline). MLTL Semantics with deadline d extends the MLTL Semantics in Definition 2. Trace $\hat{\pi}$ is defined as a trace of length $|\hat{\pi}| \geq |\pi|$ where $|\pi| \leq i + d$, the segment $\hat{\pi}[0, |\pi| - 1] = \pi$, and the segment $\hat{\pi}[|\pi|, |\hat{\pi}| - 1]$*

may be populated using prediction in order to be able to make an evaluation decision by d. We recursively define $\pi, i, d \models \varphi$ (our decision based on $\hat{\pi}$ that trace π starting from time index $i \geq 0$ satisfies, or "models" MLTL formula φ by deadline d) as

- $\pi, i, d \models$ true,
- $\pi, i, d \models p$ *for* $p \in \mathcal{AP}$ *iff* $p \in \hat{\pi}(i)$,
- $\pi, i, d \models \neg\varphi$ *iff* $\hat{\pi}, i \not\models \varphi$,
- $\pi, i, d \models \varphi_1 \wedge \varphi_2$ *iff* $\hat{\pi}, i \models \varphi_1$ *and* $\hat{\pi}, i \models \varphi_2$,
- $\pi, i, d \models \varphi_1 \, \mathcal{U}_{[lb,ub]} \, \varphi_2$ *iff* $|\hat{\pi}| \geq i + lb$ *and* $\exists j \in [i + lb, i + ub]$ *such that* $\hat{\pi}, j \models \varphi_2$ *and for every* $k < j$ *and* $k \in [i + lb, i + ub]$ *we have* $\hat{\pi}, k \models \varphi_1$

Illustrative Example. Consider the UAS example from Sect. 1. We want to deploy a parachute if the UAS's motors fail as a mitigation action to ensure a safe landing. For example, let's assume that if the MLTL formula $\varphi = \Box_{[0,6]}a \wedge \Diamond_{[0,8]}b$ evaluates to false, this indicates motor failure. Figure 5 shows the runtime trace π. Here the worst-case propagation delay is eight (i.e., $\varphi.wpd = 8$), while the best-case propagation delay is zero (i.e.,

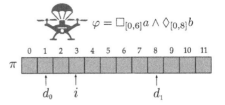

Fig. 5. Illustrative example.

$\varphi.bpd = 0$). As a result, for $i = 3$, $\pi[3, 11]$ is the maximum trace segment required to evaluate $\pi, i \models \varphi$. Let d be the deadline to trigger the deployment of the parachute, and let t_R be the current time stamp. MPRV monitors atoms a and b based on real and predicted data. If φ evaluates to false at $t_R \leq i + d$ based on real data, then the parachute is deployed at time t_R. However, there may not be enough real data at $t_R = i + d$ (i.e., because we do not have real data for the future), and the runtime monitor requires additional predicted data to make an on-deadline evaluation. In this case, MPRV incrementally queries the model predictor as needed to populate $\hat{\pi}(t_R + 1), \hat{\pi}(t_R + 2), \ldots$ with predicted values of a and b until φ evaluates to true or false. Going back to our example in Fig. 5, if we let $i = 3$, $d = d_0 = -2$, and $t_R = i + d = 1$, the model predictor will populate $\hat{\pi}(2), \hat{\pi}(3), \ldots, \hat{\pi}(11)$ until the satisfiability of $\pi, i, d \models \varphi$ is determinable, and if we let $i = 3$, $d = d_1 = 5$, and $t_R = i + d = 8$, the model predictor will populate $\hat{\pi}(9), \hat{\pi}(10)$, and $\hat{\pi}(11)$ until the satisfiability of $\pi, i, d \models \varphi$ is determinable. Parachute deployment is triggered if φ evaluates to false as $\hat{\pi}$ is incrementally populated by the predictor. Since $t_R \leq i + d$, MPRV ensures that the mitigation action is triggered before the deadline. The goal of MPRV is to produce a verdict evaluating whether $\pi, i, d \models \varphi$ holds. MPRV uses the minimum set of predicted variable evaluations needed to return a verdict; we determine this minimum set through *partial evaluation* of φ at time d.

Definition 11 *(Partial Evaluation). The partial evaluation of an MLTL formula φ over trace π starting from time index $i \geq 0$, denoted as $\varphi \mid_{(\pi,i)}$, is the evaluation of φ based on the trace segment $\pi[i, |\pi|]$. There are two cases of partial evaluation to consider: 1) $\varphi \mid_{(\pi,i)} \in \{\text{true}, \text{false}\}$, and 2) $\varphi \mid_{(\pi,i)} \notin \{\text{true}, \text{false}\}$: in this case, $\varphi \mid_{(\pi,i)}$ returns a subformula produced by standard logic rewriting rules.*

Going back to our illustrative example, we have $\varphi = (\Box_{[0,6]}a) \wedge (\Diamond_{[0,8]}b)$, $i = 0$, and $|\pi| = 6$. Let evaluations of a and b be $\pi_{\langle a,b \rangle} = [\langle 1,0 \rangle, \langle 1,1 \rangle, \langle 1,0 \rangle, \langle 1,1 \rangle, \langle 1,0 \rangle, \langle 1,0 \rangle]$. Since the subformula $\Diamond_{[0,8]}b$ is satisfied at time stamp 1, we have $\varphi\,|_{(\pi,0)} = \Box_{[6,6]}a$. To evaluate the satisfiability of φ, the value for a must be predicted for time stamp 6.

Definition 12 (*Prediction Horizon*). *Let $\hat{\pi}$ be a trace of length $|\hat{\pi}| \geq |\pi|$ where the segment $\hat{\pi}[0, |\pi| - 1] = \pi$ and the segment $\hat{\pi}[|\pi|, |\hat{\pi}| - 1]$ may be populated using prediction. The prediction horizon H_p is the length of the predicted segment of $\hat{\pi}$. The maximum prediction horizon is denoted by $max(H_p)$.*

Definition 13 (*Model Predictive Runtime Verification (MPRV)*). *Given an MLTL formula φ, a trace π, and a deadline d, MPRV produces an execution sequence $\langle T_\varphi \rangle$ (as defined in Definition 8) such that each tuple T_φ with $T_\varphi.\tau \geq i$ is produced no later than $i + d$. It populates a predicted trace $\hat{\pi}$ such that $|\hat{\pi}| \geq |\pi|$, $|\pi| \leq i + d$, the segment $\hat{\pi}[0, |\pi| - 1] = \pi$, and the segment $\hat{\pi}[|\pi|, |\pi| + H_p]$ by incrementally increasing prediction horizon H_p until $T_\varphi.v \in \{\text{true}, \text{false}\}$ as follows:*

- $d \geq \varphi.wpd$: $T_\varphi \equiv ((\pi, i \models \varphi), i)$ (*prediction is not required*)
- $d < \varphi.bpd$: $T_\varphi \equiv ((\pi, i, d \models \varphi\,|_{(\hat{\pi},i)}), i)$ (*prediction is required*)
- *otherwise:* $T_\varphi \equiv \begin{cases} T_\varphi \equiv ((\pi, i \models \varphi), i) \text{ if } \varphi\,|_{(\pi,i)} \in \{\text{true}, \text{false}\} \\ \qquad\qquad\qquad\qquad (\textit{prediction is not required}) \\ T_\varphi \equiv ((\pi, i, d \models \varphi\,|_{(\hat{\pi},i)}), i) \text{ otherwise} \\ \qquad\qquad\qquad\qquad (\textit{prediction is required}) \end{cases}$

Lemmas 1, 2, and 3 and Corollaries 1 and 2 guarantee the correctness of MPRV and establish bounds on the produced execution tuples.

Lemma 1 (Minimum Trace Length). *Given an MLTL formula φ, a trace π, and a time $t \leq |\pi|$, MPRV is guaranteed to produce all of the execution sequence tuples T_φ such that $0 \leq T_\varphi.\tau \leq t - \varphi.wpd$. In other words, the shortest trace segment starting from $\pi[0]$ that we can use to guarantee $\pi, t - \varphi.wpd \models \varphi$ is $\pi[0, t]$. Figure 6 provides a visualization of this lemma.*

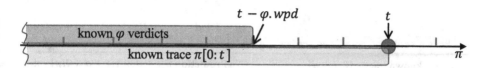

Fig. 6. Pictorial representation of Lemma 1 for *guaranteed* execution sequence elements.

Proof. The proof follows directly from induction on the structure of MLTL formula φ and Definitions 5, 6, and 7. □

Corollary 1 (Verdicts Guaranteed from Real Data). *Let t_R be the current time stamp. Given an MLTL formula φ and a trace segment $\pi[0, t_R]$, MPRV is guaranteed to produce from π (without prediction) all of the execution sequence tuples T_φ such that $0 \leq T_\varphi.\tau \leq t_R - \varphi.wpd$.*

Lemma 2 (Time Stamp Range of New Verdicts). *Let t_R be the current time stamp. Given an MLTL formula φ and a trace segment $\pi[0, t_R]$, if MPRV produces $T_\varphi.v$ from π at time stamp t_R, then $T_\varphi.\tau \in [t_R - \varphi.wpd, t_R - \varphi.bpd]$. That is, at time t_R, we know the time stamp range of any newly-produced execution sequence tuple. Figure 7 provides a visualization of this lemma.*

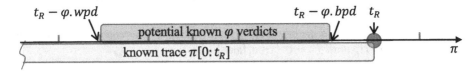

Fig. 7. Pictorial representation of Lemma 2 for range of T_φ produced at time t_R.

Proof. The proof follows directly from induction on the structure of MLTL formula φ and Definitions 5, 6, and 7. □

Corollary 2 (Verdicts from Real Data). *Let t_R be the current time stamp. Given an MLTL formula φ and a trace segment $\pi[0, t_R]$, MPRV can produce from π (without prediction) execution sequence tuples T_φ such that $0 \leq T_\varphi.\tau \leq t_R - \varphi.bpd$.*

Lemma 3 (Maximum Prediction Horizon). *Let t_R be the current time stamp. Given an MLTL formula φ, a trace segment $\pi[0, t_R]$, and a deadline d, to determine T_φ with $T_\varphi.\tau \geq i$ in at most d time steps from i (i.e., determine the satisfiability of $\pi, i, d \models \varphi$), the maximum prediction horizon $max(H_p)$ is bounded such that $max(H_p) = \varphi.wpd - d$. Figure 8 provides a visualization of this lemma.*

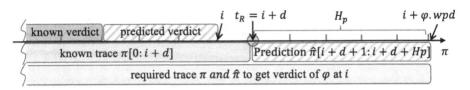

Fig. 8. Pictorial representation of Lemma 3. Note that in this case, $t_R = i + d$. Hashed regions represent predicted values, and solid regions represent known values.

Proof. If we let $t = i + \varphi.wpd$ in Lemma 1, then we are guaranteed to produce all T_φ with $T_\varphi.\tau \in [0, i]$. Given $\pi[0, t_R]$, by Definition 6, one needs to predict at most $\hat{\pi}[t_R + 1, i + \varphi.wpd]$ to determine $\pi, i, d \models \varphi$. When prediction is required, $t_R = i + d$ (as depicted in Fig. 8). Thus $max(H_p) = i + \varphi.wpd - (i + d) = \varphi.wpd - d$.   □

3.1 MPRV Algorithm

This section presents the generic MPRV algorithm (Algorithm 1). In Algorithm 1, the RV engine in lines 1, 6, and 10 can be *any* RV engine. We execute this algorithm when new sensor signals ($s_{real} \in \mathbb{R}^n$, where n is the number of sensors) are available at each time stamp (t_R). These sensor signals are converted into boolean values and represented in trace π. The sensor signals s_{real}, current time stamp t_R, and trace π are passed as inputs along with the specification details (i, d, and φ). The RV engine will update the current verdict based on the trace segment ($\pi[0, t_R]$) without prediction. If at deadline d we cannot assert true or false for $\varphi|_{\pi, i}$, the engine will continue partially evaluating the trace using prediction trace data $\hat{\pi}[0, i + d + 1], \hat{\pi}[0, i + d + 2], \ldots$ generated by *model_predict*. Once true or false can be asserted for $\varphi|_{\hat{\pi}, i}$, the verdict will be returned.

Theorem 1 (Correctness of MPRV Algorithm). *Given an MLTL formula φ, sensor signals s_{real}, trace π, deadline d, and a predictor function (model_predict) that predicts the sensor signals at a future time step, the MPRV algorithm (Algorithm 1) computes a predicted trace $\hat{\pi}$ and the execution sequence tuple T_φ by using maximum real values and minimum predicted values required to evaluate $\pi, i, d \models \varphi$ such that $T_\varphi.v = $ true iff $\pi, i, d \models \varphi$.*

Proof. We split the proof into two parts. (1) *Maximum real values and minimum predicted values:* MPRV uses all real data values from π up to deadline d (line 1–6). If before the deadline d, MPRV guarantees RV results without prediction (line 1). If at deadline d, it partially evaluates formula φ on trace π (line 2–6). If $\varphi|_{\pi, i}$ asserts true or false, it returns the result. Otherwise, $\varphi|_{\pi, i}$ returns a subformula with atomic propositions that require at least one time step of prediction to resolve the formula (follows from Definition 11). This subformula is checked iteratively at each subsequent time step of prediction until resolved, resulting in minimum predicted values (lines 7–10). (2) $T_\varphi.v = $ true $\leftrightarrow \pi, i, d \models \varphi$: (*only-if direction*) $\pi, i, d \models \varphi \rightarrow T_\varphi.v = $ true: If evaluating before deadline d, MPRV guarantees to return the current result of $\pi, i, d \models \varphi$. If evaluating at deadline d, MPRV guarantees that trace $\hat{\pi}$ contains enough data (follows from Lemma 3) to evaluate $\pi, i, d \models \varphi$, and then uses partial evaluation of the formula φ to return a final result based on available data (line 11). (*if direction*) $T_\varphi.v = $ true $\rightarrow \pi, i, d \models \varphi$: If evaluating before deadline d, MPRV guarantees to terminate and return the current result of $\pi, i, d \models \varphi$. If evaluating at deadline d, MPRV terminates and returns the final result (true or false) from the partial evaluation when the satisfiability of $\pi, i, d \models \varphi$ is determinable. Note that when at deadline d, MPRV returns verdicts only when the test condition of the while loop (line 7) evaluates to false.   □

Algorithm 1: MPRV Algorithm (Definition 13)

Input: Signals: $s_{real} \in \mathbb{R}^n$; Current time stamp: t_R; Time index: i; Deadline: d;
MLTL formula: φ; Trace: $\pi[0, t_R]$ derived from s_{real}
Output: Current verdict result for $\pi, i, d \models \varphi$

1   **if** $t_R < i + d$ **then return** $RV(\pi[0, t_R], i, \varphi)$;   // Evaluating before deadline
2   **else**   // Evaluating at deadline (i.e., $t_R = i + d$)
3 | $\hat{\pi} \leftarrow \pi$;   // initialize $\hat{\pi}$ with the real data
4 | $t \leftarrow t_R$;   // initialize t with current time stamp
5 | $s \leftarrow s_{real}$;   // initialize s with signals data
6 | $\varphi|_{\hat{\pi}, i} \leftarrow RV(\hat{\pi}[0, t], i, \varphi)$;   // RV result of $\pi[0, t_R], i \models \varphi$
7 | **while** $\varphi|_{\hat{\pi}, i} \notin \{\text{true}, \text{false}\}$ **do**   // if prediction is needed, loop
8 | | $t \leftarrow t + 1$;   // look into next prediction step
9 | | $(s, \hat{\pi}[t]) \leftarrow model\_predict(s, t)$;   // update s and $\hat{\pi}[t]$
10 | | $\varphi|_{\hat{\pi}, i} \leftarrow RV(\hat{\pi}[0, t], i, \varphi)$;   // RV result of $\hat{\pi}[0, t], i \models \varphi$
11 | **return** $\varphi|_{\hat{\pi}, i}$;   // return true or false at deadline d

---

3.2   MPRV Implementation Using R2U2

We implement the MPRV algorithm using the R2U2 RV engine framework. We first convert an MLTL formula φ into an AST offline (Sect. 2.2) and then topologically sort the nodes of the AST, denoted φ_{AST}, by arranging all child nodes before their parent nodes. This offline step creates a sequence of custom instructions that respects dependencies between instructions, as depicted in Fig. 2.

The R2U2-specific MPRV algorithm is defined in Algorithm 2. We optimize RV operations using the MLTL asynchronous observer algorithm in Algorithm 3, which does not require checking the entire trace when the trace is updated from $\pi[0, t]$ to $\pi[0, t + 1]$ (refer to [48] for algorithm details). The verification results in the form of execution sequences for each node are stored in a data structure called a Shared Connection Queue (SCQ) [34], which is a circular buffer for storing the execution sequence generated by each node of φ_{AST}. Since the circular buffer overwrites data in a circular way, only a segment of the execution sequence is kept in each SCQ. To store the necessary real and predicted data, we size the SCQs per the procedure given in Sect. 9. Before prediction begins, we must cache the local variables of the SCQ (i.e., read and write pointers). The predictive RV phase of the algorithm executes until $\varphi|_{\hat{\pi}, i}$ evaluates to true or false, which is evaluated by reading the SCQ of the root node (denoted as $\varphi.Queue$). Finally, we restore the previously cached local variables of the SCQs since the predicted values will now be outdated for the next time step. All of these tasks should be completed in one sensor sampling period to allow RV to keep pace with real-time. The algorithm terminates once $\varphi|_{\hat{\pi}, i}$ evaluates to true or false, and the verdict is returned.

Algorithm 2: R2U2-specific algorithm for MPRV (Definition 13)

Input: Signals: $s_{real} \in \mathbb{R}^n$; Current time stamp: t_R; Time index: i; Deadline: d;
MLTL formula: φ; Trace: $\pi[0, t_R]$ derived from s_{real}
Output: Current verdict result for $\pi, i, d \models \varphi$

```
/* Update φ_AST for current time stamp t_R                              */
```
1   **for** *Node g from topologically sorted node list of* φ_{AST} **do**
2       $RV\_node\_one\_step(\pi, t_R, g)$;   `// Algorithm 3`
3   **if** $t_R < i + d$ **then return** $read(\varphi.Queue)$;   `// Evaluating before deadline`
4   **else**   `// Evaluating at deadline (i.e., t_R = i+d)`
```
        /* store original RV engine state                               */
```
5   **for** *Node g from topologically sorted node list of* φ_{AST} **do**
6   Store Node g's local variables;   `// read/write pointers`
7       $\hat{\pi} \leftarrow \pi$;   `// initialize π̂ with the real data`
8       $t \leftarrow t_R$;   `// initialize t with current time stamp`
9       $s \leftarrow s_{real}$;   `// initialize s with signals data`
10      $\varphi|_{\hat{\pi},i} \leftarrow read(\varphi.Queue)$;   `// RV result of π[0,t_R],i ⊨ φ`
11   **while** $\varphi|_{\hat{\pi},i} \notin \{true, false\}$ **do**   `// if prediction is needed, loop`
12        $t \leftarrow t + 1$;   `// look into next prediction step`
13        $(s, \hat{\pi}[t]) \leftarrow model\_predict(s, t)$;   `// update s and π̂[t]`
14   **for** *Node g from topologically sorted node list of* φ_{AST} **do**
15          $RV\_node\_one\_step(\hat{\pi}, t, g)$;   `// Algorithm 3`
16        $\varphi|_{\hat{\pi},i} \leftarrow read(\varphi.Queue)$;   `// RV result of π̂[0,t],i ⊨ φ`
```
        /* restore original RV engine state                             */
```
17   **for** *Node g from topologically sorted node list of* φ_{AST} **do**
18   Restore Node g's local variables;   `// read/write pointers`
19   **return** $\varphi|_{\hat{\pi},i}$;   `// return true or false at deadline d`

3.3 Memory and Time Analysis of R2U2 Implementation

Memory Utilization Without Prediction. A system utilizing the R2U2 framework needs memory to store the instructions and SCQs. For each node g in φ_{AST}, one queue is needed (denoted as $g.Queue$). Because the SCQ overwrites data in a circular way, the queues can be viewed as sliding windows. Each sliding window takes a segment of the execution sequence generated from the corresponding child node(s). Each sliding window must store the necessary data to evaluate the satisfiability of $\pi, i \models \varphi$. The time stamp difference between the inputs of child nodes can cause an input tuple from a child node g with a higher time index τ to wait for input(s) from g's sibling(s). That is, any newly generated output from g will be stalled in g's output queue until g's siblings have the same τ. We show that the required new trace data for generating the matched time indices of the two input queues is bounded, and we use bpd and wpd to prove these bounds in Lemma 4. In [25], a similar approach is used for estimating resource usage, where they call the delay a *horizon*; however, they did not consider the best-case propagation delay or prediction.

Algorithm 3: Run RV for one time stamp on an AST node g; update g's Queue with the execution sequence $\langle T_g \rangle$, which will be propagated up as the input of g's parent node(s).

---

1 **function** $RV\_node\_one\_step(\pi, i, g)$ **is**
    Input: Trace: π; Time index: i; Node: g;
2   **if** g is an $\mathcal{AP}$ operator **then**
      /* record the value of the atomic proposition   */
3   **if** $g \in \pi[i]$ **then**
4 | $g.Queue.write((\mathsf{true}, i))$;   // write $\langle T_g \rangle$
5   **else**
6 | $g.Queue.write((\mathsf{false}, i))$;   // write $\langle T_g \rangle$
7   **else**
8     $\langle T_g \rangle \leftarrow$ evaluate MLTL operator g;   // Algorithms 3--6 from [34]
9     $g.Queue.write(\langle T_g \rangle)$;   // write $\langle T_g \rangle$

Lemma 4 (Memory Usage). *Let φ_{AST} be the abstract syntax tree generated from the MLTL formula φ as explained in Sect. 2.2. For any node g from φ_{AST}, let $\mathbb{S}_g$ be the set of all sibling nodes of g. Let $g.Queue$ be the queue for the execution sequence generated by the runtime observer of g. Then the maximum memory usage of $g.Queue$ is given by $g.Queue.size \leq max(max\{s.wpd | s \in \mathbb{S}_g\} - g.bpd, 0) + 1$.*

Proof. Refer to the appendix.

MPRV Memory Utilization. We use $g_{MPRV}.Queue.size$ to represent the size of $g.Queue$ when using MPRV. To prevent overwriting the original SCQ content with predicted data, we need $max(H_p)$ (as defined in Lemma 3) extra entries in $g.Queue$; we must prevent overwriting the original content so we can restore operations after prediction. Therefore, $g_{MPRV}.Queue.size = g.Queue.size + max(H_p)$. Algorithm 4 of the appendix further details how to determine the memory usage for each SCQ.

Each queue entry stores a tuple of a verdict and a time index. We use one bit to represent the verdict, and if we let $max(\tau)$ be the length of the mission in terms of the number of time stamps, then we need $\lceil \log_2 max(\tau + 1) \rceil$ bits to represent the time stamp. The following equation gives the total memory size (in bits):

$$total\ memory\ size = (1 + \lceil \log_2 max(\tau + 1) \rceil) \times \sum_{g \in \varphi_{AST}} g_{MPRV}.Queue.size$$

Worst-Case Execution Time (WCET). The MPRV worst-case execution time splits into two parts: the model prediction ($WCET_{MODEL}$) and RV on the trace $\hat{\pi}$ ($WCET_{RV}$). This section analyzes $WCET_{RV}$ from line 1 to line 19 except for line 13 in Algorithm 2. The WCET of line 13 are equivalent to $WCET_{MODEL}$, which depends on the chosen model predictor (refer to Sect. 5.1 for examples).

Lemma 5 (Worst-case Execution Time of RV ($WCET_{RV}$)). *Given an MLTL formula φ and the output queue size of each node in φ_{AST}, let $g.input\_Queue$ be the sum of queue sizes of direct child nodes of g, t_{exe} be the execution time for an MLTL operator node to consume one element of the input execution sequence (Algorithm 3), t_{store} be the store operation time (Algorithm 2 lines 5–6), and $t_{restore}$ be the restore operation time (Algorithm 2 lines 17–18). Then the worst-case execution time is given by $WCET_{RV}(\varphi) = \sum_{g \in \varphi_{AST}} (g.input\_Queue.size \times t_{exe} + t_{store} + t_{restore})$.*

Proof. Refer to the appendix.

4   Quadcopter Case Study

We demonstrate the utility of MPRV for a UAS quadcopter by simulating a non-linear quadcopter model [9, 13][1] whose trajectory is controlled via a linear Model Predictive Control (MPC) controller; refer to [40] for MPC algorithm details. The upper portion of Fig. 9 shows the actual position of the quadcopter compared to the planned trajectory chosen by MPC. Note that we use the same model predictor for control and for MPRV in order to save hardware resources.

Let π be a trace over atomics $a0$ and $a1$ at each time index. Table 2 specifies the atomic propositions that map system requirements to atomics $a0$ and $a1$. The specification $\varphi = (\Box_{[5]}a0)\mathcal{U}_{[10]}a1$ in Fig. 9 limits the quadcopter's vertical velocity for a future five time steps if the quadcopter keeps diverging from the planned trajectory for the next ten time steps. This specification is designed to prevent the quadcopter from crashing into the ground at high speed when diverged far off course. If MPRV returns a false verdict for φ, an appropriate mitigation strategy can be triggered (e.g., deploying a parachute).

Table 2. Quadcopter Atomic Propositions

Atomic	Atomic Proposition
$a0$	Magnitude of trajectory error ($z_{ref} - z$) ≤ 0.12 m
$a1$	Vertical speed ($\dot{z}_k$) ≥ -0.9 m/s

In the lower portion of Fig. 9, if the verdict is true, then $\pi, t \models \varphi$, where t is the corresponding time-axis value. Due to the nature of future time asynchronous observers, the evaluation of $\pi, t \models \varphi$ is not known until time t or later. We assume the required controller actuation update rate and sensor sampling rate are 50 Hz (.02 s); consequently, MPRV is run every 0.02 s. Figure 9 compares the responsiveness of $\pi, i, d \models (\Box_{[5]}a0)\mathcal{U}_{[10]}a1$ using MPRV with a deadline $d = -5$ steps (0.1 s before violation) and $d = 10$ steps (0.2 s after violation). Given the formula has $\varphi.wpd = 15$, we compute the maximum prediction horizon using Lemma 3. This results in $max(H_p) = 20$ when $d = -5$, and $max(H_p) = 5$ when $d = 10$. The green and orange bars are associated

---

[1] Specific model parameters for the quadcopter model were obtained from [26] and [42].

with a 20 and 5 step prediction horizon, respectively. The left boundary of the bar is the time when MPRV detects the formula becoming false, and right boundary is the time when a false verdict is detected without prediction. Note that for $d = -5$, the green bars maintain at least 5 time steps ahead of the corresponding false verdict (marked by red cross). Similarly, when $d = 10$, the orange bars maintain at least 10 steps after the corresponding false verdict.

In summary, the earlier the deadline, the longer the maximum prediction horizon and the earlier conclusive results are obtained. These results are in alignment with what one would intuitively expect. Note that real-world sensors and imperfect knowledge of the model limit how far one can effectively estimate the future, and the larger the prediction horizon, the more the prediction is prone to inaccuracies. While we did not account for inaccuracies in our implementation, methods have been developed to robustify MPC against model uncertainties and disturbances [12, 16].

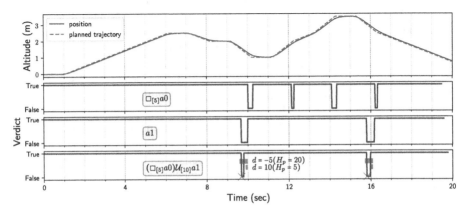

Fig. 9. The position of a quadcopter resulting from MPC and verification results of three formulas. The red × indicates motor failure. The left end of each green (orange) bar is the formula-violation detection time using MPRV with a prediction horizon of H_p. The right end of each green (orange) bar is the formula-violation detection time using RV without prediction. (Color figure online)

5   Analysis of Hardware Implementation

Our methodology is applicable across a wide range of systems and applications. When targeting a given system, users would want to deploy their own mission-specific MLTL formulas and model predictor. Users can select *any* model predictor, weighing the trade-offs between accuracy and performance. Currently, many model predictors exist in the literature. The most common method for developing system models for prediction is to derive a differential-algebraic model by analyzing the physical system's dynamics [15, 18]. Another common modeling method is system identification, which derives the model of the system by observing the system's inputs and corresponding outputs [28, 44]. Data-driven modeling via machine learning [59] or simulation-based modeling [10, 33] are a few more popular modeling techniques. Note that MPRV allows for simpler low-fidelity system models for the prediction of individual variables, and there exists a trade-off in terms of resources and computing time between low-fidelity and high-fidelity models. We provide details on determining if MPRV is feasible for an embedded platform's resource constraints and mission's performance requirements in this section.

5.1 FPGA Implementation of Model Predictive Runtime Verification (MPRV)

For experimental evaluation of our implementation, we target a modest-sized Xilinx FPGA (ZYNQ 7020) [1] and use the Vivado 2019.2 tool-chain [2] to synthesize our MPRV design. The resource usage of our quadcopter case study is shown in Fig. 10. Note that our implementation of MPRV and MPC [62] are both modular by design; several software-configurable registers allow the user to modify MLTL formulas and the MPC's control algorithm on-the-fly without having to re-synthesize the hardware. Additionally, the MPC hardware design has a trade-off between performance and resource utilization; we have maximized the MPC design to fill up the remaining resources the augmented RV engine (R2U2 with MPRV) did not use. One example of this performance and resource trade-off is in the MPC's matrix-vector multiplier (MVM). The larger the MVM, the faster the MPC can handle larger matrices, i.e., the longer the MPC's prediction horizon or the larger the number of the state variables N. For our quadcopter example ($N = 12$), Fig. 10 shows that our augmented RV engine requires additional BRAMs (2.5% of the 280 available 18Kb BRAMs) for instructions, local variables (defined in [34]), and data transmission FIFOs. When maximizing the MPC design to fill the rest of the BRAM resources, we can reach a prediction horizon $H_p = 17$.

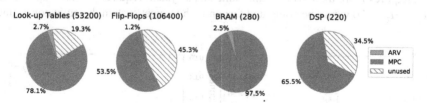

Fig. 10. Percentage of resource usage by augmented RV engine (ARV), MPC, and unused resource. The total amount of each resource available on chip is included inside the parentheses. For the BRAM, the blue corresponds to a system of 12 state variables (N) with $H_p = 17$. (Color figure online)

Recall that our implementation uses an SCQ buffer for each node in φ_{AST} as described in Sect. 3.2. Given an MLTL formula, sizing SCQs per the procedure given in Sect. 3.3 guarantees SCQs never overflow. We chose a time stamp width of 31-bits and a total SCQ size of 512 * 32 bits, which consumes one 18 Kb block RAM (BRAM) [1]. Such memory is sufficient for the example formulas with a corresponding $max(H_p)$ in Table 3. We also show the $WCET_{RV}$ of Algorithm 2 for each formula when predicting with $max(H_p)$. Example execution time of the MPC controller ($WCET_{MODEL}$) is shown in Fig. 11.

Table 3. Examples of MLTL formulas that can be supported with one 18 Kb BRAM in Fig. 10

MLTL Formula	$max(H_p)$	$WCET_{RV}$
$a0$	509	5.28 μs
$\Box_{[0,10]}\, a0$	248	47.87 μs
$\Box_{[0,10]}\, a0\, \mathcal{U}_{[0,10]}\, a1$	115	67.87 μs
$\Box_{[0,10]}\, a0 \lor \Box_{[0,10]}\, a1$	90	73.99 μs
$(a0\, \mathcal{U}_{[0,5]} a1) \lor (a2\, \mathcal{U}_{[0,10]} a3) \lor (\Box_{[0,10]}\, a4)$	41	82.16 μs

Hardware architectures exist that support online configuration of MPC for different systems, e.g., [62]. Assuming the embedded hardware-based MPC controller of [62] is acting as the model predictor of our MPRV architecture, we show in Fig. 11 our approach scales feasibly across a wide range of systems. To give a sense of the range of system complexity our approach can support, we highlight a point-mass system ($N = 2$), a quadcopter [35] ($N = 12$), and even a reduced order model of a fusion machine [14] ($N = 2700$ for full model, but $N = 30$ for reduced model at an accuracy loss of .1%). The left-hand side of Fig. 11 depicts how memory usage scales with N and H_p, while the right-hand side depicts how execution time scales. Additionally, the right-hand side of Fig. 11 illustrates how one would take into account a system's required sensor update rate to determine how far into the future we can predict (H_p). This is accomplished using the two horizontal dashed lines located at .01 s (10 ms) and at .02 s (20 ms). For example, if a system requires a sensor update rate of .01 s, then for a quadcopter system model with $N = 12$ one could have $H_p = 10$ or $H_p = 20$, but not $H_p = 50$ as computation requires more than .01 s. If this same sized system required a sensor update rate of .02 s, $H_p = 50$ would be computed fast enough to meet system dynamic constraints.

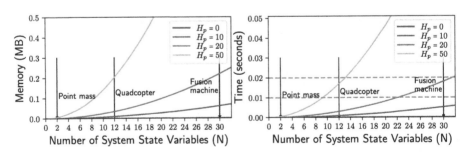

Fig. 11. Memory and execution time of MPC from [62] with FPGA clock frequency of 130 MHz.

In summary, Fig. 11 can help users determine early in a design process whether an embedded platform's memory and computing capabilities are sufficient to support MPRV and reason about system performance and resource trade-offs. For example, in our Quadcopter case study we needed a prediction horizon of 5 and 20. Regarding computing speed, our FPGA implementation can handle both cases; however, in terms of memory, the largest H_p we can support is 17 for the quadcopter model. Thus, either $H_p = 17$ would need to be sufficient for the mission, or a slightly larger FPGA would be required.

6 Conclusion and Future Work

The definition and general algorithm for MPRV are *extensible*; while we have chosen to exemplify MPRV using MLTL properties verified in the R2U2 engine with an MPC controller for a quadcopter, all of these choices can be changed or extended. Our results are promising regarding MPRV's utility for improving RV responsiveness in real-life scenarios. In particular, our implementation paves the way for better mitigation of faults by enabling evaluation of future-time requirements with enough time to trigger mitigation actions during system runtime. There is now a basis to extend MPRV to other logics (e.g., MTL [4], STL [41], MLTLM [29]), create implementations that build on other RV engines, and plug in different model predictors for when prediction steps are necessary. Investigating the trade-offs between resource demands, performance, and accuracy of different model predictors maps a valuable landscape for future MPRV design decisions.

We design MPRV to use maximum real values and minimum predicted values presuming the former is more accurate. However, this is not always the case as both real data and predicted data have their own associated error distribution (i.e., sensor noise, model parameter variation, etc.). To robustify MPRV against inaccurate distribution-valued signals, future work will include investigating techniques for robust satisfaction of MLTL specifications similar to [22,45]. While we focused on a priori known deadlines, MPRV is capable of evaluating specifications with dynamically-defined deadlines; we leave this for future work. An application for requiring a dynamically-defined deadline would be an autonomous vehicle's braking system; the time required to come to a complete stop dynamically changes based on the current velocity of the vehicle. Additionally, [23] provides an interesting direction for MPRV. This work focuses on using multiple model predictors for different components in a complex system of systems (e.g., a robotic system), but they assume the system has a shared global clock. This is not always the case, and current work has extended R2U2 to monitor different timescales through MLTLM specifications [29]. In future work, we also plan to revisit case studies of running R2U2 on real UAS [17,27,48,49,52–54] to further explore MPRV.

Appendix

Proof of Lemma 4

Proof. Figure 12 shows the pictorial representation of the execution sequence tuples inside $g.Queue$ and g's sibling nodes at the current time stamp t_R. Let the nodes g and g_1 be the child nodes of node h_1. The execution sequence tuples with the same time index τ are consumed/popped from $g.Queue$ and $g_1.Queue$ to produce the input

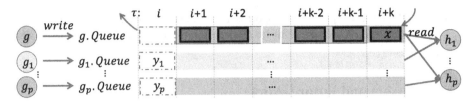

Fig. 12. Analysis of maximum execution sequence time stamp mismatch between sibling nodes. The squares are data content of $g.Queue$ and all other queues from g's sibling nodes ($g_1,...,g_p$) that share the same parent nodes (any of $h_1, h_2, ..., h_p$) with g. In $g.Queue$, each execution tuple is labeled by the execution sequence's τ value ranging from i to $i+k$. $x, y_1,...,y_p$ are the latest execution sequence tuples with the biggest time stamp in the corresponding queue.

tuples of h_1. Once these tuples are consumed by their parent node, they are dropped from the queue (marked in dashed boxes). Let x be the latest execution sequence tuple in $g.Queue$ with time index $i+k$. Let y_1 be the latest execution sequence tuple in $g_1.Queue$ with time index i, and let y_1 to have been consumed by $h_1.Queue$. Since y_1 was consumed at t_R and was not stalled by $g.Queue$, y_1 must have been produced at $t_R - 1$. According to Lemma 2, when $\pi[0, t_R - 1]$ is known, if a new execution tuple T_{g_1} is inserted into $g_1.Queue$, then $T_{g_1}.\tau \in [t_R - 1 - g_1.wpd, t_R - 1 - g_1.bpd]$. Therefore, $y_1.\tau \geq t_R - 1 - g_1.wpd$. Similarly, when $\pi[0, t_R]$ is known, if there are new execution sequence tuples T_g inserted into $g.Queue$, then $T_g.\tau \in [t_R - g.wpd, t_R - g.bpd]$. Therefore, $x.\tau \leq t_R - g.bpd$. The maximum value of k is $max(x.\tau) - min(y_1.\tau) = t_R - g.bpd - (t_R - 1 - g_1.wpd) = g_1.wpd - g.bpd + 1$. The maximum number of elements to be stored in $g.Queue$ is bounded by $g_1.wpd - g.bpd + 1$, or 1 if the difference is non-positive. The same argument follows for $g_2, ..., g_p$. Therefore, we have $g.Queue$ bounded by $s.wpd - g.bpd + 1$ for $s \in \mathbb{S}_g = \{g_1, ..., g_p\}$, or $g.Queue.size \leq max(max\{s.wpd | s \in \mathbb{S}_g\} - g.bpd, 0) + 1$. □

Algorithm for Sizing SCQs

We first derive the topologically sorted collection of all nodes from φ_{AST}. Second, we compute and record the bpd and wpd of each node in this collection sequentially (lines 1–2). Finally, we compute the output queue size for each subformula (lines 3–5).

Algorithm 4: Compute g's queue size for all node g in the R2U2 AST to optimize for storing a combination of real and predicted data for MPRV

Input: MLTL: φ; Prediction Horizon: H_p

1 **for** *Node g from topologically sorted node list of φ_{AST}* **do**

2 $\quad$ Compute $g.bpd$ and $g.wpd$;   // Definition 7

3 **for** *Node g in φ_{AST}* **do**

4 $\quad$ $g.Queue.size \leftarrow max(max\{s.wpd | s \in \mathbb{S}_g\} - g.bpd, 0) + 1$;   // Lemma 4

5 $\quad$ $g_{MPRV}.Queue.size \leftarrow g.Queue.size + H_p$;   // final queue size

Proof of Lemma 5

Proof. The $WCET_{RV}$ is the sum of the worst-case execution time of all the nodes in φ_{AST}. The time stamp of the execution sequence tuple for a unary operator node will increase when we write to $g.Queue$ in Algorithm 3. For binary operator node h, at least one of the inputs' $(g1, g2)$ time stamp will increase. The increase is bounded by the total size of the $g1.Queue$ and $g2.Queue$ (from Lemma 4). Let $h.input\_Queue.size = g1.Queue.size + g2.Queue.size$, then the $WCET_{RV}$ for node h is $h.input\_Queue.\ size \times t_{exe}$. The total execution time for all nodes in the φ_{AST} is $\sum_{g \in \varphi_{AST}} g.input\_Queue.\ size \times t_{exe}$. When we combine this with the store time (t_{store}) and restore time ($t_{restore}$) for each node, $WCET_{RV}(\varphi) = \sum_{g \in \varphi_{AST}} (g.input\_Queue.size \times t_{exe} + t_{store} + t_{restore})$. $\qquad\square$

References

1. Zynq-7000 SoC Data Sheet: Overview (2018). https://www.xilinx.com/support/documentation/data_sheets/ds190-Zynq-7000-Overview.pdf
2. Vivado design suite user guide (2019). https://www.xilinx.com/support/documentation/sw_manuals/xilinx2019_2/ug973-vivado-release-notes-install-license.pdf
3. Adolf, F.-M., Faymonville, P., Finkbeiner, B., Schirmer, S., Torens, C.: Stream runtime monitoring on UAS. In: Lahiri, S., Reger, G. (eds.) RV 2017. LNCS, vol. 10548, pp. 33–49. Springer, Cham (2017). https://doi.org/10.1007/978-3-319-67531-2_3
4. Alur, R., Henzinger, T.A.: Real-time logics: complexity and expressiveness. In: LICS, pp. 390–401. IEEE (1990)
5. Aurandt, A., Jones, P.H., Rozier, K.Y.: Runtime verification triggers real-time, autonomous fault recovery on the CySat-I. In: Deshmukh, J.V., Havelund, K., Perez, I. (eds.) NASA Formal Methods Symposium, NFM 2022. LNCS, vol. 13260, pp. 816–825. Springer, Cham (2022). https://doi.org/10.1007/978-3-031-06773-0_45
6. Babaee, R., Ganesh, V., Sedwards, S.: Accelerated learning of predictive runtime monitors for rare failure. In: Finkbeiner, B., Mariani, L. (eds.) RV 2019. LNCS, vol. 11757, pp. 111–128. Springer, Cham (2019). https://doi.org/10.1007/978-3-030-32079-9_7
7. Babaee, R., Gurfinkel, A., Fischmeister, S.: *Prevent*: a predictive run-time verification framework using statistical learning. In: Johnsen, E.B., Schaefer, I. (eds.) SEFM 2018. LNCS, vol. 10886, pp. 205–220. Springer, Cham (2018). https://doi.org/10.1007/978-3-319-92970-5_13
8. Babaee, R., Gurfinkel, A., Fischmeister, S.: Predictive run-time verification of discrete-time reachability properties in black-box systems using trace-level abstraction and statistical learning. In: Colombo, C., Leucker, M. (eds.) RV 2018. LNCS, vol. 11237, pp. 187–204. Springer, Cham (2018). https://doi.org/10.1007/978-3-030-03769-7_11
9. Balas, C., Whidborne, J., Cranfield University School of Engineering: Modelling and linear control of a quadrotor. Theses 2007, Cranfield University, School of Engineering (2007). https://books.google.com/books?id=7PIYyAEACAAJ
10. Banaei, M.R., Alizadeh, R.: Simulation-based modeling and power management of all-electric ships based on renewable energy generation using model predictive control strategy. ITSM **8**(2), 90–103 (2016)
11. Bartocci, E., et al.: Specification-based monitoring of cyber-physical systems: a survey on theory, tools and applications. In: Bartocci, E., Falcone, Y. (eds.) Lectures on Runtime Verification. LNCS, vol. 10457, pp. 135–175. Springer, Cham (2018). https://doi.org/10.1007/978-3-319-75632-5_5

12. Bemporad, A., Morari, M.: Robust model predictive control: a survey. In: Garulli, A., Tesi, A. (eds.) Robustness in Identification and Control, vol. 245, pp. 207–226. Springer, Cham (2007). https://doi.org/10.1007/BFb0109870

13. Bolandi, H., Rezaei, M., Mohsenipour, R., Nemati, H., Smailzadeh, S.M.: Attitude control of a quadrotor with optimized PID controller. Intell. Control Autom. **4**, 335–342 (2013)

14. Bonotto, M., Bettini, P., Cenedese, A.: Model-order reduction of large-scale state-space models in fusion machines via Krylov methods. IEEE Trans. Magn. **53**(6), 1–4 (2017)

15. Brown, R.G., Hwang, P.Y.C.: Introduction to Random Signals and Applied Kalman Filtering with MATLAB Exercises, 4th edn. Wiley, New York (2012). ISBN-13 978-0-470-60969-9

16. Bujarbaruah, M., Rosolia, U., Stürz, Y.R., Borrelli, F.: A simple robust MPC for linear systems with parametric and additive uncertainty. In: 2021 American Control Conference (ACC), pp. 2108–2113. IEEE (2021)

17. Cauwels, M., Hammer, A., Hertz, B., Jones, P.H., Rozier, K.Y.: Integrating runtime verification into an automated UAS traffic management system. In: Muccini, H., et al. (eds.) ECSA 2020. CCIS, vol. 1269, pp. 340–357. Springer, Cham (2020). https://doi.org/10.1007/978-3-030-59155-7_26

18. Chen, C.: Linear System Theory and Design, 3rd edn. Oxford University Press Inc., Oxford (1999). ISBN-13 978-0-19-511777-6

19. Cimatti, A., Tian, C., Tonetta, S.: Assumption-based runtime verification with partial observability and resets. In: Finkbeiner, B., Mariani, L. (eds.) RV 2019. LNCS, vol. 11757, pp. 165–184. Springer, Cham (2019). https://doi.org/10.1007/978-3-030-32079-9_10

20. Dabney, J.B., Badger, J.M., Rajagopal, P.: Adding a verification view for an autonomous real-time system architecture. In: Proceedings of SciTech Forum, pp. 2021–0566. AIAA, January 2021. https://doi.org/10.2514/6.2021-0566

21. D'Angelo, B., et al.: LOLA: runtime monitoring of synchronous systems. In: TIME, pp. 166–174 (2005)

22. Fainekos, G.E., Pappas, G.J.: Robustness of temporal logic specifications for continuous-time signals. Theor. Comput. Sci. **410**(42), 4262–4291 (2009)

23. Ferrando, A., et al.: Bridging the gap between single-and multi-model predictive runtime verification. Formal Methods Syst. Des. **59**, 44–76 (2022)

24. Ferrando, A., Delzanno, G.: Incrementally predictive runtime verification. In: CILC, pp. 92–106 (2021)

25. Finkbeiner, B., Kuhtz, L.: Monitor circuits for LTL with bounded and unbounded future. In: Bensalem, S., Peled, D.A. (eds.) RV 2009. LNCS, vol. 5779, pp. 60–75. Springer, Heidelberg (2009). https://doi.org/10.1007/978-3-642-04694-0_5

26. Förster, J.: System identification of the Crazyflie 2.0 Nano Quadrocopter (2015)

27. Geist, J., Rozier, K.Y., Schumann, J.: Runtime observer pairs and Bayesian network reasoners on-board FPGAs: flight-certifiable system health management for embedded systems. In: Bonakdarpour, B., Smolka, S.A. (eds.) RV 2014. LNCS, vol. 8734, pp. 215–230. Springer, Cham (2014). https://doi.org/10.1007/978-3-319-11164-3_18

28. Greblicki, W.: Continuous-time Hammerstein system identification from sampled data. TAC **51**(7), 1195–1200 (2006)

29. Hariharan, G., Kempa, B., Wongpiromsarn, T., Jones, P.H., Rozier, K.Y.: MLTL multi-type (MLTLM): a logic for reasoning about signals of different types. In: Isac, O., Ivanov, R., Katz, G., Narodytska, N., Nenzi, L. (eds.) International Workshop on Numerical Software Verification, Workshop on Formal Methods for ML-Enabled Autonomous Systems, vol. 13466, pp. 187–204. Springer, Cham (2022). https://doi.org/10.1007/978-3-031-21222-2_11

30. Heffernan, D., Macnamee, C., Fogarty, P.: Runtime verification monitoring for automotive embedded systems using the ISO 26262 functional safety standard as a guide for the definition of the monitored properties. IET Softw. **8**(5), 193–203 (2014). https://doi.org/10.1049/iet-sen.2013.0236

31. Hertz, B., Luppen, Z., Rozier, K.Y.: Integrating runtime verification into a sounding rocket control system. In: Dutle, A., Moscato, M.M., Titolo, L., Muñoz, C.A., Perez, I. (eds.) NFM 2021. LNCS, vol. 12673, pp. 151–159. Springer, Cham (2021). https://doi.org/10.1007/978-3-030-76384-8_10

32. Jaksic, S., Bartocci, E., Grosu, R., Kloibhofer, R., Nguyen, T., Nickovic, D.: From signal temporal logic to FPGA monitors. In: MEMOCODE, pp. 218–227, September 2015

33. Kapinski, J., Deshmukh, J.V., Jin, X., Ito, H., Butts, K.: Simulation-based approaches for verification of embedded control systems: an overview of traditional and advanced modeling, testing, and verification techniques. Control Syst. Mag. **36**(6), 45–64 (2016)

34. Kempa, B., Zhang, P., Jones, P.H., Zambreno, J., Rozier, K.Y.: Embedding online runtime verification for fault disambiguation on Robonaut2. In: Bertrand, N., Jansen, N. (eds.) Proceedings of the 18th International Conference on Formal Modeling and Analysis of Timed Systems (FORMATS), FORMATS 2020. LNCS, vol. 12288, pp. 196–214. Springer, Cham (2020). https://doi.org/10.1007/978-3-030-57628-8_12, http://research.temporallogic.org/papers/KZJZR20.pdf

35. Kurak, S., Hodzic, M.: Control and estimation of a quadcopter dynamical model. Periodicals Eng. Nat. Sci. **6**(1), 63–75 (2018)

36. Leucker, M.: Sliding between model checking and runtime verification. In: Qadeer, S., Tasiran, S. (eds.) RV 2012. LNCS, vol. 7687, pp. 82–87. Springer, Heidelberg (2013). https://doi.org/10.1007/978-3-642-35632-2_10

37. Li, J., Vardi, M.Y., Rozier, K.Y.: Satisfiability checking for Mission-Time LTL. In: Dillig, I., Tasiran, S. (eds.) CAV 2019. LNCS, vol. 11562, pp. 3–22. Springer, Cham (2019). https://doi.org/10.1007/978-3-030-25543-5_1

38. Lindemann, L., Qin, X., Deshmukh, J.V., Pappas, G.J.: Conformal prediction for STL runtime verification. arXiv preprint arXiv:2211.01539 (2022)

39. Lu, H., Forin, A.: The design and implementation of P2V, an architecture for zero-overhead online verification of software programs. Technical report, MSR-TR-2007-99, Microsoft Research, August 2007

40. Maciejowski, J.M.: Predictive Control: with Constraints. Pearson Education, London (2002)

41. Maler, O., Nickovic, D.: Monitoring temporal properties of continuous signals. In: Lakhnech, Y., Yovine, S. (eds.) FORMATS/FTRTFT -2004. LNCS, vol. 3253, pp. 152–166. Springer, Heidelberg (2004). https://doi.org/10.1007/978-3-540-30206-3_12

42. McInerney, I.: Development of a multi-agent quadrotor research platform with distributed computational capabilities. Ph.D. thesis, Iowa State University (2017)

43. Meredith, P.O., Jin, D., Griffith, D., Chen, F., Roşu, G.: An overview of the MOP runtime verification framework. STTT **14**(3), 249–289 (2012)

44. Naung, Y., Schagin, A., Oo, H.L., Ye, K.Z., Khaing, Z.M.: Implementation of data driven control system of dc motor by using system identification process. In: EIConRus, pp. 1801–1804 (2018)

45. Pant, Y.V., Abbas, H., Quaye, R.A., Mangharam, R.: Fly-by-logic: control of multi-drone fleets with temporal logic objectives. In: 2018 ACM/IEEE 9th International Conference on Cyber-Physical Systems (ICCPS), pp. 186–197. IEEE (2018)

46. Pellizzoni, R., Meredith, P., Caccamo, M., Rosu, G.: Hardware runtime monitoring for dependable COTS-based real-time embedded systems. In: RTSS, pp. 481–491 (2008)

47. Pinisetty, S., Jéron, T., Tripakis, S., Falcone, Y., Marchand, H., Preoteasa, V.: Predictive runtime verification of timed properties. J. Syst. Softw. **132**, 353–365 (2017)

48. Reinbacher, T., Rozier, K.Y., Schumann, J.: Temporal-logic based runtime observer pairs for system health management of real-time systems. In: Ábrahám, E., Havelund, K. (eds.) TACAS 2014. LNCS, vol. 8413, pp. 357–372. Springer, Heidelberg (2014). https://doi.org/10.1007/978-3-642-54862-8_24

49. Rozier, K.Y., Schumann, J., Ippolito, C.: Intelligent hardware-enabled sensor and software safety and health management for autonomous UAS. Technical Memorandum NASA/TM-2015-218817, NASA, May 2015

50. Rozier, K.Y., Schumann, J.: R2U2: tool overview. In: Proceedings of International Workshop on Competitions, Usability, Benchmarks, Evaluation, and Standardisation for Runtime Verification Tools (RV-CUBES), vol. 3, pp. 138–156. Kalpa Publications, Seattle, WA, USA, September 2017

51. Schumann, J., Moosbrugger, P., Rozier, K.Y.: R2U2: monitoring and diagnosis of security threats for unmanned aerial systems. In: Bartocci, E., Majumdar, R. (eds.) RV 2015. LNCS, vol. 9333, pp. 233–249. Springer, Cham (2015). https://doi.org/10.1007/978-3-319-23820-3_15

52. Schumann, J., Moosbrugger, P., Rozier, K.Y.: Runtime analysis with R2U2: a tool exhibition report. In: Falcone, Y., Sánchez, C. (eds.) RV 2016. LNCS, vol. 10012, pp. 504–509. Springer, Cham (2016). https://doi.org/10.1007/978-3-319-46982-9_35

53. Schumann, J., Rozier, K.Y., Reinbacher, T., Mengshoel, O.J., Mbaya, T., Ippolito, C.: Towards real-time, on-board, hardware-supported sensor and software health management for unmanned aerial systems. In: PHM, pp. 381–401, October 2013

54. Schumann, J., Rozier, K.Y., Reinbacher, T., Mengshoel, O.J., Mbaya, T., Ippolito, C.: Towards real-time, on-board, hardware-supported sensor and software health management for unmanned aerial systems. IJPHM 6(1), 1–27 (2015)

55. Selyunin, K., Nguyen, T., Bartocci, E., Nickovic, D., Grosu, R.: Monitoring of MTL specifications with IBM's spiking-neuron model. In: DATE, pp. 924–929, March 2016

56. Selyunin, K., Nguyen, T., Bartocci, E., Grosu, R.: Applying runtime monitoring for automotive electronic development. In: Falcone, Y., Sánchez, C. (eds.) RV 2016. LNCS, vol. 10012, pp. 462–469. Springer, Cham (2016). https://doi.org/10.1007/978-3-319-46982-9_30

57. Tiger, M., Heintz, F.: Stream reasoning using temporal logic and predictive probabilistic state models. In: TIME, pp. 196–205. IEEE (2016)

58. Todman, T., Stilkerich, S., Luk, W.: In-circuit temporal monitors for runtime verification of reconfigurable designs. In: DAC, pp. 50:1–50:6. ACM, New York, NY, USA (2015)

59. Torabi, A.J., et al.: A survey on artificial intelligence-based modeling techniques for high speed milling processes. IEEE Syst. J. 9(3), 1069–1080 (2015)

60. Yoon, H., Chou, Y., Chen, X., Frew, E., Sankaranarayanan, S.: Predictive runtime monitoring for linear stochastic systems and applications to geofence enforcement for UAVs. In: Finkbeiner, B., Mariani, L. (eds.) RV 2019. LNCS, vol. 11757, pp. 349–367. Springer, Cham (2019). https://doi.org/10.1007/978-3-030-32079-9_20

61. Yu, X., Dong, W., Yin, X., Li, S.: Model predictive monitoring of dynamic systems for signal temporal logic specifications. arXiv preprint arXiv:2209.12493 (2022)

62. Zhang, P., Zambreno, J., Jones, P.H.: An embedded scalable linear model predictive hardware-based controller using ADMM. In: ASAP, pp. 176–183. IEEE (2017)

63. Zhang, X., Leucker, M., Dong, W.: Runtime verification with predictive semantics. In: Goodloe, A.E., Person, S. (eds.) NFM 2012. LNCS, vol. 7226, pp. 418–432. Springer, Heidelberg (2012). https://doi.org/10.1007/978-3-642-28891-3_37

Author Index

© The Editor(s) (if applicable) and The Author(s), under exclusive license
to Springer Nature Switzerland AG 2023
L. Petrucci and J. Sproston (Eds.): FORMATS 2023, LNCS 14138, p. 181, 2023.
https://doi.org/10.1007/978-3-031-42626-1

Printed in the United States
by Baker & Taylor Publisher Services